G000279747

MADAME TUSSAUD'S CHAMBER OF HORRORS

Two hundred years of crime

By Pauline Chapman

Madame Tussaud, Waxworker Extraordinary
(with Anita Leslie)

Madame Tussaud who died in 1850, aged eighty-nine.
According to Tussaud family tradition this portrait
was done by her younger son Francis.

Pauline Chapman

MADAME TUSSAUD'S CHAMBER OF HORRORS

Two hundred years of crime

Constable · London

First published in Great Britain 1984
by Constable and Company Limited
10 Orange Street London WC2H 7EG

ISBN 0 09 465620 7
Set in Linotron Plantin 11 pt by
Rowland Phototypesetting Ltd
Bury St Edmunds, Suffolk
Printed in Great Britain by
St Edmundsbury Press
Bury St Edmunds, Suffolk

Contents

Illustrations

Acknowledgements

My thanks are due first to Michael Herbert, Chief Executive of Madame Tussaud's, for allowing me unrestricted use of the archives in order to write this book; also to Juliet Simkins, Head of Press and Publicity, for her support and suggestions, and to Undine Concannon, my successor as Archivist to Madame Tussaud's, for her help, particularly with the picture selection.

The librarians of Local History Libraries in the towns visited by Madame Tussaud during her travelling years (1802–1835) have been unfailingly helpful during my many years of research into this period.

The literature of crime is vast ranging from contemporary newspaper reports and broadsheets to hundreds of books, series such as the more than eighty titles of *Notable British Trials*, many crime anthologies, and countless volumes dealing with individual cases and trials. It is impossible to list the many sources to which I have referred in order to summarize the facts and circumstances of the crimes I have mentioned, which are only a very few of those which over such a long period have earned their perpetrators the macabre distinction of a place in the Chamber of Horrors. To all those writers whose work has helped me in the study of these crimes I owe gratitude.

Foreword

It is a remarkable fact, that although appalling scenes of violence, bloodshed and horror are commonplace today on television, in the cinema, and in press photography, the effigies of criminals standing in silent sinister company in Madame Tussaud's Chamber of Horrors still exercise the same inexorable fascination on the public as they did when people flocked to see their original counterparts in Paris in 1783.

Two hundred years ago the forerunner of the Chamber of Horrors, the *Caverne des Grands Voleurs* (the Cavern of the Great Thieves) was founded by Madame Tussaud's teacher and mentor, Dr Philippe Curtius. He set it up as an adjunct to his already celebrated wax exhibition which portrayed personalities who were, or had been, famous and in the public eye. His new venture immediately drew crowds of people eager to gaze also at wax representations of notorious criminals who had paid the penalty for their crimes.

Nineteen years later Madame Tussaud decided to include a selection from the *Caverne* founded by the late Dr Curtius—who had made her his sole heiress—among the wax figures she brought with her to England in the winter of 1802. She opened her exhibition at the Lyceum Theatre, showing this special group as a separate section. Throughout the long years of touring which followed she maintained this division in her exhibition using a 'Separate Room' for its display whenever circumstances permitted.

In 1835 she settled with her exhibition in London, and it was here, in 1846 that the Separate Room acquired the name 'Chamber of Horrors' which became indelibly printed on the public mind.

Visitors from all over the world entered the Chamber. As time went on full-size examples of some of the instruments of punishment, the guillotine and the gallows, and 'relics' of crimes were acquired and shown with the wax portraits. Nonetheless neither Madame Tussaud nor her descendants ever succumbed to the temptation of showing more sensational horrors. They totally eschewed such displays as mock torture chambers, dungeons, horrific figures or tableaux. Madame Tussaud adhered absolutely to the principles she had learned from Dr Curtius. All her portraits, whether of famous people or of murderers, were accurate likenesses. She presented them in such a way that the visitors who gazed at them could derive a historical or moral lesson.

Curtius had taught her to take life and death masks with fine plaster of Paris. When submitting to the former the semi-recumbent sitter breathed through straws or quills inserted in the nostrils, and any facial hair such as whiskers was flattened with pomade.

But a clay squeeze taken from a mask could never give the 'nearest approximation to life' which was the aim of Curtius and his pupil. An exceptionally observant eye, a retentive memory, the ability to take careful measurements, to sketch and make detailed notes were also necessary. Above all the modeller had to possess the unique artistic talent for translating all this into a portrait which communicated the essence of the subject's personality as well as being an accurate likeness.

From the finished clay head a piece-mould was made into which the hot wax was poured. Experience only could judge the right moment for the piece-mould to be removed. Then the wax features were given their final delicate sculpting with special tools, colouring was applied and eyes and hair inserted.

In the course of time Madame Tussaud's sons would abandon the life mask and clay squeeze in favour of a clay portrait head modelled from sitter, bust, or picture, and subjected to the same careful and detailed procedures. In the mid-nineteenth century the development of photography provided an additional aid for the modeller. The daguerreotype became popular and sometimes studio photographs could be obtained, even of criminals if they had sat to a photographer at some time before they were apprehended by the police. Madame Tussaud's great-grandson, John Theodore, was himself a keen photographer having studied the new art from its earliest stages, and he used his skill to help him in his work. Today, of course, detailed photographs play an essential part in creating the portrait.

Throughout the decades, while wrong doers executed or severely punished for their crimes continued in waxen effigy to exert the same irresistible fascination as they had in Curtius' original *Caverne*, the attitudes of society towards criminals and punishment were gradually undergoing radical change. In Madame Tussaud's day the death penalty was imposed for many crimes, and few people concerned themselves with ideas of rehabilitating malefactors and trying to render them fit to take their place in the community as law-abiding and useful citizens.

The extraordinary history of the Chamber of Horrors from its inception in 1783 demonstrates that in spite of social changes the fascination exercised by criminals and punishment has never diminished. Crowds still surge through the Chamber of Horrors. Of course, during two centuries it has undergone change and modification, yet it has always remained true to those principles that Madame Tussaud learned from Dr Curtius in Paris. Its story, spanning the last years of the *ancien régime*, the French Revolution and the reigns of eight British monarchs, has no parallel.

[1]

La Caverne des Grands Voleurs and the French Revolution

'As soon as Justice has despached someone he [Curtius] models the head and puts him into the collection, so that something new is always being offered to the curious, and the sight is not expensive for it only costs two sous'.

Thus wrote the Paris chronicler de Bachaumont in his *Mémoires Secrètes* on 11 May 1783. He was describing a new kind of wax exhibition, *La Caverne des Grands Voleurs* (The Cavern of the Great Thieves), that had recently opened on the Boulevard du Temple. The proprietor-modeller who introduced the innovation of a room filled with the waxen effigies of notorious criminals who had suffered the death penalty was Dr Philippe Curtius, the teacher and mentor of Marie Grosholtz who later became Madame Tussaud.

Curtius already owned a famous and flourishing *Salon de Cire* in the Palais Royal, where one might gaze upon 'waxen coloured figures of celebrated characters in all stations of life'. German-born Curtius had arrived in Paris from Berne some twenty years earlier. He came under the patronage of the Prince de Conti, a cousin of the King of France.

A medical doctor turned wax-modeller, a talented sculptor and artist, Philippe Curtius was also a man of unquenchable drive with a flair for showmanship and a journalist's nose for what is new. With the Prince's support and encouragement he quickly made a reputation in the French capital as a clever exponent of the fashionable art-form of portraiture in wax.

Dr Philippe Curtius, Madame Tussaud's 'uncle', who opened the forerunner to the Chamber of Horrors, the *Caverne des Grands Voleurs*, in 1783.

After working for private clients for a few years he opened his first public exhibition in 1770, renting premises in the Palais Royal.

Under the arcades of the Palais Royal were shops, galleries and studios. Its gardens, open to the public, were always thronged. Curtius' *Salon de Cire* was an immediate success always kept up-to-date with portraits of people in the public eye. It attracted not only French visitors but tourists from abroad and amongst those who crowded the exhibition were the nobility and members of the French and foreign royal families.

A few years previously, in 1767, Curtius had sent to Berne for his housekeeper, Madame Grosholtz, and her six-year-old daughter Marie. Widowed Madame Grosholtz and her daughter were both Strasbourg-born, but had gone to Berne and joined the household of Dr Philippe Curtius before the Prince de Conti, visiting Switzerland incognito, noticed the doctor's talents and invited him to Paris. Curtius, always shrewd, maintained his home in Berne until he felt himself firmly established in Paris.

Six-year-old Marie showed a talent for modelling which interested Curtius. He was fond of the child and began to train her in the techniques and skills of wax modelling. By the time she was seventeen she was sufficiently proficient to undertake the modelling of important 'subjects'—she modelled Voltaire, old and sick, in 1778—and she helped her teacher, who she called 'uncle', to run the exhibition and to show round people of special distinction who visited it. Thus, about the year 1780, she attracted the attention of Madame Elizabeth, sister of King Louis XVI. The Princess was artistic and felt she would like to learn modelling in wax. Marie was invited to come to Versailles and instruct Princess Elizabeth in the capacity of art tutor.

This was an offer that could not be refused, especially as in spite of her duties in Madame Elizabeth's household Marie was still able to visit her 'uncle' and mentor and do some work for his *Salon de Cire*. For example she modelled Benjamin Franklin in 1783.

In spite of the partial loss of the skills of his young pupil and assistant Philippe Curtius' driving energy and his liking for money and publicity urged him to seek something new to attract even more people. The *Salon de Cire* had been established for more than ten years. Its famous tableau of 'The Royal Family at Dinner' and the always updated collection of portraits of the famous were as attractive to the public as ever. But something quite different was needed for additional premises Curtius had acquired at 20 Boulevard du Temple in the lively, bustling show-business area of Paris—something that would attract all classes of visitor.

The already famous wax-modeller and showman did not have to look far for inspiration. In eighteenth-century Paris, as elsewhere in Europe, the greatest, the never-failing crowd-puller was the public execution of a felon. Curtius during twenty years in the capital had the opportunity of witnessing many such occasions. As de Bachaumont had remarked, there was always 'something new' in the area of public punishment since those who 'Justice despatched' were many and various. When the French Revolution broke out in 1789 there were well over a hundred offences that carried the death penalty. Only the King could grant a pardon and he granted few, while the judges were for the most part not open to corruption.

Punishment of the convicted criminal, whether his offence were petty or heinous, was most frequently inflicted in public, in market places, public squares or at street corners. Even lesser punishments which did not end in death attracted people as spectators, while an execution was the most popular occasion of all. The wealthy came in carriages or sedan chairs, reserving places if they could in windows overlooking the place of execution. The rest, the crowd of ordinary people, arrived mostly on foot getting the best viewpoint they could. Some did not get a viewpoint at all, some were squeamish and seldom took advantage of these 'entertainments'.

From Curtius' point of view there were many hundreds in all these categories who would be interested in having a close look later on at the more notorious of the executed or severely punished criminals if they were displayed in the form of portrait figures created in wax with their features taken from life before punishment, or from death masks after execution had taken place.

These figures could be effectively set out in the spacious rooms of the newly acquired house in the Boulevard du Temple. A new exhibition of this kind would certainly not be lacking variety either as regards the nature of the crime or the penalty suffered. The old pillory still stood in the Halles and had a succession of fraudulent bankrupts and similar malefactors; flogging was now towards the end of the eighteenth century mostly carried out in private but there were certain types of offender, pickpockets for example, who were still flogged at the cart-tail.

When it came to the death penalty, medieval cruelty still prevailed and the dreadful fates of executed criminals promised added interest for the visitors who gazed at their wax portraits. For Curtius attendance on occasions likely to produce suitable 'subjects' was no problem at all. The majority of public executions were carried out in the Place de Grève which was conveniently accessible to his place of work and residence, an important consideration for a busy man now almost single-handed in his studio and exhibition.

The methods of execution that would produce these 'subjects' for Curtius consisted mainly of drawing and quartering; breaking on the wheel; and hanging. Decapitation, in spite of being the privilege of a noble who incurred the death penalty had fallen into disuse. The axe had been discarded in the reign of Louis XIII, and executioners had lost the art of severing an exalted head at one blow with a sabre. The guillotine did not come into use until 1792.

However, the methods of execution at the time when Curtius conceived the notion of his new exhibition involved cruel suffering. Drawing and quartering, though not an infrequent sentence, was unpopular with the executioner since it was complicated and expensive. He had to pay men to assist him. The executioner himself tied the criminal's legs and arms to four horses, but several men were needed to drive the horses in different directions until the victim, in excruciating agony, was torn asunder. This could take over an hour to accomplish.

What was known as the 'wheel' was commonly used. The prisoner was stretched out and bound on to a large wheel laid flat while the executioner broke his limbs with a heavy iron bar. The dexterous manipulation of wheel and bar was appreciated and applauded by the onlookers.

The ancient permanent gibbet outside the city walls had given place to newly-built streets, so when hanging was the penalty imposed, gallows were set up in some public place for each occasion and dismantled afterwards. For economy's sake three or four criminals were often hanged together. The hangman was paid twenty five livres for each criminal but he had to provide the rope which cost six livres and could only be used twice.

Everyone knew the dates of public executions which were about to become so important to Curtius. They were announced by public criers who also distributed copies of the decree ordering the penalty. On the day—the day on which Curtius would have to obtain his likeness—the prisoner was taken to the place of execution in a cart. Enormous crowds including women and children arrived early. The sight of blood did not dismay them. It was a familiar sight anyway. In the narrow streets of crowded and fetid central Paris, butchers' premises periodically unloosed a flood of blood into the gutters when they were slaughtering animals brought in on the hoof. In hot weather it became infected but people were used to it. When the Revolution brought the new guillotine into action it was not surprising that the blood shed by the instrument was regarded with indifference by the thousands who watched. What with long previous experience of public executions and the butchers' shops it meant little. Nor were the crowds that watched the guillotine at work a new phenomenon. They had been the inspiration in 1783 for Curtius' *Caverne des Grands Voleurs*.

Continuously supplying the *Caverne* with 'something new' necessitated the co-operation of those who inflicted punishment, particularly executioners. This was not at all an insurmountable problem. For some years before Curtius conceived his new idea, the executioners of France had considered their financial lot an unhappy one. This situation made the quick practised taking of a death mask after execution, or a life mask shortly before punishment, something that was quite easy to arrange.

Executioners had been well-off financially until their chief source of income apart from fees was removed from them by a Royal Decree of 1775. This decree, dated 3 June, deprived them of an emolument called the *havage* which was a tax on grain and fruit and other foodstuffs which were sold in the executioner's 'ward'. The executioners were entitled to collect this levy from the sellers, and when their right to the tax was suppressed their losses were heavy. The chief executioner of Paris, Charles-Jean Baptiste Sanson, was reckoned to have lost some 60,000 livres of annual income from his large ward.

In place of *havage* executioners were given wages out of public funds and nearly all received additional fees for executions performed, as well as certain allowances, but the financial position of these public servants was severely worsened.

The Sanson family of Paris were particular sufferers on account of their personal circumstances. Charles-Jean Baptiste Sanson, official executioner in 1775, had been ill for many years after becoming seriously paralysed in 1754. His son Charles-Henri, whose co-operation Curtius needed in 1783, had been obliged to take over from his father when a young man and had, in fact, performed his father's duties without pay until 1778 when the old man died and Charles-Henri was finally appointed officially to the post of Chief Executioner. Sanson had in his ward some 600 jurisdictions and for years, even after the Revolution, complained bitterly of the expenses involved in the job which, since the loss of *havage*, he said he could not afford. Any extra earnings were welcome.

In addition there is evidence that Charles-Henri Sanson though not very well educated liked to consider himself something of a philosopher and tried to break down the prejudices about his job that made his fellow-citizens shun him. Dr Curtius, on the other hand, knew everyone of interest it seemed, and entertained liberally; friendship with Curtius could therefore benefit Sanson the executioner in other ways apart from financial gain.

The *Caverne des Grands Voleurs* opened in auspicious circumstances to instant popularity. Mercier tells us that people fought to get in to view the scoundrels in waxen effigy. When twenty years later Madame Tussaud (the former Marie Grosholtz) came to England she never mentioned her uncle's *Caverne des Grands Voleurs* but she cannot have failed to know a great deal about the project from its inception. When the *Caverne* opened in 1783 she was esconced in Madame Elizabeth's household at Versailles and certainly could not have given Curtius any assistance in obtaining the life or death masks of criminals needed for the innovation. However, on her visits to Paris to see her mother and 'uncle' and to do some work for the exhibition, the modelling of executed heads in Curtius' studio cannot have escaped her notice.

He showed, too, portrait figures of earlier murderers whose features she could have helped her 'uncle' to reproduce without risking her position at Versailles. The 'barker' at the door of 20 Boulevard du Temple shouted to passers-by to come in and see the figures of Desrues who had killed a woman in 1777 and the woman Lescombat who in 1775 had made her lover murder her husband. The latter portrait was probably modelled from an engraving which still survives showing Madame Lescombat in her prison cell holding a baby's bonnet, for she was pregnant and her execution was postponed though she paid the penalty after the child's birth. It seems that even in this forerunner of the Chamber of Horrors the public liked to look at portraits of murderers whose crimes had been committed years earlier; no doubt their names had become a kind of folk-lore for later generations.

During the next six years the *Caverne des Grands Voleurs* expanded and retained its popularity. As well as the effigies of murderers and other criminals there was a display of 'curiosities' and 'relics'. These included an Egyptian mummy and the bloodstained shirt worn by Henry IV of France when he was assassinated in 1610. The two objects aroused such sustained popular interest that when Madame Tussaud came to England in 1802 she brought them with her. The shirt actually remained in the exhibition until destroyed in the fire of 1925 which burned the Marylebone Road premises to the ground.

Curtius gave up his rooms in the Palais Royal and the *Salon de Cire* was established under the same roof in the Boulevard du Temple as the *Caverne* for which a separate charge was made.

In the early months of 1789 Dr Curtius was well aware of a

threatening political situation. He petitioned for Marie's release from royal service so that she might return to the shelter of his roof. By then the likenesses of punished or executed criminals were almost as familiar to her as the celebrated and often exalted occupants of the *Salon de Cire*. Curtius had always kept a hospitable table and Marie had now to accustom herself to a new kind of dinner-guest for Curtius' politics, either from conviction or expediency, had veered away from support of the royal and aristocratic whose patronage he had enjoyed for so long, and turned with intense enthusiasm to the new revolutionary ideas of equality, liberty and fraternity. It was as well that Marie could not foresee that some of these guests, such as Marat and Robespierre, who expounded and argued so vehemently at the dinner-table, would, in the not so far distant future, take their places in the *Caverne*, their dead features modelled by Marie herself.

Curtius' innovation had proved both popular and profitable. It was soon to become even more popular, and Marie, released from any connection with the Court of Versailles, was free to work as closely as before with her 'uncle'. Her skills were put to full-time use again and, however reluctantly, her small fingers (she was a very small woman) would soon assist in tasks less agreeable than those she had undertaken hitherto. She was twenty-eight now, back at home in the exhibition which, apart from the interlude at Versailles with Madame Elizabeth, had literally been her life since childhood. Dr Curtius, his *Salon de Cire* with its macabre adjunct, and his relations with the famous and infamous were known throughout Paris as the turn of political events was to demonstrate.

It was about midday on 12 July 1789 that the people of Paris learned that the King had dismissed Necker the Finance Minister who favoured reforms. They heard also that the liberal-minded and popular Duc d'Orléans was threatened with exile. Crowds in the Palais Royal gardens, which were a centre for political oratory, gathered round the speakers declaiming against the King. Someone suggested that the two well-known wax busts of the heros Necker and Orléans should be taken from Curtius' *Salon de Cire* and paraded through the streets in protest.

Curtius saw the mob approaching and closed his gates but opened them again when he realized its purpose. He handed over the two busts but persuaded the excited crowd not to take a full-length figure of the King on the grounds that it was too awkward to handle. The men agreed, shouting 'Bravo Curtius, bravo!' and departed with the busts of Necker and the Duc d'Orléans elevated on small pedestals and draped with crêpe. This protest ended with the first bloodshed of the Revolution, for troops were called out and opened fire killing and wounding several of the mob.

Two days later on 14 July the ancient prison-fortress of the Bastille was attacked, a symbol of oppression though in fact it had only contained very few prisoners for a long time past. The Governor, de Launay, was seized. Curtius, who had joined the newly-formed National Guard and commanded a company, was there. He claimed to be among the first to enter the Bastille.

Governor de Launay was dragged by the mob to the Hôtel de Ville. Flesselles, the Provost of Merchants, was also seized and finally the infuriated rioters cut off both their heads in the Place de Grève, scene of so many of the public executions which had supplied Curtius with new occupants for the *Caverne des Grands Voleurs*.

Where better to take the heads of these two enemies of the people than to 20 Boulevard du Temple to be modelled and placed with those of other criminals? It was Philip Astley, owner of the famous circus located near Curtius' premises, who saw Marie Grosholtz (her uncle was absent, busy with his company of the National Guard) seated at her door rapidly taking death masks of these two decapitated heads. However familiar the heads of executed criminals may have become to Marie during the past six years, this was her first horrible experience with decapitated heads. She made a good job of them, however, no matter what her feelings, for Philip Astley bought duplicates from Curtius and showed them at his London spectacle, prominently advertising his purchase. The

Caverne was taking on a new aspect as showcase for the political 'criminals' of the Revolution.

Another candidate for the *Caverne*, horrible in appearance, was not a criminal but a released prisoner from the Bastille. This was an emaciated old man known as the Comte de Lorge though his true identity is uncertain. The unhappy creature, said to have been imprisoned for thirty years, almost a skeleton, with a long beard, could not face the outside world and begged to be taken back to prison. This was refused and he died within a few weeks. He was not forgotten for over 150 years to come, for Madame Tussaud brought the Comte de Lorge's portrait to England with her and his emaciated features peered out in the Chamber of Horrors until recent times.

A few weeks later the head of a neighbour was carried past on a pike. Marie saw it and either she or Curtius undertook the gruesome task of modelling it. This was the head of Foulon, made Intendant in the Finance Ministry shortly after the dismissal of Necker. He had once unwisely said that if the people were hungry they could eat hay. This became known and he retired from the Ministry, giving out that he had died. No one believed this. He was found in the country, brought back to Paris and hanged from a lamppost, his mouth stuffed with hay. Later the mob cut off his head. (His head was one selected by Curtius and Marie in the early months of 1794, when they were preparing a collection of wax figures to be taken to India for exhibition by an Italian called Dominick Laurency. It was advertised in the *Calcutta Gazette* and was evidently a grisly representation. 'The blood seems to be streaming from it and running on the ground', in the same way no doubt as it had appeared when the public of Paris gloated over it in Curtius' establishment.)

Curtius became extremely involved politically. He had joined the Jacobin Club at the end of 1789 and its records show that he was an active member. He went on a mission for the Jacobins and voluntarily assumed responsibility for Austrian army deserters who made their way to the Jacobin Club as a refuge. As an officer of the National Guard he was frequently on duty.

Increased responsibility fell on Marie and it was she who had to undertake much of the work resulting from the horrors of the Revolution. Had not the *Caverne des Grands Voleurs* been an established success and widely known as a repository for likenesses of criminals long before the fall of the Bastille, it is unlikely so many severed heads would have passed through her hands.

It was not until the terrible month of September 1792 that the Paris mob, now swelled by cohorts from Marseilles, brought yet another head to Marie. The September Massacres lasted for three days. The *sans-culottes*, enraged because they felt reforms were too slow in coming, broke into monasteries, convents and prisons, indiscriminately slaughtering the inmates. The Princesse de Lamballe, Superintendent of the Queen's Household, had been taken to La Force prison in August. She was dragged out and horribly mutilated, her head cut off and raised on a pike. It was immediately taken to the Boulevard du Temple, and in the words of Madame Tussaud in her *Memoirs and Reminiscences of France* 'the savage monsters stood over her' while she took the likeness. They were not interested in the portrait except as an addition to be shown with the other severed heads in the exhibition. The mob departed to the Temple prison, where the royal family were incarcerated, to parade the head before the eyes of the hated Queen Marie Antoinette. It was the last head to enter the exhibition in such a way. Henceforward it would be the guillotine and not the mob which was the instrument of death—with one exception, Marat, who was assassinated by Charlotte Corday.

As early as 10 October 1789, Dr Guillotin, a physician with humane views in advance of his time, who sat as a deputy in the revolutionary National Assembly, had appealed to his fellow deputies to adopt a single method of execution to be used in all cases where the death penalty was imposed. He suggested a mechanism (later to be nicknamed *la guillotine*) by which the fall of a heavy blade on the neck of the victim would cause instant and relatively painless decapitation. His suggestion was not immediately accepted, but as a result of his continued campaign the first guillotine was set up and claimed its first victim, a pickpocket, in April 1792.

The good doctor could not foresee how many thousands of heads would be severed from shoulders by his humane machine during the nationwide revolutionary Terror which ended in 1794 when its instigator Robespierre's own head fell beneath its blade. The death heads in the Chamber of Horrors are just six from those thousands which rolled throughout France from Dr Guillotin's invention which, horrible though it seems, was indeed comparatively humane.

In January 1793 King Louis XVI was informed of the death sentence passed on him by a majority of five in the National Convention (formerly known as the National Assembly). Marie Grosholtz had come into contact with the King personally when she was attached to Princess Elizabeth's household and he had always treated her with informal kindness. On that January day when the King was taken from his prison in the Temple to the guillotine set up in the Place de la République (now the Place de la Concorde) Curtius' *Salon de Cire* was closed and shuttered as were all places of entertainment, shops, and windows of private houses in central Paris. Curtius, as captain of a company of the National Guard, must have been stationed somewhere along the route. The journey took one hour and a half, a silent procession of some thousands of men armed with guns and pikes following the carriage in which Louis XVI rode through mist and rain, the silence only broken by the rolling of drums.

After the execution performed by Charles-Henri Sanson, whose co-operation had for the past ten years enabled Curtius to keep his *Caverne des Grands Voleurs* supplied with 'subjects', the King's head and body were taken to the Madeleine cemetery. Marie took a death mask of the guillotined head 'by order of the National Assembly'. It is not known where she took it, nor if she took it alone or assisting Curtius, but it is certain that if the revolutionary Government wanted a death mask of King Louis XVI, Curtius, who for years had been modelling the heads of executed criminals, would be the obvious choice for the job; or if he were unable to carry out the task on account of his duties with the National Guard, then Marie, who had been home and working with her 'uncle' in the exhibition for the past four years, was a fully competent substitute. Even if the National Convention did not give the order, and it was Curtius who wanted to acquire the death mask, his connection with Sanson of many years standing would have made the necessary arrangements an easy business.

There are many well-authenticated stories of people who had none of Curtius' connections being able to retrieve relics of relatives who had died on the scaffold by paying the attendants at the cemetery. A Government order, however, seems the more likely for we know that Curtius did not immediately put the King's head on display as was his usual practice. A month later he was castigated by the violently revolutionary journalist Prudhomme for *not* showing the execution of Louis XVI in his *Caverne*. Instead he was giving pride of place to a wax model of the body of an assassinated deputy, Lepelletier, who had voted for the death of the King. This regicide had been struck down while at dinner in a restaurant by the hand of a former royal guardsman named Paris who had made good his escape. The journalist Prudhomme mentions the substantial number of *écus* Curtius had garnered by showing such criminals as the murderer Desrues and his wife, effigies still evidently on display in the *Caverne*. 'Why does Curtius not show the criminal King?' raged Prudhomme.

In July of the same year Marie modelled her most famous revolutionary figure, that of the assassinated Marat, killed while writing in his bath in which he sat to relieve the irritation of his chronic skin disease. He was stabbed by Charlotte Corday, an idealistic young woman from Caen who believed Marat to be responsible for the September Massacres and the plight of France. She was twenty-five and fully aware of the penalty she would pay for killing the man she regarded as a dangerous tyrant.

Directly the National Convention heard of Marat's death an order was sent to Marie Grosholtz to take a mask from his face. She did so while he still lay in his bath. Charlotte Corday went to the guillotine as she had expected. Marie visited her in prison where she spent her last brief hours, and later at the Madeleine cemetery made a mask from her decapitated head.

The defunct Marat became a cult immediately. Curtius exhibited the wax cast of his dead face in a tableau depicting the assassination. Again crowds fought to get in as they had done when the *Caverne des Grands Voleurs* was first opened, Robespierre amongst them. As he left, Robespierre paused to harangue the people standing on the steps of the exhibition as he spoke. Curtius took twenty-five livres a day, so anxious were Parisians to look on Marat's hideous dead features. Madame Tussaud brought the moulds of both Marat and Charlotte Corday with her to England and today Marat is still a focus of attention in the Chamber of Horrors.

As the Revolution ran its course and Robespierre, who believed that an organized and controlled Terror was the only way to prevent periodic bloody killings like the September Massacres, rose to power, the heads of his enemies began to roll. Marie's next gruesome task was to take a death mask from the head of Queen Marie Antoinette whose path she had so often crossed at Versailles. On 16 October 1793 the tumbril bearing the now grey-haired and emaciated but still proud Queen made its way to the guillotine. Again crowds lined the route and the National Guard was out. The National Convention gave the order for a death mask to be taken and Marie performed the work as before.

In December of the same year Curtius himself modelled a guillotined head of particular interest to the population of Paris. Madame du Barry, last mistress of old King Louis XV, met her death on 16 December. She had been able to pay several visits to England during the Revolution thanks to her popularity with the tenants on her estate at Louveciennes where she was regarded as a kind and generous lady. In 1793 she was engaged in a London lawsuit connected with jewels which had been stolen from her house in Paris, when she heard that she had been denounced in France by a man she did not know and indeed had never seen, who had arrived on her Louveciennes

The guillotined heads of Marie Antoinette and Louis XVI modelled by Madame Tussaud in 1793 shortly after each of their deaths.

estate. Government seals were put on her château and she was posted as an emigrée. Fearing confiscation of her property she returned to Paris against all advice. Her trial and condemnation followed. Almost to the last she could not believe her fate and her piteous screams on the scaffold disturbed the waiting crowd which was accustomed to victims of the guillotine meeting their end with stoicism.

There are several accounts of Curtius' visit to the Madeleine cemetery in the chill December dusk where he awaited the arrival of the carts with the bodies. Sorting out the head he needed with practised fingers he smoothed out the distortion of the still beautiful face of Madame du Barry, oiled the features, and applied the plaster mask before the head was tossed to join the others in the common grave. Soon the wax likeness was arousing much interest in Curtius' exhibition.

Hébert, the infamous editor of the paper *Le Père Duschene*, bitter attacker of Marie Antoinette, opposed Robespierre and was guillotined in March 1794. His death head was 'officially' modelled by Marie. He had screamed more loudly on the scaffold than the unfortunate Madame du Barry.

Marie's own head was briefly in jeopardy in the early summer of 1794 when the Terror was at its height and unsupported denunciations sent many to their doom. Marie and her mother were suddenly arrested on a charge of Royalist sympathies. She never knew who denounced her, but believed it was a man who worked in the small theatres of the Boulevard du Temple. He made a living by amusing people during intervals in the performances. He came on stage and pulled grotesque faces and was known as 'le grimaçier'.

Curtius was away in the Rhineland on a mission for the Government and unable to protect his family. Marie and her mother were thrown into prison but saved, as were so many others, by the fall of Robespierre. She was released in time to take a death mask of Robespierre after his execution.

Curtius was still away in the Rhineland when Robespierre fell from power because the people of France had grown sick of the Terror. Robespierre and four supporters were indicted and led

The exact replica of the guillotine with victim and executioner in the Chamber of Horrors today with three of the death heads, Fouquier-Tinville, Robespierre and Hébert, modelled by Madame Tussaud shortly after death in the background.

away to confinement, Robespierre finally arriving at the former Hôtel de Ville. About two o'clock on 27 July 1794 an armed force led by one of Robespierre's opponents entered this building. There was a fracas. Robespierre was either shot or shot himself. He did not die but his jaw was shattered. The next day Robespierre, the instigator of the Terror, himself mounted the guillotine, his wounded jaw bandaged. He uttered a piercing scream as executioner Sanson tore away the dressing. Twenty-five of his followers were also guillotined after him. Robespierre's remains were taken as usual to the Madeleine cemetery, where Marie, under orders as before, took a mask from the head with its shattered jaw—a mould of which she brought with her to London later on.

A few months later Marie had to meet and overcome an immense personal loss. Philippe Curtius died in October 1794 at the comparatively early age of fifty-seven. He had been ill for some months. Marie believed he had been poisoned during his Rhineland mission, a contention which is possible though there is no evidence to support it. A man like Curtius, while skilfully keeping on the right side of those who successively held power, cannot have failed to make enemies. He left Marie Grosholtz as his sole inheritor. In his will, made in the August before his death, he referred to her simply as 'my pupil in my art'.

She continued to run the exhibition on the lines she knew so well, and which had proved so popular during thirty years of political and social change. We do not know whether she continued to model ordinary executed criminals when the Terror had ceased its bloodshed. Marie did, however, have two more guillotined political heads in her hands.

Carrier, a Commissioner of the Terror in the provinces, responsible for mass drownings in the Loire at Nantes in 1793, met his end on the guillotine in 1794, and again the official order to take a mask was sent to Marie. The last of these death masks that she took was on 7 May 1795, when the anti-Terror swing of public opinion brought Fouquier-Tinville, former dreaded Public Prosecutor, to the guillotine. This man smiled as he regarded the crowd though he was seen to tremble.

In September 1795 Marie Grosholtz married. Her husband was François Tussaud, a civil engineer eight years younger than herself. It was not a satisfactory marriage. François proved irresponsible with money and in addition to financial difficulties Marie had to keep up the popularity of the *Salon de Cire* in a much-changed post-revolutionary world. She also bore three children, a daughter who died in infancy and two sons, Joseph and Francis born in 1798 and 1800 respectively, an added responsibility which, with a feckless husband and ageing mother, she had to cope with single-handed. In spite of pursuing Curtius' tried policy and modelling from life political and other notabilities of the day including Napoleon as First Consul in 1801, Marie realized that the popularity of the *Salon de Cire* was on the decline. There is no mention of the *Caverne des Grands Voleurs*. After the executions of the Revolution the appeal of portraits of those 'whom justice had despatched', once so strong a crowd-puller, had no doubt lost much of its fascination for the time being.

In 1802 an unexpected opportunity presented itself. During the Terror, Curtius had saved the life of a showman friend called Philipstal by intervening with Robespierre when Philipstal was arrested, accused of Royalist sympathies. Now he was presenting a kind of magic lantern show called the Phantasmagoria, and in 1801 had a successful season at the Lyceum Theatre in London.

He decided to embark on another London season, and subsequently to take his show to Scotland and Ireland. He invited Madame Tussaud to join him as partner with her *Salon de Cire*. The prospect of finding an entirely new public in England was attractive, and she signed an agreement which she realized too late was heavily loaded in Philipstal's favour, giving him an unfairly large share of profits and control.

[2]

Madame Tussaud's Travelling Years

When she decided to recoup her fortunes by bringing her exhibition to London, Madame Tussaud did not forget that the *Caverne des Grands Voleurs* had brought the crowds flocking during Curtius' lifetime. Ordinary French criminals meant nothing in the British Isles but, in spite of the ten years which had elapsed since Louis XVI had lost his head, the Revolution and its victims were still fresh in the public mind in England. She carefully chose those death-head moulds most likely to fascinate the new public she sought.

She selected Marat, Hébert, Robespierre, Carrier and Fouquier-Tinville to form the nucleus of a 'Separate Room' if people proved to be interested in seeing them. She included the death heads of the King and Queen of France too, though it would be in bad taste to exhibit these when the royal family of France were in exile, and they would not be put on show for many years to come. She also picked out the portrait of the emaciated Comte de Lorge, victim of the Bastille.

Other items that she planned to introduce to her new public were two models of the Bastille, one showing the fortress in its entire state, the other showing it being pulled down stone by stone by the people of Paris, also a model of the guillotine to the scale of three inches to the square foot 'accurately measured from that by which many thousand celebrated characters suffered in the Place de Grève'. She also included Curtius' Egyptian mummy and its case together with 'a vast number of other curiosities fully specified in the handbills', one of which was the bloodstained shirt of Henry IV. It was her long experience of how people would gaze fascinated at the horrible which influenced her decision to take all these macabre exhibits, a decision that led finally to the famous Chamber of Horrors.

The moulds and wax casts of the guillotined heads were carefully packed amongst the other moulds, casts, leather straw-stuffed bodies and carved wooden arms and legs that Madame Tussaud brought to London for the launching of her exhibition at the Lyceum Theatre. She set off for London taking her four-year-old son Joseph with her but leaving two-year-old baby Francis with her mother and husband in Paris. The more curious items passed through the ports of exit and entry with the rest and excited no comment during transit. Fanny Burney (Madame d'Arblay), who visited France after the Treaty of Amiens was signed in 1802, remarks in her diary on the indifference of customs officers on both sides of the Channel. Madame Tussaud had taken good care that her documents were in order. As an alien she now had to show her certificate of origin to the chief magistrate of any town she visited.

Madame Tussaud's exhibition at the Lyceum Theatre in London was a success. She had superior talents, was French and had been connected with the Court of Versailles and the French Revolution, and experienced the early successes of the rising star Napoleon Bonaparte, all of which helped her to compete with other well-known and competent wax-modellers who showed in England. But none, not even Mrs Salmon's famous wax works in Fleet Street, nor Mrs Bullock's 'Beautiful Cabinet of Wax Figures', offered anything to compare with Madame Tussaud's exceptional examples which combined the historic and the horrible in so striking a manner.

It was the 'death heads', models and historic relics that gave Madame Tussaud's exhibition at the Lyceum Theatre its unique flavour. She never showed freaks of nature or anatomical specimens such as one might observe in fairgrounds and other shows. Her separate collection which developed into the Chamber of Horrors was always based like the *Caverne des Grands Voleurs* on real malefactors and relics which had historic as well as gruesome impact.

It was on account of this special aspect of her exhibition that Madame Tussaud was asked when she had only been at the Lyceum Theatre a couple of months or so to model another decapitated head, a commission which must have convinced her she had been right in bringing a selection from her 'uncle's' *Caverne* to London. It was the head of no ordinary criminal that she was asked to model, although, before the much-publicized trial and condemnation to death of the gentleman in question, few members of the public and certainly not Madame Tussaud had heard of him or his tragic story.

Colonel Edward Marcus Despard came of a good Irish family. He joined the army at the age of sixteen and became an honoured and respected officer. During service in Jamaica he met and served under Nelson accompanying him on various military expeditions into Nicaragua during the American War of Independence which ended with the Peace of Paris signed in 1783.

In 1784 Despard was appointed Superintendent of His Majesty's affairs in Honduras. He settled there with his negro mistress, who was known as Mrs Despard and became accepted as his common-law wife. She had a son regarded and brought up by Despard as his own.

Friction arose between British logwood cutters already established in Honduras and new settlers who arrived in much larger numbers to cut the timber. Boundary disputes flared up, and Despard was accused by the early settlers of favouring the newcomers.

In 1790 Despard was recalled to London and officially absolved of any blame for the settlers' disputes in Honduras but told that the post of Superintendent that he had held was now abolished. In spite of his record of honourable service he was offered neither compensation nor a new post.

As the years went by Despard became an embittered man and his protests against his treatment by the Government were

A sketch taken at the trial of Colonel Despard, the traitor whose decapitated head Madame Tussaud was asked to model in London in 1803.

increasingly loud and violent. In spite of the support of friends and of the reforming Member of Parliament, Sir Francis Burdett (modelled from life by Madame Tussaud for the Lyceum exhibition), Despard could not gain a hearing. Such were his outbursts that he was imprisoned several times for short periods. His name was associated with that of Wolf Tone the

Irish rebel and with an Irish priest who was caught carrying a document advising the French how to act politically after a successful invasion.

In 1800 Despard began actually plotting with low-class soldiers and labourers against the British Government. This culminated in an insane scheme to seize the Tower of London and the Bank of England and to assassinate King George III.

Despard, some of whose plottings were already known, was 'shopped' on his final desperate scheme by a soldier who had been recruited to the cause but had no intention of being involved in trouble. Despard was arrested with about forty labouring men and soldiers when they were meeting at the Oakley Arms, a pub in Lambeth, in December 1802.

The one-time Colonel and fine officer was brought to trial on 8 and 9 February 1803 at the Sessions House at the New Gaol in Horsemonger Lane, Newington. The trial aroused great public interest. Madame Tussaud was well established at the Lyceum Theatre and although her English was still deficient its repercussions could not have escaped her ever-alert attention.

Despard's friends and Mrs Despard, all of whom believed he had become deranged through bitterness and frustration, made every effort to save him. Admiral Lord Nelson was called on for help and appeared in person at the trial and as hero of the Battle of Copenhagen this made news. He testified to the bravery and loyalty of the man he had got to know well twenty-four years ago, but had not seen since those Nicaragua days (as prosecution lawyers pointed out). Nelson's testimony was to no avail. Colonel Despard was found guilty of high treason. The jury recommended mercy on account of Despard's former good character, but he was sentenced to be hanged, drawn and quartered and beheaded: a savage sentence which when she heard of it must have carried Madame Tussaud back to the medieval-style cruelties in the Place de Grève.

The trial and sentence made Colonel Despard famous. He who for thirteen years could never get a hearing for his grievances was now talked about everywhere. He petitioned for a pardon which was not granted. On Saturday, 19 February 1803, warrants for the execution of Despard and six of his associates were delivered at Horsemonger Gaol.

Two small mercies were permitted to them all. King George III remitted the disembowelling and quartering. The prisoners would be hanged and then beheaded. Their bodies need not lie in a felon's grave. Despard's common-law wife, who was overwhelmed with grief, would be allowed to take away his remains for burial where she pleased and a like privilege was granted to relatives of the others.

Huge crowds assembled at Horsemonger Lane where the scaffold had been set up on the flat roof over the entrance lodge of the prison. The *Gentleman's Magazine* reported that all parts that had a view of the scaffold were completely jammed. 20,000 people were estimated to be present. Detachments of military were deployed to control any disturbance but the crowds were orderly and quiet.

Colonel Despard and his six fellow-conspirators were dragged across the prison courtyard on a hurdle, a low cart with the wheels removed in which trusses of clean straw were laid. It was drawn by two horses. Despard behaved with great calmness and composure. He expressed astonishment at the size of the crowd and was allowed to deliver a lengthy address which was received by most of those who could hear it with silence though there were a few scattered handclaps.

The crowd stood with heads bared while the executioner performed his work, and the seven bodies were left hanging on the scaffold for about half an hour. Then they were carried behind the scaffold and the beheading carried out with an axe. The crowd gave a gasp of horror when the executioner stepped forward and held up Despard's head shouting 'Behold the head of a traitor, Edward Marcus Despard!' Flimsy coffins had been prepared in which the bodies were placed. The six fellow-conspirators were taken for burial in one grave in the vault of a chapel in London Road, St George's Field, but Mrs Despard and her friends had arranged for Despard's remains to be removed to an undertaker's premises in Mount Street, Lambeth. She was awaiting the arrival of her son from France.

We can only speculate whether Madame Tussaud's services had already been retained, or whether the idea occurred to the grieving widow and Despard's supporters during this waiting period. Madame Tussaud did not, as she had been accustomed to in Paris, take the death mask immediately after the execution but at the undertaker's premises.

Sir Francis Burdett made the arrangements for an impressive funeral. It was on Tuesday, 1 March, that the crowds again assembled to watch the funeral procession. Madame Tussaud quietly gathered up her tools and materials and made her way across the river to Lambeth. *The Times* made a full report on the funeral and noted that 'an artist it is said took a cast of Mr Despard's face a few moments before the lid of the coffin was screwed down'. Madame Tussaud's practised fingers only required a few moments and then she left the undertaker's premises and slipped discreetly back to the Strand. It was very like her unobtrusive visits to the Madeleine cemetery a decade earlier.

Colonel Despard made his last journey across Blackfriars Bridge in a cortège surrounded by constables which passed between silent crowds who watched as it wended its way to St Paul's Cathedral. The hearse was drawn by four horses and followed by three mourning coaches each containing four gentlemen. Sir Francis Burdett had arranged for Despard to be interred in part of the burial ground of the ancient medieval church of St Faith's, long demolished, which was included in the Cathedral's precincts. Edward Marcus Despard, spared a felon's grave by the King's mercy, was interred in a grave fourteen feet deep in the shadow of the great walls. Here, deep down and forgotten, still lie the bones and skull of the last decapitated head modelled by Madame Tussaud's fingers.

Colonel Despard remained in wax effigy in Madame Tussaud's exhibition for many years to come. He joined Marat and the guillotined heads. Curious crowds showed how right Madame Tussaud had been to perpetuate her 'uncle's' *Caverne des Grands Voleurs*. Henceforward, she would always have a separate section—the public wanted it.

In April 1803 Madame Tussaud closed her exhibition at the Lyceum Theatre and in accordance with the plans of her partner Philipstal she took ship with her crates of portrait figures and their accessories, the relics, and all the paraphernalia of the exhibition, and sailed for Edinburgh. In spite of the long journey and unknown Scotland which lay ahead, Madame Tussaud was not unwilling to quit London and depart to the North. The Treaty of Amiens signed in March 1802 and always fragile was obviously about to collapse (it ended on 17 May 1803). She was an alien, a Frenchwoman, and with England at war with Napoleon, Scotland was a safer haven for her than the invasion-vulnerable south of England.

After a stormy and alarming journey she was fortunate in finding large and suitable premises in Edinburgh and lost no time in setting up the exhibition with its splendid *coup d'oeil*—a brilliant vista lit by scores of candles—and the separate section. This contained those French Revolution items she had already displayed in London and her portrait of the decapitated Colonel Despard. Her advertisements made it clear that the latter had been modelled in London from the head and 'by request'. She also advertised her willingness to make portraits from life of any visitors who fancied their likeness in wax, and in addition she announced 'the artist can model from the dead body as well as from animated nature'—a fact made obvious by the exhibits in what she began to call her 'Second Salon' when she reached Glasgow after a highly successful Edinburgh season.

Madame Tussaud stayed in Scotland until February 1804 and though execution of criminals must have taken place in both Edinburgh and Glasgow during the period none attracted the attention of her skilful fingers. It is significant that *The Hangman's Record* (published 1907), which lists all the principal executions throughout the British Isles with details of the more sensational items since the late seventeenth century, found nothing worth recording for Scotland during the months of Madame Tussaud's stay.

She was not interested (nor had Curtius been interested) in taking the likenesses of executed criminals just in order to introduce horror for horror's sake. Madame Tussaud was essentially a journalist in wax and she liked to point a historical or moral lesson too. Only when there was genuine public interest did Madame Tussaud model for the Second Salon.

After Edinburgh and Glasgow, Philipstal instructed Madame Tussaud to follow him to Dublin where he was introducing his Phantasmagoria. She was reluctant to take this step fearing another sea journey and the inclement climate she felt she would meet in Ireland. However, she had no choice and in February 1804 she and her small son, Joseph, landed in Dublin. She was to spend four successful years in Ireland showing in Waterford, Kilkenny, Cork, Belfast and many smaller garrison towns as well as the capital. The British troops stationed there in large numbers and the Irish people themselves were equally eager for entertainment in a period of comparative political and economic calm after long experience of active rebellion, turmoil and poor potato harvests.

The exhibits in Madame Tussaud's 'Second Division' (as she named it in her Irish advertisements) were the same as those she had shown in Scotland with the exception of the head of Colonel Despard. He remained packed away in concealment. The political climate might be quieter but it was still extremely sensitive. Eight men had been executed for treason in Dublin the previous September. The unfortunate Colonel had met his fate on account of conspiracy against the King and Government of England and his trial had indicated earlier association with Wolf Tone the Irish rebel and others active against England. No one could appreciate better than Madame Tussaud, seasoned as she was by her experiences in the French Revolution, what potential trouble could arise if she displayed the executed Colonel Despard to the British soldiery and the Irish population.

During her four years in Ireland Madame Tussaud modelled a number of prominent Irishmen such as Henry Grattan the statesman, but she did not add to her Second Division. She wrote to her family in Paris that people flocked to the exhibition to see 'the famous and infamous', but the infamous were confined to portraits that were now of historical rather than contemporary interest.

Madame Tussaud's success in Dublin following her satisfactory months in Edinburgh and Glasgow enabled her to buy out her partner Philipstal in 1804. Ever since Madame Tussaud's arrival in London there had been bitter disputes between them over money. The ill feeling was not eased when Madame Tussaud's wax figures proved to be more popular with the public than Philipstal's Phantasmagoria, which does not appear to have made any impact on Dublin. It had taken two years for Madame Tussaud to find enough money to pay off her partner. Possibly he was glad to take the money, be rid of this woman who was always demanding her fair share of the money she brought in, and make his return to the Continent.

From now on, as Madame Tussaud wrote to her family, she worked entirely for herself and her children. Having gained freedom to run her business as she wished and for her own profit, she took another fateful decision. She would not return to her husband in Paris but would remain and make her own way henceforward, with only her small son Joseph for company and assistance. 'We can each go our own way', she wrote to François Tussaud at 20 Boulevard du Temple.

Madame Tussaud never gave any indication of what brought her to this final and as it proved irrevocable decision to leave her irresponsible husband, split from the family in Paris that she undoubtedly loved and remained devoted to, especially her younger son Francis, now four years old.

'If only I had my darling Françison with me I could ask for nothing more', she wrote in the same letter that gave her husband his *congé*, while urging him to look after her mother.

However, make the crucial break she did, and henceforward managed her exhibition single-handed until Joseph was old enough to give really effective help. Her policies remained firmly based on the precepts of her 'uncle' Curtius which were reinforced by her own touring experience. The exhibition would always be presented with the maximum splendour; it would provide education as well as entertainment; it would always be kept updated; and it would always include a section that would appeal to and satisfy the eternal craving of the public for something macabre, for the shudder of terror. Though here too she would keep her standards and never sink into sensationalism.

While retaining Curtius' policies Madame Tussaud took another important decision. When she arrived in Belfast in May 1808 she no longer advertised the exhibition under the name of 'The Great Curtius of Paris' while she remained anonymous mentioned only as 'the artist'. She now appeared as:

MADAME TUSSAUD

ARTIST OF THE GREAT EUROPEAN

CABINET OF FIGURES

MODELLED FROM LIFE

By the end of July 1808 Madame Tussaud was back on Scottish soil and opened her exhibition at the Masons' Hall, Greenock, where she had made a brief appearance a few years earlier before sailing for Dublin. In what had now become the 'Separate Room' she had still, in spite of the rigours of touring in Ireland, all the exhibits she had brought from France and the portrait of Colonel Despard which she could display again. This would remain on show for a further ten years before public interest in the traitor finally faded. Colonel Despard had his last entry in the catalogue of 1818.

After spending a successful month in Greenock Madame Tussaud announced in the press that she was leaving for London. In fact she embarked on what proved to be a twenty-seven year marathon of touring England and Scotland. At the beginning general conditions were far from easy for her. She and her little son were aliens and England and France were still at war. However, since her arrival in London six years earlier

Madame Tussaud had steadily built up her image as a French Royalist emigrée, an image that was reinforced by the more gruesome revolutionary items in her exhibition as well as the elegant French portrait figures that dated back to her Versailles days.

Travelling was difficult enough in itself at the beginning of the nineteenth century. A contemporary writer described the highways over which her fragile figures had to be jolted as 'at once loose, rough and perishable; expensive and rough to travel on'. At this time the work of the great road-builders Telford and MacAdam had not yet improved road surfaces. In spite of the hazards of these roads Madame Tussaud was now experienced in the mechanics of touring and never stayed long enough in one place to exhaust local interest, nor did she make too frequent visits to larger towns and cities. But experience could not eliminate, though it might ease, the heavy load of taking down and putting up the exhibition, fitting the figures, the settings, the clothes, all the impedimenta into closed wagons, repairing breakages at every stop, modelling new heads, making new clothes for the figures. Strong though she was in body and character Madame Tussaud's stamina was tested to the utmost point. She might hire help as she went along, but her only real support was her little son Joseph, who to the extent of his growing strength and ability worked alongside his mother.

Madame Tussaud had the journalist's flair for what is news and her exhibition was indeed a travelling newspaper in many parts of the country where people seldom saw any kind of journal. Where there was a local press there were few illustrations. News circulated, but often by word of mouth. People heard famous names but had no idea what their bearers looked like. When Madame Tussaud's exhibition arrived they could not only see but could inspect them closely. Posters, handbills, catalogues to inform and educate were a vital adjunct to the exhibition, and Madame Tussaud never failed to have them well set out and ready.

Being thus constantly on the move, criss-crossing the country, it was virtually impossible for Madame Tussaud to update the Separate Room. When famous and upright 'subjects' were concerned she could arrange for a sitting or observation from life, and travel to get it at a suitable time. For example the Prince Regent was 'taken' in 1812, Napoleon on the 'Bellerophon' in 1815, Alexander I of Russia in London in 1814. Sometimes it was possible to approach a celebrity locally. One such was Dr Soloman whose remedy for a multitude of ills, Balm of Gilead, was a household word. She took the Doctor's likeness from life at his home when she was on her first visit to Liverpool, in 1813. If these methods proved impossible there were busts and portraits to which she could gain access for the likeness.

On the other hand condemned criminals could only be *accurately* modelled if she could observe them closely as they stood public trial or, as in the case of Colonel Despard, take a mask from their features after death. Madame Tussaud never permitted imaginary portraits or portraits based on insufficient data to appear in the exhibition.

Trials and executions took place in many gaols in different counties. It was impossible for her to leave her work in order to pursue the likenesses of condemned criminals all over the country. It was very different from the time when Curtius had opened his *Caverne* in Paris where the Place de Grève, principal place of execution, was literally almost round the corner and contacts with gaolers and executioners were easily made and cemented.

During twelve years following her departure from Ireland Madame Tussaud was unable to make any additions to her Separate Room. It was a frustrating situation. There were executions for almost every imaginable crime—murder for gain, jealousy, revenge or illicit passion; child-killing; arson; poisoning horses; robbery; rape; unnatural acts; sacrilege; forgery; fraud.

Even a crime such as stealing a sheep carried the death penalty and hangmen were kept busy the length and breadth of the British Isles. Yet Madame Tussaud was unable to obtain likenesses of any criminals whose misdeeds attracted general interest, no matter how much her public would have liked to see such portraits.

There were many felons suitable for the Separate Room who could provide a moral or social lesson as well as an appeal to people's craving for the macabre. For example there was Mary Bates executed in York in March 1809 (Madame Tussaud was in London) for poisoning and fraud. Described in *The Hangman's Record* as 'one of those despicable hags called fortune-tellers', the woman also dispensed nostrums to unfortunate young women to procure abortions. She dispensed a few nostrums too many and went to the gallows.

Social history would have been recorded in the Separate Room in 1813 when nine Luddites were hanged, also at York, for rioting—they were unfortunate men who misguidedly believed that by smashing the newfangled machines of the expanding industrial revolution they could preserve their livelihood. In the same year there was a spectacular mail robbery when the Leeds mail coach was halted and plundered by three men, one already known as an expert cracksman. All three were hanged. In 1817 three pirates met their doom at Execution Dock on the Thames, and their bodies were hanged in chains on the Isle of Dogs. Their bodies were allowed to hang until five tides had overflowed them.

Always there was public curiosity to know what notorious criminals looked like, but Madame Tussaud could not satisfy it. Nonetheless with her customary tenacity and her journalist's awareness of people's tastes she held on firmly, using what she had, to the original concept of the *Caverne des Grands Voleurs* as a separate exhibition that would arouse shock and horror yet retain educational overtones.

Wherever she went, Edinburgh, Newcastle, Hull, Cambridge and dozens of other towns and cities, her posters gave liberal space to the 'Remarkable Characters—Objects' and the 'curios and interesting relics' that comprised this special group. Indeed as the years went by Madame Tussaud seemed to lay more and more emphasis on this aspect of the exhibition as evidenced by her handbills and posters. In her catalogues a special extra page was allocated to introduce the Separate Room.

> The following highly interesting FIGURES AND OBJECTS in consequence of the peculiarity of their appearance are placed in an ADJOINING ROOM and form a SEPARATE EXHIBITION well worthy of the inspection of artists and amateurs.
> Admission to the above 6d.

Full details were given on subsequent pages.

Mere sensation-seekers got no encouragement to enter, but occasional anecdotes 'leaked' to the press stimulated interest in the Adjoining Room. In 1819 when Madame Tussaud was touring East Anglia it was reported that a Lincoln man had ordered a small replica to be made of her model guillotine (this replica was, it was said, constructed by Madame Tussaud's own carpenter). The gentleman concerned made his unfortunate servant experiment with it, who, as a result, had a forefinger chopped off.

In the summer of 1820 Madame Tussaud was established in the Saloon of the Music Hall at Leeds. She had not been there since 1812 and was having particular success with background music which enhanced the vista and grouping and the promenade concerts which took place very evening as visitors wandered among the figures.

It was here that she dramatically introduced the first 'new blood' since Colonel Despard into the Separate Room. In June 1820 she advertised in the *Leeds Intelligencer*:

EXHIBITION

Saloon, Music Hall, Leeds

By Particular Desire

NEW ADDITION

'Madame Tussaud, Artist, has the honour most respectfully to inform her numerous friends and the Public of Leeds and its vicinity that at the particular request of several families of Distinction she will continue her splendid Exhibition THREE DAYS LONGER, Monday, Tuesday and Wednesday, 12th, 13th, 14th instant upon which will be exhibited a likeness of the celebrated notorious ARTHUR THISTLEWOOD taken from life.'

The notorious Cato Street Conspirator Thistlewood was, like Colonel Despard, a traitor. To obtain this likeness Madame Tussaud had to travel from Wakefield in Yorkshire, where her exhibition was located in April, to Newgate Prison in London. She performed her task between Thistlewood's conviction and sentence to be hanged which took place on 12 April and the execution which was carried out on 1 May. Arthur Thistlewood died with fourteen fellow-conspirators and, while he was publicly decapitated after hanging, he was spared the gruesome quartering which was part of a traitor's fate unless the King granted remission. Unlike Colonel Despard, Thistlewood was buried in a felon's grave in the precincts of Newgate.

Arthur Thistlewood had started his life quietly enough as the son (said to be illegitimate) of a Lincolnshire farmer who had the boy trained as a land-surveyor. The young man was politically-minded and a reader. In the opinion of neighbours his mind became unsettled by reading the works of Thomas Paine, whose *The Rights of Man* was adopted, by those in England who sympathized with the French Revolution, as a manifesto.

Thistlewood, an extremist, was obsessed with revolutionary zeal. He went to France and after the fall of Robespierre returned to England firmly convinced that the first duty of a patriot was to massacre the Government and overturn all existing institutions.

From this time onwards Thistlewood was continually involved in and organizing revolutionary plots against the King and Government and was constantly watched by the authorities. In December 1816, when Madame Tussaud was in London, showing at the Magnificent Mercatura in St James's, Thistlewood and his colleagues, determined to inaugurate revolution in England, organized a great public meeting at Spa Fields in London. It must have seemed to Madame Tussaud that the clock was turning backwards. However, this was England not France and the meeting was dispersed and broken-up quite peacefully. Warrants were issued for the arrest of Thistlewood and his principal co-revolutionary James Watson who escaped to America.

Though brought to trial Thistlewood was let off this time but he continued his plottings. These culminated in a scheme to assassinate the Prime Minister and other ministers at a Cabinet dinner and take over the government of the country himself. During January and February 1820 a store of arms, bombs and hand grenades was accumulated by Thistlewood and his followers in a loft over stables in Cato Street. What came to be known as 'The Cato Street Conspiracy' was hatched but the authorities were watchful. On 23 February the conspirators were apprehended in the very act of arming themselves at Cato Street for a murderous assault on Lord Harroby's house where the Prime Minister and Cabinet were dining. In the mêlée that followed Thistlewood added to his crime by killing a police officer with his sword. His trial took three days and aroused intense public interest. Condemnation as a traitor was inevitable.

When Madame Tussaud entered the condemned cell she saw a tall man of military appearance. She spread her plaster over a long sallow face and noted the dark hair and hazel eyes with arched eyebrows. It was over a month before the portrait of traitor Arthur Thistlewood joined that of traitor Despard in the Separate Room in the Music Hall, Leeds. However public interest in the Cato Street Conspiracy soon waned. George III had died on 29 January 1820 and the new King George IV, in the throes of pressing for divorce from his estranged wife Queen Caroline, was the centre of interest.

Madame Tussaud never retained portraits that no longer attracted public attention and a surviving catalogue of 1822 printed in Manchester makes no mention of Thistlewood or Despard. The death heads and Marat and the 'relics and curiosities' still stimulated people to spend an extra sixpence. Mirabeau, a likeness which had been taken from his face shortly before he died a natural death in 1791, was moved in to join the other French revolutionaries and there was also a portrait figure of the assassin Ravaillac to accompany the bloodstained shirt of Henry IV of France.

For the next thirteen years Madame Tussaud continued her relentless touring, suffering shipwreck when she attempted to take her exhibition to Dublin again for the King's state visit in 1822. Fortunately her store of moulds had been left in Liverpool and she did not take the occupants of the Separate Room with her for this joyful occasion, so they all survived. In the same year she welcomed her son Francis, now twenty-two, who came to England to join her and work in the exhibition with Joseph until his death.

Space was an ever-recurring problem for the Separate Room, but Madame Tussaud always managed to find it. In 1823 when she hired the Town Hall in Coventry and stayed for about three months she used the Mayoress's parlour for the purpose. It was reported when she showed at the Minor Theatre, Hull, in 1825 that owing to lack of space 'Figures and objects' could only be placed in an adjoining situation.

Madame Tussaud was in Scotland showing at the Old Assembly Rooms, Dumfries, in April 1828 when in distant Suffolk the murdered body of Maria Marten was dug up in the Red Barn (it had a red-tiled roof) at Polstead near Bury St Edmunds. Madame Tussaud knew Bury St Edmunds for she had taken her exhibition there in 1818 and 1825.

Basically it was an ordinary enough murder—a man growing tired of a young mistress importuning for marriage though not at all what he wanted for a wife, and ridding himself of her by killing in the hope that he could safely conceal his crime. However, there proved to be some unusual circumstances about the case and it aroused unprecedented public interest. It was not a crime that Madame Tussaud could afford to ignore during the three months that elapsed before the trial while she worked her way slowly southward by way of Carlisle and Penrith.

When Maria Marten's body was dug up from the earth floor of the Red Barn, William Corder, a prosperous young man from the Polstead neighbourhood, was swiftly arrested and charged with murder. He had promised marriage to Maria, daughter of a farm labourer, under pressure after the birth of a child. She was twenty-five years old. Nearly a year before her body was found, Corder had told Maria to meet him at the Red Barn, which was situated on his land, from where they would proceed to Ipswich and be married the next day. Maria, who in spite of her liaison with Corder, had continued to live with her parents, was not seen again after she left her home to keep the tryst.

Corder soon wrote to Maria's parents to say that in the end they had been married in London and that she was now living happily as a married woman in the Isle of Wight. As weeks and months passed the parents became suspicious as they had had no communication from their daughter herself. Moreover, it was later disclosed, Mrs Marten had repeated vivid dreams that her daughter's body lay buried in the Red Barn, a supernatural experience that was to catch people's imagination. It was at Mrs Marten's insistence that at last, in April 1828, her dreams were heeded and investigations started. Maria's body was found in the Red Barn as her mother had dreamt. She had been shot through the head and stabbed through the heart.

William Corder was traced and arrested. It came to light that after Maria Marten had gone to the Red Barn *en route*, as she believed, to the promised marriage and had vanished, her lover had travelled to London. There he advertised for a wife. In the early nineteenth century spinsterhood was considered, and indeed often was, a most unenviable lot. No less than forty-five young women hopeful of improving their status by matrimony responded to Corder's advertisement. The bride he selected was a highly respectable schoolmistress and he married her without delay.

When the case came to trial William Corder pleaded not guilty to murdering Maria Marten. He claimed that Maria had committed suicide and he had buried the body in an agony of fear lest he should be accused of killing her. By now popular interest was so intense that *The Times* devoted no less than six columns to the two-day trial. Corder was found guilty and an estimated 10,000 assembled to watch his execution at Bury St Edmunds on 11 August.

This time it was not necessary for Madame Tussaud in person to obtain a likeness from Corder's face before or after his execution, nor did she pay the guinea an inch which the hangman is reputed to have charged for the rope. William Corder's body was handed over to Mr George Creed, surgeon at the hospital at Bury St Edmunds where a death mask was taken. Madame Tussaud modelled her portrait on a cast from this. Corder's wax likeness remained in the Separate Room and then the Chamber of Horrors for many years, while the story of Maria Marten's murder in the Red Barn became almost folklore. Nor did the remains of William Corder disappear entirely from view. His skeleton was preserved in the hospital and in the year of his execution the publisher Kelly produced a history of the crime and trial written by J. Curtis and bound in Corder's skin which surgeon George Creed had specially tanned for the purpose. This volume was kept at the Athenaeum, Bury St Edmunds. Corder's skeleton finally finished up in the Royal College of Surgeons in London, and the book, death mask, and part of his scalp in the Moyses Hall Museum in Bury St Edmunds.

While tanning the skin of an executed criminal for bookbinding might be considered carrying matters too far, the problems of qualified surgeons teaching anatomy in hospitals or wishing to pursue medical research in order to identify and alleviate the diseases of the human body were genuine and long-standing.

As early as 1506 the town council of Edinburgh had granted a charter to the Incorporation of Barbers and Surgeons for the supply of 'one condempnit man after he be deid to make anatomes of'. An annual one-body allocation was even then totally inadequate. As centuries passed and demand for anatomical research intensified and medical investigation opened up new areas of knowledge to be explored, the situation became acute.

In the early nineteenth century the supply of bodies for the anatomist's work and teaching was extremely limited. The majority of executed criminals were given burial, some like Colonel Despard, by relatives and friends who obtained permission, or some, like Arthur Thistlewood, in a lime-filled grave within prison precincts. Others lay in churchyards, their burial places unmarked, such as many who died on the scaffold at Tyburn and were interred in the churchyard of St Giles-in-the-Fields, the church which they passed on their way to Tyburn and where they were offered a last calming and probably soporific bowl of ale.

It was a situation of supply and demand which led to a steady increase in the gruesome practice of 'body snatching' from graveyards. The first indicted case of body snatching in London was in 1777 for the theft of a corpse from the shared churchyard of St George and St George the Martyr in Bloomsbury.

Robbing of graves developed into a profession and those who practised it for a livelihood were nicknamed 'resurrectionists'. In spite of fines, imprisonment or transportation an ever-growing demand encouraged the body snatchers to carry on their work with zeal. Even rural graveyards were not safe and often guardians were appointed by relatives or parish councils to watch over the burial places. But surgeon-anatomists had to teach and students to learn so bodies fetched good prices. Hospitals asked no questions and by the early nineteenth century body snatching had reached its zenith.

It was inevitable that this demand should encourage some men to hasten the death of poor, destitute, friendless people in order to obtain supplies for hospital dissecting rooms. Two such men were Burke and Hare who recognized the advantages of not having to violate graves. They became in 1829 perhaps the most famous ever occupants of Madame Tussaud's Chamber of Horrors and her portraits of these two atrocious murderers remain a focus of attention there today.

William Burke and William Hare were Irish labourers living

Burke and Hare, the body snatchers, modelled in 1829. Burke was executed. Hare saved his life by turning King's evidence.

ANATOMY
AND
Physiology.

DR KNOX, F.R.S.E. (*Successor to* DR BARCLAY, *Fellow of the Royal College of Surgeons and Conservator of its Museum,*) will commence his ANNUAL COURSE OF LECTURES ON THE **ANATOMY** AND **PHYSIOLOGY** of the Human Body, on Tuesday, the 4th November, at Eleven A. M. His Evening COURSE of LECTURES, on the same Subject, will commence on the 11th November, at Six P. M.

Each of these Courses will as usual comprise a full Demonstration on fresh Anatomical Subjects, of the Structure of the Human Body, and a History of the Uses of its various Parts; and the Organs and Structures generally, will be described with a constant reference to Practical Medicine and Surgery.

FEE for the First Course, £3, 5s.; Second Course, £2, 4s.; Perpetual, £5, 9s.

N. B.—*These Courses of Lectures qualify for Examination before the various Colleges and Boards.*

PRACTICAL ANATOMY
AND
OPERATIVE SURGERY.

DR KNOX'S ROOMS FOR **PRACTICAL ANATOMY** AND **OPERATIVE SURGERY,** will open on Monday, the 6th of October, and continue open until the End of July 1829.

Two DEMONSTRATIONS will be delivered daily to the Gentlemen attending the Rooms for PRACTICAL ANATOMY. These Demonstrations will be arranged so as to comprise complete Courses of the DESCRIPTIVE ANATOMY of the Human Body, with its application to PATHOLOGY and OPERATIVE SURGERY. The Dissections and Operations to be under the immediate superintendance of DR KNOX. Arrangements have been made to secure as usual an ample supply of Anatomical Subjects.

FEE for the First Course, £3, 5s.; Second Course, £2, 4s.; Perpetual, £5, 9s.

N. B.—*An Additional Fee of Three Guineas includes Subjects.*

*** *Certificates of Attendance on these Courses qualify for Examination before the Royal Colleges of Surgeons, the Army and Navy Medical Boards, &c.*

EDINBURGH, 10. SURGEONS' SQUARE,
25th September 1828.

An advertisement for Dr Knox's anatomy class

in Edinburgh in squalid lodgings run by two disreputable women with whom they associated. When another lodger, old and ill, finally died Burke and Hare put the old man's body in a sack and took it to the Edinburgh Hospital where Dr Knox, one of Edinburgh's most famous anatomists, held his classes.

Burke and Hare were well paid and decided that here was an opportunity to go into business in a regular way. However, old and ailing lodgers likely to die quickly did not occur frequently. The two men took to prowling the wynds and closes of old Edinburgh in search of feeble, friendless, destitute creatures who might be persuaded into their lodgings and, after being made insensible with drink, assisted into the next world. In the course of nine months they delivered sixteen bodies to Dr Knox's dissecting rooms.

Finally a penniless couple who were lodging with Burke and Hare became curious about the disappearance of an old woman who had participated in a drinking party the previous night. They rummaged about and found the old woman's body under a tarpaulin. Shocked and horrified, they summoned up the courage to go to the police.

William Hare and one of the women associates, Maggie Laird, decided to turn king's evidence. William Burke and the second woman, Nell MacDougal were committed for trial which was fixed for the somewhat curious date of Christmas Eve, 24 December 1828.

In the words of the *Caledonian Mercury* of 25 December 1828, 'No trial in the memory of any man now living has excited so deep, universal and (we may almost add) appalling an interest as that of Burke and his female associate.' Not only were there the horrible details of the murders but the curtain was torn from the whole problem of body snatching and the involvement in it of highly respected medical men such as Dr Knox, and the students and staff of the hospitals at which they practised and taught.

The ventilation of the situation resulted in 1832 in the passing of the Anatomy Act, which authorized those who had legal custody of a body, that is to say a relative or a public authority if no relatives could be found, to send it to a medical school so that before it was buried it could be used for the study of anatomy and the practice of surgical operations.

William Hare and the woman Maggie Laird of course went free after the trial, having turned king's evidence. Hare is thought to have died a beggar in London about 1860. As regards the accused pair, a Scottish verdict of 'not proven' was found for Nell MacDougal, but Burke was found guilty and hanged in Edinburgh on 28 January 1829 before an enormous crowd of spectators.

Madame Tussaud was exhibiting in Preston when Burke's trial began, but in the New Year she moved to Liverpool. On 16 January she announced her opening at the Pantheon, Church Street, for the following Monday. She had not been in Liverpool for eight years—it was her third visit—and she planned a stay of several months for visitors could be drawn from an extensive surrounding area. The trial and conviction of William Burke provided her with exactly the opportunity she needed to bring fresh life to the Separate Room. On Friday 13 February she made her first announcement:

NEW ADDITIONS

BURKE THE MURDERER

Exhibition, Pantheon, Church Street

'Madame Tussaud has the honour to announce she has completed the figure of Burke which she hopes will meet with the approbation of her friends and the public although the introduction of such a character to her exhibition may be considered improper by *some* yet as it is done merely in compliance with the public curiosity she trusts it will be received with satisfaction. It represents him as he appeared at his trial and the greatest attention has been paid to give as good an idea as possible of his personal *appearance*.'

Presenting this as her personal work Madame Tussaud must have travelled to Edinburgh to sit in Court herself, observing, noting, sketching, while her sons transferred the exhibition from Preston to Liverpool. The public demanded a portrait of Hare as well and for this Madame Tussaud did not go to Edinburgh herself. Hare was free and would have to be tracked down, a time-consuming operation better performed by Joseph or Francis. By March she was able to present:

NEW ADDITION

THE INFAMOUS, THE DIABOLICAL, HARE.

The Associate of the Monster Burke.

Her advertisement went on to explain, 'In consequence of numerous enquiries for a figure of the wretch HARE, she sent her Son to Edinburgh to procure a good likeness of him . . . the likeness of Hare was taken a short time previous to his leaving Edinburgh and the countenance is fully indicative of his character.'

At the same time whichever of Madame Tussaud's sons visited Edinburgh also acquired a cast taken from Burke's face three hours after execution, and this plaster bust was shown with the new figure of Hare and the figure of Burke that Madame Tussaud had herself modelled from observation during the trial.

Public interest in the Separate Room was enormously stimulated by the entry of these two criminals certainly equal in their iniquity to any that Curtius had modelled for his *Caverne des Grands Voleurs*. In the same year the attractions of the Separate Room were augmented again and this time by the appearance of the first woman criminal to find a place there since Madame Tussaud's arrival in England. On 19 August, once again in Edinburgh, a man whose real name was Bradfoot, though he called himself Stewart, was hanged with his wife for poisoning and robbing the captain of a trading vessel. He was alleged to

A *Punch* magazine cartoon of the Chamber of Horrors, 1849

have caused the death of nine victims in all, first drugging and poisoning them with laudanum and then robbing them. Mrs Stewart aided him.

Madame Tussaud was not one to sympathize with weakness in her own sex, but she seems to have felt some compassion for Mrs Stewart though a cast of her face, taken like her husband's three hours after execution, was put on display in the same way. But Madame Tussaud took the trouble to print in her catalogue an extract from the *Edinburgh Evening Post* published a few days before the execution. The reporter wrote: 'The fate of the wife though in a legal point of view she is equally criminal with her husband excited comparatively a degree of compassion in the breasts of those acquainted with the circumstances in which she had long been placed with regard to Stewart. Attached by him in an infatuated degree she received every kind of abuse at his hands and yet she continued to act as his coadjutor and to serve him faithfully as if he had behaved to her with incessant kindness.'

For the next six years, while Madame Tussaud continued tirelessly to tour the country, Burke and Hare together with the unfailingly popular revolutionary death heads were the star attraction of the Separate Room. There were a few additions from time to time which kept the display updated. While exhibiting at Brighton in 1833 Madame Tussaud was presented by an unnamed donor with the original cast of the executed head of wife-murderer Holloway. Princess Augusta, sister of George IV, came with Prince George of Cambridge during this Brighton visit, but such unpleasantness was not for royal eyes.

One of the new additions though more pathetic than horrible was Dennis Collins, who hurled a stone at King William IV at Ascot Races in June 1832. The miserable Collins, a former sailor, had been pensioned off after losing a leg in an accident and had been admitted to Greenwich Hospital. Obviously mentally as well as physically afflicted, he was expelled from that haven after repeated instances of misconduct and additionally punished by having his pension cancelled. Mid-nineteenth-century attitudes did not include sympathy for such social misfits, and thereafter the wretched, half-starved, disabled ex-sailor stumped the countryside on his wooden leg vainly petitioning at intervals for the return of his tenpence a week pension.

The jagged flint that he hurled at his monarch hit the King's hat but could have caused serious injury if it had struck his temple or eye. Collins was hustled off to Reading Gaol. Madame Tussaud was fortunate enough to be showing her exhibition in Reading and hastened immediately to take a mask of the would-be regicide's features. She noted the tattered sailor's garb he wore and dressed her portrait figure accordingly. The wretched man disclaimed any intention beyond calling attention to his grievance and was sentenced not to death but to transportation for life. He was spared further misery for he died on the way and was buried at sea. Regicides already had a historic place in Madame Tussaud's Separate Room and Dennis Collins, later joined by others, remained in the exhibition for nearly 150 years.

In 1834 Madame Tussaud arrived in London to spend some time in various locations in the metropolis. She did not know it then, but her travelling years were about to end. She would settle permanently in London. The Separate Room that she had so tenaciously kept together for thirty-two years under such difficult conditions would begin to expand and to rival its progenitor, Curtius' *Caverne des Grands Voleurs*, and develop into the Chamber of Horrors whose name became a household word.

[3]

The Exhibition is Established in London – *Punch* Magazine Names it The 'Chamber of Horrors'

It was in March 1835 after more than a year spent showing the exhibition in a number of different locations in and around London that Madame Tussaud and her sons took over the lease of spacious premises in a building known as Bazaar. This was conveniently and centrally situated at the corner of Baker Street and Portman Square.

There was a very large long room on the upper floor with some small buildings jutting out from it, and in front, facing on to Baker Street, was a private house to accommodate the family. This was to be the home of the exhibition for forty-nine years and in this permanent location Madame Tussaud could, for the first time since she left Paris, develop her exhibition to its full potential. A splendid gilded and ornamented 'Golden Corinthian Salon' was the setting for the main display of portrait figures and there was also space in an 'adjoining situation' for the Separate Room to be expanded, and strikingly arranged and lighted.

In a contemporary book, *London Interiors*, the author Mead ends his account of the impressive spectacle with the remark, 'On leaving the exhibition Madame puts your courage to the test to ask if you would like to see the Separate Room . . . few persons, such is the love of the marvellous, decline the invitation.' Mead mentions the 'bleeding and dying heads' of the French revolutionaries and various 'horrible relics'. A newspaper account, while praising the exhibition in the highest terms, refers to the Separate Room as 'that ghastly apartment into which ladies are advised not to enter'. Madame Tussaud could feel satisfied that its impact had not waned with the years.

Great personalities as well as ordinary citizens flocked to the new premises. The Duke of Wellington was among the famous visitors. He permitted Madame Tussaud to model him from life and paid his first visit (reported in the *Morning Herald*) in July 1835. He repeated this visit many times in years to come.

The Duke's favourite figures were those of Queen Victoria and Napoleon lying in state on his deathbed and he could always give a passing glance at his own portrait in the group 'Great Men of the Late War'. He was amongst the many who accepted Madame Tussaud's invitation to enter the Separate Room. When he requested Joseph Tussaud to let him know quickly when any new figure of special interest was added he particularly emphasized that the denizens of the Separate Room should be included. Joseph expressed some surprise that such persons were of interest to the great Duke, who replied with his usual uncompromising common sense 'Well, do they not represent *fact*?'

The Duke was right. Madame Tussaud never wavered from her policy. She did not show imaginary portraits whether of the famous or criminals. She insisted on an accurate likeness. Nor did she include in the Separate Room any objects merely because they were gruesome. Everything had factual and often historical value. Educational lessons could be derived from them. This provided an excuse for many visitors who might otherwise have hesitated to enter the 'ghastly apartment' without scruples of conscience. They could feel that the extra sixpence it cost was well spent. Variety was also important. This was exemplified by the would-be regicide Guiseppe Fieschi, and the 'diabolical' Greenacre as he was called on one of Madame Tussaud's posters.

The Corsican Fieschi, a rabid conspirator, attempted in the summer of 1835 to assassinate Louis Philippe, King of the French who, identified with the liberal opposition, had ascended the throne after the revolution of 1830. Anti-monarchist Fieschi constructed an 'infernal machine' consisting of a number of gun barrels loaded with metal fragments which he mounted on a wooden frame. From an upper window in the Boulevard du Temple (where Madame Tussaud had lived for so long at number 20) he planned to kill the King and his sons as they rode in cavalcade with their suite to inspect the National Guard.

He fired the machine with disastrous effect. Though the King and his sons escaped some nineteen persons were killed outright or mortally wounded and many others injured. Fieschi was tried and condemned on 28 July 1835 though he was not guillotined until February the following year. Madame Tussaud and her sons started work on his portrait figure within a couple of weeks of the trial. A life mask was procured from Paris though it is not known whether this was commissioned or whether Joseph or Francis made the journey across the Channel to take it personally. Ledger entries on 18 August record payments for Fieschi's boots and wig and for gun barrels to make a reproduction of the 'infernal machine'. On 1 September a carpenter was paid for constructing a framework to support the barrels. The completed figure was in a dramatic pose depicted in the act of igniting the gunpowder that fired the deadly metal-filled barrels. Guiseppe Fieschi made a remarkable contrast with the pathetic figure of Dennis Collins holding in his hand the stone he had hurled at King William IV.

James Greenacre was representative of an entirely different type of criminal to be found in the Separate Room. A callous murderer, he killed a washerwoman named Hannah Brown to whom he had promised marriage after she had been unwise enough to hint that she had savings of several hundred pounds when Greenacre was in financial difficulties. The case aroused great public interest because, after committing the crime, Greenacre carved up his victim's body and hid the pieces in various parts of London, where Hannah lived in the Paddington area. The remains came to light one by one after a labouring man had made the initial discovery of Hannah's headless and limbless trunk tied up in a sack and concealed beneath a large paving stone in Edgware Road. James Greenacre's execution took place on 2 May 1837 and some 20,000 people waited outside Newgate Gaol to witness it.

In March 1843 Madame Tussaud and her sons opened two Napoleon Rooms for which they had been purchasing relics and pictures for some time including the famous Waterloo Coach. The rooms were elaborately decorated, the ceilings and picture frames being particularly splendid. The first, the Golden Room, contained the 'Shrine of Napoleon' while the Waterloo Coach occupied the second room.

The charge of sixpence extra for the Separate Room was extended to cover the two Napoleon Rooms so different in their concept and contents. It was in the special catalogue printed to describe the new Napoleon Rooms that the name the 'Chamber of Horrors' appeared for the first time though in the ordinary catalogues it was still called the Separate Room.

At this time the new name did not catch public notice. It was not until three years later that the magazine *Punch* made it a household word. *Punch* had previously made a number of references to the exhibition calling Madame Tussaud 'one of the national ornaments of the feminine species' and remarking in an article entitled 'The Temple of Fame' that 'both the regal ermine and the murderers' fustian obtain their enviable niche in her display'. Then the wrath of the editor of *Punch* was aroused by a special attraction introduced for the 'season' of 1846. This was:

> 'A magnificent display of Court Dresses of surpassing richness comprising 25 ladies' and gentlemen's costumes intended to convey to the MIDDLE CLASSES an idea of ROYAL SPLENDOUR, a most splendid novelty and calculated to display to young persons much necessary instruction.'

It was the year of the repeal of the Corn Laws following disastrous harvests in England and Ireland which brought hunger and misery to the poor. Madame Tussaud's snobbery, which her public always loved, proved too much for the editor of *Punch*. Under the heading 'A Great Moral Lesson at Madame

Tussaud's' the article criticized her for so lavish a display at such a time:

> 'The collection should include specimens of the Irish peasantry, the hand-loom weavers and other starving portions of the population all in their characteristic tatters; and also the inmates of the various workhouses in the ingnominious garb presented for them by the Poor Law. But this department of the exhibition should be contained in a separate Chamber of Horrors and half a guinea entrance should be charged for the benefit of the living originals.'

This time the name struck home and henceforward the Separate Room was registered in the public mind as the 'Chamber of Horrors'.

One of the most extraordinary murderers to enter the Chamber of Horrors during Madame Tussaud's last years was James Blomfield Rush, perpetrator of a double murder in which, according to Tussaud family tradition, Queen Victoria herself took a particular interest. John Theodore Tussaud, great-grandson of Madame Tussaud, related the origins of the tradition as he had learned it from his grandfather.

Since 1839 the Royal Smithfield Cattle Show had been held annually in the large open area behind Bazaar which had formerly been used for the sale of horses and carriages. Successful from the start, the Cattle Show brought an influx of visitors from the country. It was patronized by the Prince Consort who showed fine beasts bred on the royal farms at Windsor, and Queen Victoria herself used to visit it. It was in November 1848, the time of the winter cattle show, that the murder took place of Mr Isaac Jermy, Recorder of Norwich, who lived at Stanfield Hall, near Wymondham in Norfolk. John Theodore Tussaud related the story of a Norfolk farmer who came to London to visit the Cattle Show and found himself in a remarkable situation.

> 'After,' said the farmer, 'I had been to the show and examined the beasts, I thought I would devote a spare hour to

Madame Tussaud's celebrated exhibition. Accordingly I presented myself at the door and paid my money.

'On entering I was surprised to find that I was the only spectator. Undisturbed for some time I wandered about looking with astonishment at the waxen figures habited in their gorgeous apparel.

'In a few moments some ladies and children arrived and standing next to one of the former I said what ugly, grim-faced people some of the Kings and Queens were. The lady smiled and said "I perfectly agree with you; they are!"

'My attention was soon arrested by hearing one of the party, pointing to a figure, mention Lord Nelson, when, proud of being born in the same county as the illustrious sailor, I could not help exclaiming "Ah, he was from my neighbourhood!" Upon which one of the ladies advancing said to me "Are you from Norfolk? Pray can you tell me about poor *Mrs Jermy* with whose melancholy fate I so deeply sympathize. Have you any information differing from that which has appeared in the public papers?"

'To this I replied "No, Madame, for I have been some days from home".

'Scarcely had the conversation ended than Madame Tussaud herself entered and seeing me there asked how I got in and if I did not know that she had forbidden entrance of anyone. I replied that I did not, having paid my money and walked in as a matter of course.

'Judge of my surprise, therefore, when she informed me that I had had the honour of speaking to none other than our good and gracious Queen, and that the lady whose tender anxiety has been so warmly expressed for the injured widow of Stanfield Hall was the same illustrious person . . . the party which accompanied the Queen were the royal children and her attendants.'

Even without the Queen's interest the crime committed by James Blomfield Rush assured him of the place that he occupied in the Chamber of Horrors for over 120 years. On 28 November

A contemporary drawing of James Blomfield Rush who was executed in Norwich in 1849.

1848 Mr Isaac Jermy of Stanfield Hall near Wymondham, a barrister and Recorder of Norwich since 1837, was shot dead at his home. His son, Jermy Jermy, was also shot and killed and Mrs Jermy and a servant were badly wounded by the same attacker. The background to this multiple crime was friction and ill will over land tenancies. Both James Blomfield Rush and his stepfather before him were tenant farmers on the substantial estates of the Jermy family.

James Blomfield Rush had an unusual mother. He was the illegitimate son of Mary Blomfield, daughter of a farmer who was also a miller and a baker. She was engaged to a gentleman farmer in the neighbourhood. He broke off the engagement but had already seduced Mary Blomfield who was pregnant.

Unlike most girls of the period who found themselves in her unhappy position Mary did not accept shame and disgrace. She sued her former fiancé for breach of promise and obtained substantial damages. A son, James Blomfield, was born and when the boy was two years old the substantial dowry Mary had obtained for herself through her breach of promise suit enabled her to marry John Rush, a tenant farmer on the Stanfield Hall lands.

John and Mary Rush had no children of their own but he proved a kind and generous stepfather to his wife's illegitimate offspring, giving the boy his name and a good education. There was nothing, apart from the circumstances of his birth, that could account for the subsequent behaviour of James Rush, for he had a good start in life.

In 1824 James Blomfield Rush began farming on his own account. He made a good marriage with a local girl and moved to a new farm, spending considerable sums on improving it. Trouble began during this tenancy. A wheat stack was set on fire and James was accused of arson (the stack was said to be insured) but he was not brought to trial. He was again in trouble in 1830 when some of his farm men, acting with their master's approval, rescued from custody a group of farm-workers accused of destroying threshing machines. The introduction of machinery on farms, like the introduction of new machinery in the industrial Midlands, was bitterly opposed by workers who feared for their livelihood. This time Rush was brought before the magistrates but discharged under an order to keep the peace.

Six years later Mr Isaac Jermy's elderly father wished to cut down on his farming activites. He vacated Stanfield Hall which he had occupied and leased it to James Blomfield Rush who installed his family there. Soon after this the old man died. Though there were several other claimants to the inheritance Isaac Jermy staked his rights and wished to move into Stanfield

Hall as heir. His legal knowledge enabled him to declare that the lease of the Hall given to Rush was illegal and invalid, and he rescinded it. Rush and his family had to move out and go into another farm on the estates. Ill feeling between Isaac Jermy and his tenant James Blomfield Rush had begun.

This was to get worse when both wanted a small property, Potash Farm, which came on the market. Rush, in addition to farming, had established himself as a land agent and auctioneer. He was instructed by Isaac Jermy to bid for Potash Farm with a ceiling price fixed. Rush did bid, but he bought the farm himself. He did not have the money to pay for it and by a curious arrangement borrowed this and other sums from Isaac Jermy, undertaking to repay by 30 November 1848.

Meanwhile Rush's domestic circumstances had undergone a change. In 1842 his wife, who had borne him nine children, died. Rush engaged a young woman named Emily Sandford, daughter of a respectable clerk in London, to act as governess to his large brood. The inevitable happened. He seduced Emily who bore him a child that died, but, though he was a widower and free to marry, he did not take Emily Sandford as his wife. Instead Rush set her up as his mistress in London lodgings located in Pentonville. Here he made frequent visits, staying several days and in the evening seeking entertainment in the Angel Inn, the Grecian Rooms, and Sadler's Wells Theatre.

In addition to these pleasures Rush held meetings at the Pentonville lodgings with disgruntled claimants to the Jermy estates, encouraging them to pursue their rights in the face of Isaac Jermy's establishment of himself as heir. Emily Sandford was present at these meetings. She made copies of documents and several times signed as witness to Rush's signature. Meantime Isaac Jermy continued his occupation of Stanfield Hall as rightful owner of the estates.

In 1848 Emily was again pregnant. From time to time she stayed at Potash Farm ostensibly as housekeeper and passing as a widow, Mrs James. Rush only spent short periods at this small farm. His children were installed in the larger farm into which he had moved when ousted from Stanfield Hall by his landlord, Isaac Jermy, whose tenant he still was.

Emily paid one of her visits to Norfolk in October 1848. This time she did not go straight to Potash Farm. James Rush put her into lodgings in Norwich. The landlady discovered she was pregnant which did not accord well with her status as widowed Mrs James, and she was asked to leave. She went to Potash Farm.

Thus on the evening of 28 November 1848 when the shocking murders at Stanfield Hall took place Emily Sandford and James Blomfield Rush were both in residence at Potash Farm. The daily servant went home when her work was done. Emily Sandford was the only person who could give an account of Rush's movements on that fatal evening.

The shooting of Isaac Jermy and his son Jermy Jermy, both of whom died immediately, and the serious wounding of Mrs Jermy and a lady's maid Eliza Chestney took place soon after eight o'clock in circumstances so incredibly dramatic that they seemed more like fiction than reality.

After dinner the Jermy family were sitting in the drawing-room: the Recorder, his wife, his son and young daughter. Isaac Jermy heard an unusual sound and left the drawing-room to go and investigate at the front door. The family heard the sound of a shot, and the son Jermy also left the room by way of a door leading to a dark passage to see what had happened. He came face to face with an extraordinary figure, a man wearing a voluminous cloak and a red and black mask holding two pistols. Jermy Jermy fell to the ground mortally wounded not knowing that his father lay dead at the front door.

Mrs Jermy hearing the second shot rushed out and her arm was shattered by a bullet. The little girl ran shrieking across the entrance hall as Eliza Chestney, the lady's maid, emerged from the domestic quarters. Eliza was shot through the thigh and fell. The butler who was following close behind her faced a brace of pistols, turned tail and sought refuge in the pantry. The assassin, threatening the servants with destruction if they emerged, scattered some papers in the hall and fled.

While these scenes were taking place inside the Hall a groom in the stables at the back heard the shots and screams. He waded the moat that surrounded the house and stableyard and ran to the nearest farm where he raised the alarm. Then he took horse for Wymondham where he roused various gentlemen and the Norwich police were summoned 'by telegraphic despatch'. Meanwhile the groom and the gentlemen hastened to Stanfield Hall where they found Isaac Jermy and his son dead, and Mrs Jermy and Miss Chestney 'deluged in blood'.

Suspicion immediately fell on James Rush. The ill will between him and the Recorder was public knowledge and Eliza Chestney identified his shape and aspect in spite of the cloak and mask. Rush was of course familiar with the lay-out of Stanfield Hall as he had lived there for some time and he was known to the staff as a visitor. The substantial sum of money Isaac Jermy had lent him to buy Potash Farm was due for repayment on 30 November.

The police went to Potash Farm where they questioned 'Mrs James' the housekeeper (Emily Sandford). She made a statement that she and Rush had spent the evening together at the farm. However, subsequently Emily Sandford had second thoughts. She made another and quite different statement revealing her real identity to the police. She described how Rush had left the house, his agitated behaviour, his order that she should spend the night in her own room whereas she usually shared his bed. She told of his return, his clothing, his wet boots. The police searched Potash Farm. They found a voluminous cloak and a wig. They did not find any pistols.

James Blomfield Rush was arrested. He pleaded not guilty to the murders and woundings, declaring he had only left Potash Farm for some ten minutes during the evening when a noise outside made him suspect poachers. He alleged that Stanfield Hall had been attacked by claimants to the estates who were responsible for the shootings and had scattered the papers found in the hall, stating their intention to take Stanfield Hall by force, after the assassin had fled.

Rush was not believed. His trial opened at the Shire Hall, Norwich, on 29 March 1849. He conducted his own defence

Emily Sandford, Rush's mistress, in court. Her evidence conclusively sent Rush to the gallows in 1849.

and the chief witness against him was his mistress, Emily Sandford. She alone could confirm Rush's statement that he had scarcely left Potash Farm on the evening of the murders as she had said in her first statement to the police. Or she could take her revenge on the lover who refused to marry her in spite of repeated promises to do so, leaving her disgraced with an illegitimate child.

Emily entered the witness box looking weak and dejected, her oval face framed in ringlets. She wore black satin and a crêpe veil. During the trial she wept much and on account of her recent confinement a medical attendant stood by throughout. Rush cross-examined her at great length attempting to blacken her character and prove that she lied in the second statement she had made to the police.

Emily Sandford may have looked weak, turned faint, wept, and frequently turned her eyes to the prisoner, but her will to take revenge was iron. Nothing could shake her story of Rush's behaviour and absence on that fatal evening.

Throughout the trial the public seats were packed with 'ladies and gentlemen of great respectability'. When the trial came to an end the jury were out for only six minutes before returning a verdict of guilty. The six-day trial had caused such excitement throughout the country that the Norwich newspapers which normally appeared weekly were published daily and sackfuls specially despatched through the mail to other cities and towns.

James Blomfield Rush was hanged on a scaffold outside Norwich Gaol on 11 April 1849. Emily Sandford and her infant son vanished into obscurity. Widowed Mrs Jermy whose plight had aroused the interest and sympathy of Queen Victoria recovered from her injuries, though too weak to appear at the trial; Eliza Chestney was carried to it on a stretcher. Mrs Jermy did not remain a widow long for she married a baronet in December 1850. James Rush's portrait in wax 'taken from life at Norwich' speedily entered Madame Tussaud's Chamber of Horrors and was 'by general consent looked on with the most painful interest'. He was dressed as he appeared at the trial and Madame Tussaud also acquired the architect-constructed and realistically painted models of Stanfield Hall and Potash Farm which had been used at the trial.

Even Madame Tussaud's extraordinary stamina was now yielding to the weaknesses of old age. Rush was the star attraction of the Chamber of Horrors during her last year of life together with the notorious couple Frederick and Maria Man-

CHAMBER
OF
HORRORS.

MADAME
TUSSAUD & SONS,
Anxious to introduce every Character that interests the Public, to their COLLECTION, respectfully announce that they have added
PORTRAIT MODELS
OF
MANNING
AND HIS
WIFE,
TAKEN DURING THEIR TRIAL,
Representing them dressed as they appeared on that occasion. Also a Model in Plaster of their Victim,
Mr. O'CONNOR,
(From recollection), by a Gentleman who knew him well, acknowledged to be a good Likeness. Also a
PLAN OF THE KITCHEN
WHERE O'CONNOR WAS MURDERED.
The Models of Manning and his Wife are placed in the Dock, with the Portrait Figure of
RUSH
Taken from Life at Norwich,
Dressed as he appeared at his Trial, and which has been by general consent looked upon with the most painful interest, in conveying a perfect resemblance of the greatest CRIMINAL (with the exception of the Mannings), that has yet been brought to justice. Models of
STANFIELD HALL,
The Seat of the late J. JERMY, Esq., and
POTASH FARM,
The Residence of RUSH, are placed in the Chamber of Horrors,

EXHIBITION,
BAZAAR, BAKER STREET,
Portman Square.

ADMITTANCE - ONE SHILLING.
CHAMBER of HORRORS, 6d. extra.
Open from 11 in the Morning till Dusk, and in the evening from 7 o'clock till 10.

J. W. PEEL's Steam Machine, 74, New Cut, Lambeth

Madame Tussaud's poster in 1849 advertising the recent addition of portrait models of the Mannings which had joined the portrait figure of Rush.

ning who were executed at Horsemonger Lane Gaol (where Colonel Despard had met his end so many years ago) in November 1849.

The Mannings, wanting money, murdered a comfortably-off retired customs officer with whom they were friendly and buried his body under their kitchen floor. Maria Manning, Swiss-born, formerly a lady's maid, chose to go to her death wearing a black satin dress. This caused consternation among middle-class housewives who aspired to a black satin dress as a symbol of respectable prosperity. It was reported that sales of the material slumped for a considerable period and few cared to appear in the dress they were accustomed to don for 'Sunday best'. Charles Dickens chose to witness the Mannings' execution, the first and only public hanging he attended. The Mannings' crime had aroused enormous popular interest and the scenes at their execution caused Charles Dickens to protest violently against the barbarity of hangings carried out in public. Madame Tussaud's visitors were less squeamish and flocked to see the criminals in effigy. For good measure they also saw a model in plaster of the victim and a scale model of the kitchen in which he was murdered and buried.

Madame Tussaud was eighty-nine when she died in April 1850, active in body almost to the last and with her mind unclouded. Madame Tussaud during her long life had equalled and surpassed her uncle's *Salon de Cire* in the Boulevard du Temple. During the fifteen years since she had settled in London, she had also established the fame of her own successor to Curtius' *Caverne des Grands Voleurs*, the Chamber of Horrors. Her instinct when she had tentatively picked out the French Revolution death heads, the portrait of the assassinated Marat and other gruesome but historical items, and carried them with her to England in 1802 had not been at fault. Her sons, to whom she left her exhibition with a last injunction 'Do not quarrel', were equally convinced that the Chamber of Horrors, as well as the splendid main exhibition combining entertainment and education, had a long future ahead.

[4]

The Victorians and the Macabre

Madame Tussaud's sons Joseph and Francis were trained to carry on her policies. Of course the Chamber of Horrors had its critics. The magazine *Punch* remarked with disapproval 'There seems to be a sort of fascination in the horrible', while Thackeray, writing as 'Goliath Muff' in *The Sights of London*, was particularly offended by the effigies of the notorious Mannings:

> 'Should such indecent additions continue to be made to this exhibition the "horrors" of the collection will surely predominate. It is painful to reflect that although there are noble and worthy characters really deserving of being immortalized in wax, these would have no chance in the scale of attention with thrice-dyed villains.'

Joseph and Francis were undeterred by criticism. They continued to add 'noble and worthy' characters to the main halls, while new Chamber of Horrors 'subjects' were equally carefully modelled and displayed. With the Great Exhibition of 1851 promising an influx of visitors the Tussaud brothers decided that the exhibition must be enlarged. The Bazaar premises were on lease, but they obtained the landlord's permission to extend and remodel. A new 'Hall of Kings', a spectrum of British monarchy, was the project for the main exhibition which would add prestige, colour and magnificence to the already splendid array of figures set out in the Golden Corinthian Salon.

A new and larger room for the Chamber of Horrors was included in the plans. When this was completed Joseph and Francis explained why they had given this additional space and importance to 'the horrible'. In the catalogue dated 1851 they told their public:

> 'The sensation caused by the crimes of Rush, the Mannings, etc was so great that thousands were unable to satisfy their curiosity. It therefore induced Madame Tussaud & Sons to expend a large sum in building a suitable room for the purpose, and they need scarcely assure the public that so far from the exhibition of the likeness of criminals creating a desire to imitate them, experience teaches that it has a direct tendency to the contrary.'

A poster issued at the time draws attention to the 'good ventilation' of this new and larger Chamber which was no doubt much appreciated by any visitors who felt faint at the sight of so many murderers portrayed in wax.

Even though Joseph and Francis felt it necessary to stress the deterrent and educational aspects, the Chamber of Horrors was not at all at variance with social attitudes of the period. Certainly respectability and morality were firmly established with the exemplary family life of Queen Victoria and the Prince Consort and would remain entrenched for the rest of the Queen's long reign, but behind the solid and prosperous façade the epoque wore another face.

The Victorians had a taste for the morbid, a preoccupation with the macabre and sordid that showed itself in such forms as a fascination with death, and the double lives led by many Victorian gentlemen whose virtuous and respectable domesticity gave no indication of the low-class mistress perhaps ensconced in a small house tucked away in a secluded area like leafy St John's Wood.

Only a few reformers concerned themselves with child prostitution, drunkenness, gin palaces, sweatshops, grinding proverty, hideous slums and child labour. Brutal sports like prize-fighting drew crowds and public executions which had so shocked Charles Dickens in 1848 were not abolished until 1868.

The Chamber of Horrors catered for these tastes, while offering the excuse of a moral lesson for those who might otherwise scruple to inspect it. This is emphasized in a poster for the 1864 Madame Tussaud's season: 'The proprietors assure the public that so far from the exhibition of the likenesses of criminals creating a desire to imitate them, experience teaches that it has a direct tendency to the contrary.' In the 1870s Joseph Randall Tussaud, Madame Tussaud's grandson, endeavoured to reinforce the educational and historical aspects of the Chamber by renaming it 'The Chamber of Comparative Physiognomy', thus adding a touch of scientific interest as well. He advertised it as such but his efforts were of no avail. The Chamber of Horrors was what people knew, liked, and wanted. The Chamber of Horrors it remained.

Charles Dickens may have recoiled from public hanging, but he was one of those who were fascinated with the waxen criminals who had suffered it. Between 1854 and 1860 there were a number of articles about the 'Horrors' in his magazines *Household Words* and *All the Year Round*. 'But what a horrible place!' he exclaimed as he noted the criminal likenesses taken from death masks, the cold, sinister light that pervaded the new large room and even the faint smell of wax which permeated the air and seemed to add to the sinister atmosphere. He was struck by the indifference of some visitors to the macabre and chilling ambience:

> 'What shall be said of the man who could stand at the door of the Chamber of Horrors *eating a pork pie*? Yet such a one there was—your Eyewitness saw him; a young man from the provinces . . . His eye was on the model of Marat as assassinated in a bath and with this before him he could eat an under-done pork pie! It is the last straw that breaks the camel's back; it was this last horror that sent your Eyewitness out of Madame Tussaud's as fast as his legs would carry him!'

Additional space gave more opportunity for the display of 'relics', especially those with the historical connotation that Madame Tussaud had always considered so important. In March 1854 Joseph Tussaud went to Paris on a thirteen-day visit, the main purpose of which was to visit Clément-Henri Sanson, grandson of Charles-Henri Sanson, executioner of so many illustrious personages during the period of the Terror, and the man whose co-operation had been vital to Curtius when he set up his first *Caverne des Grands Voleurs* in 1783.

Clément-Henri Sanson had succeeded his father as Chief Executioner of Paris in 1840. He inherited not only the job which had passed from father to son for a number of generations but also a collection of items connected with the profession which he kept together in a room and was willing to show to interested persons and journalists. However, Clément-Henri, unlike his forbears, did not hold his position until his death for he managed to get into debt so severely that in 1847 his creditors had him thrown into Clichy Prison. As a result he was dismissed from his post and, his only child being a girl, there was no son to follow him.

He remained impoverished and in time was ready to dispose of his 'museum'. Joseph Tussaud paid £220 in English money—a considerable amount at the period—for Sanson's drawings of the guillotine so that a full-scale model could be constructed for the Chamber of Horrors with complete accuracy. It replaced the small model that Madame Tussaud had brought to England with her. Joseph also acquired the lunette and guillotine blade that had held and severed the royal heads along with those of many hundreds of other victims, and a chopper that had also formed part of the guillotine's equipment during the Revolution.

Soon the full-size guillotine, complete with baskets to receive the heads and bodies, was a new centre of attention in the Chamber of Horrors adding fresh interest to the death heads of the revolutionaries. The guillotined heads of Louis XVI and Marie Antoinette were still not publicized in catalogues or posters. Madame Tussaud had felt it would be in extremely bad taste and at variance with her image as a survivor of the *ancien régime* to draw attention to the particularly unpleasant tasks she had been obliged to perform in 1793 when she took masks from the dead faces of the King and Queen of France.

It was not until Joseph died in 1865, leaving his younger brother Francis in control, that the royal death heads were publicly recorded in the catalogue. Although Madame Tussaud had never discriminated between her two sons and they both got on well all their lives, Joseph was the closest to her for he had worked with her since the age of four. Francis was a grown young man before he joined her and once complained in a letter to his father that Joseph was the favourite since he had been with his mother since he was little. While Joseph lived his mother's policy was strictly adhered to but by the time of his death in 1865 many years had passed since Madame Tussaud's departure and the terrible events of 1793 had grown remote and passed into history.

In 1878, the English instrument of execution, the gallows, took its place in the Chamber of Horrors. Francis had died in 1873 and it was his son, Joseph Randall, who purchased the gallows, which had been for over fifty years in Hertford Gaol, which was now to be demolished. The first person to be executed on this gallows in 1824 was one John Thurtell found guilty of the murder of a solicitor, William Weare, to whom he owed a large gambling debt. The new gallows was of an improved design to which Thurtell himself is said to have contributed while awaiting his trial. He was arrested at the end of October 1823, tried on 6 and 7 January 1824 and executed two days later. While awaiting his trial he had expressed his repugnance towards the method currently in use by which the condemned man was driven under the gibbet in a cart. The felon stood on the cart while the rope was fixed round his neck, and the cart was then driven from beneath his feet. The short drop did not always result in instant or humane death. The new type of gallows had a high raised platform and trapdoor with oiled bolts providing a long drop. When Joseph Randall set up the gallows in the exhibition he modelled a figure of John

Thurtell from contemporary portraits to go with it. The gallows is still in the Chamber of Horrors today.

The acquisition of the gallows led to the modelling for the first time of the official hangman, a figure who had disappeared from public gaze with the abolition of public executions in 1868. William Marwood was appointed hangman in 1874 on the retirement of bootmaker Calcraft. Marwood willingly agreed to sit for his portrait and asked no recompense.

John Theodore Tussaud, great-grandson of Madame Tussaud, was now a young man of sixteen and got to know Marwood well. He recalled how the executioner would visit the studios from time to time when he felt depressed, smoke a pipe and sip a glass of gin and water. He then liked to stroll round the Chamber of Horrors looking at the effigies of those he had despatched from this world and had no objection to his own effigy being in their company. Usually he was accompanied by his old dog, a grizzled terrier, 'that has played with my ropes, that has caught rats in my business bags'. One day on a visit to the Chamber of Horrors he was alone and sadly mentioned that his old dog was dying. A bystander, recognizing the executioner, overheard this remark. 'Why not hang him?' he callously enquired. Marwood was reproachful. 'No, no. Hang a man, but my dear old dog, never!'

Marwood's successor Berry was an entirely different character. While he seemed pleased to have his effigy placed in the Chamber, unlike Marwood who sat for no reward, he demanded a substantial fee.

When opportunity arose small 'relics' connected with crime were acquired and displayed alongside the 'subject' concerned. One of these which has survived to modern times is the leather 'poison case' of Dr William Palmer, the notorious Rugeley poisoner, whose wholesale destruction of victims aroused intense interest on the Continent as well as throughout the British Isles when he was brought to trial in 1856.

William Palmer was a member of the Royal College of Surgeons and a house-surgeon at St Bartholomew's Hospital before he set up as a general practitioner at Rugeley in Stafford-

William Marwood who sat to John Theodore Tussaud when he was appointed official hangman.

shire at the end of 1848. The following year he married Ann, illegitimate daughter of a colonel who lived in Stafford. She produced five children of whom only the eldest survived. Dr Palmer's medical practice was limited. He preferred the excitements of the Turf and both owned and bred racehorses, a pursuit which landed him in serious financial difficulties.

Palmer's wife Ann died in September 1854 of a 'bilious cholera'. Though he had only a limited life-interest in her property, her death was extremely beneficial for Palmer who had taken out insurance policies on her life to the extent of £13,000—monies which were paid to him without question by the insurers. However, when William Palmer's brother died suddenly the following year, his life having been insured for a similar sum, the insurance company refused to pay.

A few months later Palmer was arrested and accused of having poisoned a betting friend who had been taken ill and died after a get-together at the Talbot Arms at Rugeley. The bodies of Palmer's wife and brother were exhumed and traces of strychnine or antimony poisoning found. The coroner's inquest decided they had been wilfully murdered. The case aroused great excitement locally. It was commonly reported that Dr Palmer had altogether disposed of as many as fourteen victims including his brother-in-law whose money had passed to his wife, creditors and illegitimate children who had conveniently died.

On account of local feeling it was decided Palmer must stand trial at the Old Bailey in London. To achieve this a special Act of Parliament, the 'Palmer Act', was passed permitting an accused person to be tried in London if it appeared he was unlikely to get a fair trial in his own county. Palmer was duly found guilty and condemned to death, being taken back to Stafford for the execution. A death mask taken after execution still survives at Stafford.

Madame Tussaud's managed to acquire what was known as 'Dr Palmer's poison case' which was shown with the wax portrait placed in the Chamber of Horrors. It still exists, a small

Dr William Palmer, the Rugely poisoner, whose gambling debts on the Turf brought him to the gallows in 1856.

leather case fitted with glass phials which were said to have contained the poison powders Palmer administered to his victims. He was only thirty-two at the time of his death by hanging. His plump frock-coated figure with a smart black satin stock round a high white collar, fresh-complexioned and far from villainous looking, remained in the Chamber of Horrors for over a century; one of England's most notorious poisoners, an object lesson on the fate of those who love to gamble and an example of how deceptive appearances could be. Dr Palmer was a perfect inmate for the Chamber.

Variety was added in 1864 when effigies of the '*Flowery Land* Pirates' appeared in the Chamber of Horrors. Madame Tussaud's catalogue announced 'A more diabolical crime can scarcely be found in the annals of maritime history' and indeed it was a fearful story of multiple murder at sea.

Late in July 1863 the vessel the *Flowery Land* left London docks bound for Singapore with a crew of ten and one passenger. The crew seems to have showed symptoms of insubordination in the early stages of the voyage, but it was not until early September that a sudden murderous attack was made. The mate, taken by surprise, was struck with handspikes and in spite of cries for help and mercy was so severely beaten about the head that his features were obliterated and his body flung overboard. As the captain hastened to the scene, having heard the noise, he was stabbed with daggers on the companionway. His brother who tried to escape the mutineers was brutally beaten and, as he was never heard of again, his body presumably went overboard too. Only the captain's body received any kind of burial rite. The second mate, a man named Tiffin, begged to be allowed to sew it up in canvas and say the last office as it was thrown into the sea.

The mutineers plundered the ship and Tiffin, the only one left who knew anything about navigation, was forced to sail the vessel to ten miles off the coast of Brazil where it was scuttled. As the cook and steward struggled in the water they were beaten to death; the remaining survivors took to the boats. Once on land Tiffin managed to escape from his companions and lodged information about the bloody happenings that had preceded the sinking of the *Flowery Land*.

The mutineers were arrested and eventually found themselves in the dock of the Old Bailey charged with the murder of the captain, though they had killed at least four others as well. A John Lyons seems to have been the only one of the accused with an English name. There were four Spaniards, a Turkish subject and a Greek. All were found guilty. The Greek, Carlos, stood a second trial for scuttling the ship and was sentenced to ten years penal servitude. The rest were condemned to death though one sentence was commuted to imprisonment for life. Five went to the gallows on 22 February 1864. It was a bizarre group of vicious brutal seamen whose effigies appeared in the Chamber of Horrors and public interest in this frightful crime lasted for ten years. If the single passenger escaped alive he had a unique traveller's tale to tell!

Ever increasing use of rail travel brought more and more visitors to the metropolis and increasing numbers included Madame Tussaud's exhibition in their sightseeing. To those of them who braved the Chamber of Horrors the effigies of the men who carried out the first two murders committed in British railway carriages were of particular interest. Sixteen years lay between these two murders but both were committed to obtain trivial spoils so that a shuddering traveller who gazed at the portraits might well feel apprehension on his return journey about his fellow-occupants of his compartment. The first crime occurred in 1864.

A young German tailor working in London perpetrated this railway murder. Franz Müller entered a first-class compartment whose sole occupant was one Thomas Briggs, chief clerk of a London bank. The murder was committed on the short stretch between Hackney Wick and Bow. Thomas Briggs was battered with his own walking-stick and thrown out on to the line after being robbed of his gold watch and chain and the paltry sum of thirty shillings.

The twenty-five year old tailor made two mistakes which sent him to the gallows. Having bundled his unconscious victim, who died later, out of the carriage door he took the wrong silk hat, leaving his own on the carriage seat. He also exchanged the chain of the gold watch for a new one at a Cheapside jeweller's shop and the jeweller had sharp eyes. The police acted quickly, checking on City jewellers to see if the watch had been sold or pawned. From one of them they got the story of the exchanged watch-chain, and the description of the man who brought in watch and chain.

It was through this description and an advertisement about the hat that Franz Müller was identified. They went to his lodging but the bird had flown. He had used the thirty shillings to complete the purchase money for a place on an immigrant ship bound for New York. Immigrant ships were slow and police officers boarded a faster vessel. They were waiting for Franz Müller when he landed wearing the stolen gold watch and a cut-down silk hat. Müller had done this to change the hat's appearance. Müller was arrested and stood trial at the Old Bailey in October. The cut-down silk hat, identified as the one the victim had worn, and the gold watch were regarded as conclusive evidence by the jury who only took ten minutes to reach a verdict of guilty. This verdict aroused some protest and the King of Prussia sent a personal message to Queen Victoria to try and save this obscure young German from the gallows. The Queen took no action and Müller was hanged before a large crowd on 14 November. Before he died he confessed his guilt. It was typical of the Victorian instinct towards the macabre that for some time after this execution a cut-down silk hat was popular with fashionable young men about town.

Travellers had no further cause for alarm until 1881 when a twenty-two-year-old unsuccessful journalist who called himself Percy Lefroy (his real name was Mapleton) murdered for equally trivial gain. In June of that year he attacked an elderly retired merchant and dealer in coins who was alone in a railway carriage travelling from London Bridge to Brighton. His name was Isaac Frederick Gold and his body was found on the line near the entrance to Balcombe Tunnel. He had been shot in the neck and knifed. The attack took place earlier for, while the train passed through Merstham Tunnel, passengers in adjoining coaches had heard sounds like shots. There was no corridor.

Percy Lefroy Mapleton made no efforts to protect himself from suspicion. He left the train at a station on the outskirts of Brighton with his clothes bloodstained and a watch-chain hanging from his shoe. The ticket-collector noticed his appearance and held him for questioning. Lefroy told a bizarre story that there had been three passengers in the carriage. When the train entered the darkness of Merstham Tunnel he heard a shot and was knocked unconscious, awaking later to find himself alone in the carriage. The police did not believe this tale. They searched him and found some German coins of the kind Mr Gold was found to deal in.

Lefroy was arrested but asked to be allowed to go to his lodgings in Croydon. He was permitted to do this under escort by a police officer. Lefroy dodged through the front door and escaped at the back. He went into hiding but was foolish enough to send a telegram to his employer asking for his wages. Rearrested and kept in custody, Lefroy was tried and convicted and hanged on 29 November 1881. Like his predecessor in railway murder, Percy Lefroy Mapleton made a full confession before his execution. His effigy, that of a not very tall, meagre, chinless man, is still in the Chamber of Horrors over a hundred years since he committed his crime.

The last figure to enter the Chamber of Horrors during the lifetime of Madame Tussaud's surviving son, Francis, was that of a woman murderer. Mary Ann Cotton, a three-times-married former nurse aged forty, was convicted at Durham for poisoning a young stepson with arsenic but suspected of fourteen or fifteen other murders committed to get small sums of insurance money or to facilitate another marriage. Indeed no less than twenty-one deaths of persons connected with her had occurred over a period of twenty years. Madame Tussaud's catalogue emphasized dramatically 'crimes for which no punishment in history could atone. The child she rocked on her knee today was poisoned tomorrow. Most of her murders were committed for petty gains; and she killed off husbands and children with the unconcern of a farm-girl killing poultry.' Mary Ann Cotton, a fitting subject in every way to satisfy the Victorian taste for the horrific, was hanged in March 1873.

In August of the same year Francis, Madame Tussaud's younger son, died at the age of seventy-three. Neither he nor his brother, who had predeceased him by eight years, could match their mother's stamina and longevity though both had inherited her talent as a sculptor and steadfastly maintained her high standards of presentation and showmanship.

The family continuity in the exhibition was not broken. Joseph's only son had died when still in his twenties, a young man gifted as a sculptor and musician but a victim of consumption which killed him while he was in Rome seeking health in a warmer climate. Francis fortunately left two sons who worked in the exhibition all their lives. The elder, Joseph Randall Tussaud, took over the artistic side of the exhibition and was a clever modeller while Francis Curtius Tussaud devoted himself to promotion and public relations. Younger talent was coming on too. Joseph Randall's eldest son, John Theodore, was now fifteen and had already modelled a successful portrait figure for the Grand Hall, that of King Milan of Serbia.

Members of royal families and foreign notabilities continued to fit in a visit to Madame Tussaud's when they were staying in London, joining the throng of ordinary visitors who passed through the halls. One who did so much enjoyed the Chamber and was long remembered. He was the Shah of Persia who came to London in 1878. So pleased was he that he left a note of appreciation written in Persian in his own hand on a piece of Madame Tussaud's notepaper.

Young John Theodore, who was twenty, accompanied his father who escorted the Persian royal party round the exhibition. In the main halls it was the Shrine of Napoleon showing the great man lying in state on his simple camp-bed that caused the Shah to linger for some time, but when it came to entering the Chamber of Horrors it was the guillotine that focussed his attention.

Perhaps the Shah viewed it as a possibility for punishing

criminals in his own country. He wanted a demonstration. Young John Theodore never forgot the looks of genuine fear and apprehension that swept over the faces of the royal suite when the Shah suggested it would add realism if one of his officials had his neck fixed in the lunette while someone ran the heavy blade up and down. The Shah was persuaded to desist from this desire.

The following year, 1879, brought one of Britain's most notorious criminals, Charles Peace, burglar and murderer, to take his place in the Chamber of Horrors. His wax effigy has never left it since. Charles Peace was born in Sheffield in 1832, and his exploits as a criminal are the more remarkable since he was partly crippled as a boy in an accident which left him with a limp. He was twenty when he began to burgle and thieve, adopting crime as a lifelong career. He wandered from town to town and was not entirely successful as he was caught and jailed four times. In 1859 he married a widow with a son but it was not till 1872 that he went back to Sheffield and set up as a picture-framer and gilder, also dealing in old musical instruments and bric-à-brac. Peace himself had a talent for the violin which he sometimes played in public. He used an old violin-case to carry his burgling tools, and burglary was his main business.

In 1876 he committed two murders within four months. He was not caught in connection with the first to which he confessed when in jail under sentence of death. Another man suffered for this crime and Charles Peace sat in the gallery and watched his trial. Peace was surprised by a policeman when he was about to burgle a group of well-to-do homes in the Manchester area. Peace fired at the constable and the ball struck him in the chest. 'I got away which was all I wanted,' said Peace later. Two Irish brothers were accused of the crime and one of them was sentenced to death. He was not executed but imprisoned. Peace maintained silence until his confession 1878, after which the Irishman was pardoned and compensated.

At the same time he was pursuing with his attentions the young wife of a Sheffield neighbour, Arthur Dyson. His atten-

Charles Peace, burglar and murderer, who played the violin and used a violin-case to carry his burgling tools.

tions were unwelcome. He was a small slight man, looking older than his age, grey haired, with a peculiar kind of speech impediment. But he was strong and agile as a monkey, and his ability to contort his rubber like features into all kind of expressions had helped as disguise in his career as a burglar. In the summer of 1876 the situation with the Dysons boiled up with Peace threatening to blow out the brains of both husband and wife. A magistrate's warrant for his arrest was taken out but Peace and his family fled to Hull and the matter was dropped.

The Dysons hoped for tranquillity and moved in October to another neighbourhood in Sheffield. Charles Peace turned up as they moved in. The next month he appeared on the doorstep one evening and a violent scene ensued. While Arthur Dyson was pursuing Peace down a passage and on to the pavement two shots were fired. Dyson was hit in the head and died almost instantly.

Peace fled and for the next two years was on the run, with a reward on his head. He moved from town to town, making full use of his uncanny ability to disguise himself. On one occasion he called on his startled wife wearing a black suit, velvet waistcoat, and top hat, and leading a small fox-terrier. He escaped recognition and finally came South, establishing himself in a villa in Peckham with his wife and his mistress, a situation which Mrs Peace appears to have accepted though the two women quarrelled ceaselessly. Here he posed as a gentleman of independent means, interesting himself in his hobby as an inventor. He was known as Mr Thompson and attended church regularly with his wife. They entertained. Mr Thompson played his violin for the guests. At night however Mr Thompson carried out successful burglaries. During the day he drove round in his pony and trap locating suitable properties to be burgled. People knew all about the series of burglaries, but none connected respectable, hospitable Mr Thompson with them. Peace used to say that anyone who wore really good clothes was never suspected of misdemeanour.

On 10 October 1878 flickering light in a house in prosperous

Blackheath attracted the attention of PC Robinson as he patrolled in the early hours of the morning. Summoning colleagues, he investigated. A figure jumped out of the drawing-room window and ran. PC Robinson gave chase and five shots rang out, the last hitting him in the arm. None the less PC Robinson and his colleagues caught and arrested the burglar, who gave his name as John Ward.

At the Old Bailey, in spite of a long and whining plea for mercy, the judge sentenced John Ward to penal servitude for life. Worse was to come for Charles Peace as either his wife or his mistress, probably under police pressure, revealed the true identity of John Ward and of the vanished Mr Thompson. Peace was charged with the murder of Arthur Dyson.

The magistrate's hearing was in Sheffield. When Peace was taken from Pentonville on the early morning train in convict's garb and accompanied by two warders, he managed to throw himself out of the open window, presumably in the hope of killing himself. A warder caught his foot as he disappeared but the boot came off and Peace fell to the track, sustaining injuries but not fatal ones. He appeared in Court swathed in bandages and moaning and complaining loudly.

Peace was removed to Armley Gaol to await trial for murder at Leeds Assizes. The jury took only twelve minutes to reach a verdict of guilty and the death sentence was passed. While awaiting execution Peace made a full confession of all his crimes. He wrote his own memorial and constructed an elaborate model of a Victorian mausoleum out of cut paper which Madame Tussaud's was able to acquire along with one of his violins.

For those visitors to the Chamber of Horrors who wished to draw a moral lesson on the misuse of natural gifts, the wax effigy of Charles Peace provided an excellent example. He was talented and versatile, interested in theatricals, music, and versifying and could probably have made himself an outstanding name on the music halls of the Victorian age, had he not preferred the plunder of the cat-burglar, the thrill of moving his agile frame swiftly and smoothly over roof-tops and the pleasure he derived from his spoils as a natural thief who did not hesitate to murder.

With the start of the 1880s a new era opened for Madame Tussaud's exhibition and its essential component, the Chamber of Horrors. The lease of the premises where it had expanded and gained renown for almost half a century was running out. Now the exhibition was regarded as a London institution, but there were problems over a new lease. Madame Tussaud's grandsons decided they could now afford to build for themselves the kind of specially designed and worthy edifice that they needed for further expansion, improvement, and greater splendour.

A suitable site was available in Marylebone Road conveniently near at hand. It was purchased and excavations began in 1882. Two years later, the massive task of transporting the exhibition to its new and magnificent home began. On 14 July 1884, the new Madame Tussaud's exhibition opened its doors on the site where it stands today.

From the Chamber of Horrors fifty-six sheeted figures made the journey up Baker Street to their new home, together with the guillotine, the gallows, and numerous relics and 'objects'. In addition, and still at the heart of the Chamber of Horrors, were the portraits Madame Tussaud had selected from the *Caverne des Grands Voleurs* and brought with her to England eighty-two years earlier.

[5]

The Chamber of Horrors Expands in New Premises in Marylebone Road

There were seven halls in the spacious new building awaiting their wax population, and with one exception they were splendid with painted panels, ornate plasterwork, gilding and brilliant lighting. With such a stupendous task of carrying, unwrapping, setting-up and arranging, it was not surprising that when the press were invited for a preview on 12 July 1884 the Chamber of Horrors, now located in the basement beneath the richly decorated Napoleon Rooms, was not quite ready.

The reporter from the *London Weekly* viewing the new apartment thought that:

> 'Peace the burglar and Orsini the conspirator looked very funny with their forms swathed in white sheets, whilst Burke, as he lolled at an angle against the wall, seemed as if he had been making merry with his companions over the fact of removal from the close quarters of the old Chamber of Horrors to the broad, well-ventilated apartment in which they are henceforth to be domiciled.'

Other newspapers were less jocular, finding the new Chamber in keeping with the character of its occupants. Below ground level, at the back where the noise of traffic did not penetrate, the eerie silence was emphasized by the almost total absence of natural cheerful daylight. The *Morning Post* commented '. . . in the basement being the Chamber of Horrors in which alone of all the rooms the light comes dimly from the sides possibly with a view to adding to the lugubriousness of its general appearance'. It offered, said another reporter, a singular contrast with the agreeable contents of the general collection.

The big room was lofty, its roof supported on iron pillars. The man from *The Globe* was impressed. 'True to their custom of doing nothing by halves, Messrs Tussaud have given us a Chamber of Horrors which, except on the question of air and cleanliness, could hold its own against anything the old Bastille contained.'

Victor Tussaud, another of Madame Tussaud's grandsons, now working with his brothers in the exhibition, gave an interview to the *Pall Mall Gazette* on the subject of the inmates of this subterranean and creepy place. He told of the changes that had come about since the Chamber of Horrors had first been set up in England by his grandmother.

> 'In these days we may not visit criminals in their cells. Some of the casts have been done after execution of course or from sketches made in the cell. But now my brother (Joseph Randall) goes to the trial of anyone we wish to place in our museum. He takes pencil and sketch-book and from his notes we produce what you see. Nor do we put ourselves out to buy the clothes of the dead men. If they are brought to us we may buy them, but we do not look for them.'

Everything in the Chamber of Horrors was in order two days later for the grand opening reception. Even though the more recent portraits were not taken like the earlier ones from heads after execution, there was at least one person at the reception who found his nerves needed support in order to stand up to the sinister atmosphere of the Chamber. Since the distinguished company invited included dukes, numerous lords, and a bevy of MPs, the Tussaud brothers enlisted the help of the police to look after the safety of their guests. One police officer was put in charge of the Chamber of Horrors, but was given permission to stroll through other parts of the building including the refreshment room. The reception went on until after midnight and when the last guest had been ushered out the constable from the Chamber of Horrors was assumed to have taken his departure also—until the morning when heavy snores were heard issuing from one of the 'docks' in which some of the criminal effigies were arranged.

This police constable whose fall from grace is recorded by John Theodore Tussaud in *The Romance of Madame Tussaud* is probably the only person who has ever spent a night in the Chamber of Horrors. The Tussaud family were always at a loss to know how and where the rumour started that a reward would be paid to anyone who was brave enough to endure this ordeal.

John Theodore himself thought it arose from the writings of the journalist G. R. Sims (who also used the pen name 'Dagonet'). Sims, a friend of the family, and himself modelled for the exhibition, was fascinated by the Chamber and often mentioned it. In 1891 he himself decided to test his courage and failed. He wrote about his experience.

> 'I have been penetrating the secrets of Tussaud's lately and had a specially quiet half hour with the murderers in the Chamber of Horrors just to see what it was like.
>
> 'The idea came to me when I had been sitting late to John Tussaud. I wanted to see what it would feel like to be alone with these awful people with only one jet of gas lighting up their fearful features.
>
> 'After the door was shut I walked about and stared defiantly at William Corder and James Blomfield Rush and even went so far as to address Dr Eyraud in French. But wandering around in the semi-darkness I stumbled and fell and when I got up and looked round I found I was in Mrs Pearcey's kitchen.
>
> 'Then I made one wild rush at the closed door and hammered on it till the kindly watchman came and let me out. *I never want to be shut up alone at night in the Chamber of Horrors as long as I live!*'

Even those most closely associated with the Chamber and its inmates were not insensible to its atmosphere. John Theodore Tussaud always remembered the sudden shock and fright he experienced one evening walking through the 'Horrors' when it was empty and the lights dimmed. He saw a nearby murderer move and apparently lean forward as if to grab him. He was momentarily horrified—in the sinister, quiet room for an instant this seemed possible even to him. Investigation showed that the fastening holding the figure had worked loose and the vibration of a heavy goods train on the Metropolitan line had shifted and caused it to lean menacingly forward just as John Theodore was within reach.

Every now and again some incident would give fresh impetus to the story. In 1909, for example, a play entitled *The Whip*, which included a scene set in the Chamber of Horrors, was put on in the West End. On the opening night handbills were distributed offering £100 to anyone who would spend the night in the Chamber of Horrors, a piece of publicity which caused much waste of time at Madame Tussaud's where a spate of enquiries had to be answered. Even today the story is not dead and people enquire from time to time about the reward. However, no one but the inebriated policeman and G. R. Sims are known to have attempted spending the midnight hours locked in there.

Less than six months after the opening of the new building, Madame Tussaud's set up in the Chamber of Horrors a portrait model with one of the most bizarre and unusual stories that ever lay behind a crime. It aroused widespread and intense public controversy and argument. The portrait was of Captain Dudley, captain of a yacht called the *Mignonette*, and the charge against him was murder and cannibalism on the high seas. The jury were faced with a tale that must have seemed outside reality.

Early in 1884 an Australian lawyer purchased in England a yacht named *Mignonette* which he wished to have sailed on his behalf to Sydney, New South Wales. There was nothing unusual in this procedure which is frequently followed today. A purchaser buys a yacht and hires a crew to sail it to the port of his choice, often in another hemisphere.

The skipper chosen was Captain Thomas Dudley, an experienced sailor. He took as crew Edward Stephens, who acted as mate, and a man called Brooks, both also experienced seamen. The inevitable 'ship's boy' was a lad of between seventeen and eighteen years, Richard Parker, no doubt thrilled at this opportunity to sail the world.

The *Mignonette* was of English build and English registration, a sound vessel. The party sailed from Southampton and pursued their course normally until, when some 1,600 miles off the Cape of Good Hope, they encountered a severe storm in which the yacht foundered and the crew of four were obliged to take to their boat. They only carried one boat.

Either through overconfidence that they would run into no trouble or sheer carelessness, inexcusable in an experienced crew, this single boat had not been provisioned. It contained no drum of water, and the only food consisted of two eleven ounce tins of turnips which someone must have snatched up as they left the sinking yacht.

The yacht had been blown off sailing lanes, and sighted no ship. For three days the three men and the boy eked out the tins of turnip. On the fourth day they were lucky enough to capture a small turtle on which they survived until the twentieth day of their shipwreck. Now they had literally nothing to eat, and the only water they had consumed came from rain showers caught in their oilskin capes. The last of these showers had fallen three days earlier.

It was in these circumstances that Captain Dudley and mate Stephens discussed their plight with seaman Brooks. They reckoned they were 1,000 miles from land, off the sea lanes. The boy was not included in the talk when the two senior men suggested to Brooks that someone would have to be sacrificed if all their lives were not to be lost. Brooks dissented.

However, on 24 July Captain Dudley suggested that lots should be drawn to decide who should be put to death to save the lives of the others. The boy Richard Parker was not consulted, and again Brooks refused to consider any such plan. The next day both Dudley and Stephens spoke of their families, and Dudley put forward that it would be best to kill Richard Parker if they had sighted no vessel by the following morning.

On 25 July there was no sail in sight. Dudley suggested that Brooks should have a sleep while indicating that the time had now come to kill the boy. Brooks still held out though Stephens assented. The unhappy boy, even if he realized what was being proposed, was beyond protest. He lay helpless in the bottom of the boat extremely weak from famine and from drinking sea-water. He could offer no resistance, nor did he agree to sacrificing what remained of his life in order to save his companions.

Captain Dudley then offered a prayer for forgiveness if they were tempted to a rash act and that their souls would be saved. With Stephen's agreement he went to the prostrate boy, telling him his time had come, and straight away cut his throat. Brooks still did not assent.

For three days the men fed upon the body of Richard Parker. On the fourth they were sighted by a barque and rescued alive though in a state of extreme prostration. Finally the barque landed the three men at Falmouth where, their story being made known, Dudley and Stephens were committed for trial at Exeter on a charge of murdering Richard Parker on the high seas. Brooks was not charged though it later came out in the evidence that, the boy having been killed, he joined his companions in partaking of the flesh in order to save his life.

The trial took place before Baron Huddleston on 7 November 1884. The case obviously aroused both public interest and emotion. Finally the judge directed the jury to return a special verdict which enabled the case to be transferred to the Royal Courts of Justice in London. The defence had argued that in the circumstances it had appeared to the accused that there was no hope of rescue and unless they fed on the boy or on themselves they would die of starvation, and that as the boy was weak he would in all probability have died first anyway. Finally the case was decided by a panel of five judges. The verdict was guilty and the death sentence automatically passed.

Joseph Randall Tussaud had sat long hours in Court and the portrait of Captain Dudley, convicted of murder and cannibalism on the high seas, immediately joined the ranks in the Chamber of Horrors. Controversy raged round the facts of the case and the culpability of men placed in the frightful circumstances that faced the three sailors.

The Weekly Despatch commented that to put Captain Dudley's figure in Madame Tussaud's showed questionable taste, but other newspapers disagreed. Both the *Morning Advertiser* and the *News of the World* found the likeness excellent, and remarked on the large crowds that flocked in who were much more likely to have been attracted by Captain Dudley than by the effigy of Mrs Eliza Gibbons who had been found guilty of murdering her husband and entered the Chamber at the same time.

In the event neither Captain Dudley nor Stephens went to the gallows. The Crown soon commuted their sentence to six months imprisonment. Captain Dudley retired into obscurity and his wax effigy also disappeared quietly after one of the shortest stays ever recorded in the Chamber of Horrors. Mrs Eliza Gibbons did not hang either for her sentence was commuted to life imprisonment. However, a woman who had done away with her husband always had a public attraction and she held her place for three years to come.

After accomplishing the stupendous task of moving the exhibition from Baker Street to Marylebone Road Madame Tussaud's grandson, Joseph Randall, decided to retire from his controlling position in studio and management in 1885. In spite of having played a full part since his youth he had always battled against ill health. He was much given to colds and moods of deep depression and the recent death of his beloved wife Nellie who had borne him thirteen children caused him deep grief which he could not overcome. Although Joseph Randall lived on for seven years after his retirement he took no active participation after his withdrawal.

Even if Joseph Randall had not inherited the robust health, drive and resilience of his grandmother, she had passed these qualities on in full measure to Joseph Randall's son, John Theodore, who now took the helm as artistic director. He had contributed his first wax portrait figure to the exhibition when he was only fourteen, and now at twenty-six was fully trained. Other members of the family were also training and would join studio, wardrobe and management.

As regards the Chamber of Horrors, John Theodore Tussaud, as principal modeller, would attend the trials of criminals judged suitable for inclusion. John Theodore's exceptional energy and skill enabled him to produce a remarkable output of work both for the main exhibition and the Chamber of Horrors. He kept up standards and developed into a martinet to whom, like his great-grandmother, the maintenance of the exhibition, its interest, its quality and its innovation was the ruling passion of his life. Amongst the 'subjects' he modelled during his first year as head of the studio was a murderer who achieved social notoriety because three attempts to hang him after the death penalty had been passed failed to produce any result.

The convicted murderer, John Lee, always proclaimed his innocence. He was a lad of nineteen and worked as a footman in the household of an old lady, Miss Emma Keyes, who had once been a maid to Queen Victoria and now, retired, lived at Babbacombe in comfortable circumstances. Miss Keyes, though not short of money, was a strict and parsimonious mistress. In November 1884 she was found dead, lying on her dining-room floor, and the room was on fire. She had been brutally murdered with head injuries and her throat cut.

There was no direct evidence but suspicion fell on the young footman John Lee who, it was discovered, had already served a sentence for stealing. Also he was known to have been angered because the strict Miss Keyes had reduced his already small wage on account of some trivial misdemeanour.

Though the evidence was purely circumstantial the jury thought it sufficiently convincing to find him guilty of murder and the death penalty followed. When Berry the hangman came to perform his duty all the grim routine procedures were carried out normally. The hooded prisoner stood on the trap waiting for the hangman to pull the lever which would release it and send the convicted man to eternity.

Berry pulled the lever. Nothing happened. The trap refused to budge. It is said the executioner even stamped on it furiously. The condemned man (who said he had dreamed he would not hang) was removed while the mechanism was examined and tested. It worked perfectly. John Lee was replaced on the trap which again refused to drop. Further checks were made which showed the mechanism apparently in perfect working order. All those present were horrified when for the third time the prisoner was placed on the drop and for the third time the trap refused to fall.

John Lee was taken back to his cell and within hours the death sentence was commuted to life imprisonment. This extraordinary failed hanging made the effigy of Lee and that of the executioner Berry, whose figure was already in the Chamber of Horrors, a focus of interest, and he kept his place in the Chamber for nearly twenty years—the man they could not hang. John Lee himself remained in prison until 1907. On his release he married and emigrated to America where he lived until his death in 1933.

The notorious case of Mrs Maybrick was another which brought John Theodore's modelling powers particularly into the public eye. She was an attractive woman, a striking subject. American-born Florence Maybrick was tried at Liverpool in 1889 for the murder of her husband, an English Liverpool merchant. He was twenty years her senior, a hypochondriac given to dosing himself with drugs and medicines.

When the Maybricks settled in Liverpool they lived in some style. It was six years after their marriage that Florence discovered that her husband had a mistress, and also that they were in financial difficulties. Many a respectable middle-aged Victorian gentleman had a mistress, a situation that most wives accepted without exhibiting undue resentment, preferring to keep quiet. Florence reduced her expenditure and sought consolation with a friend of her husband with whom she rather unwisely spent a weekend in London. Maybrick discovered this escapade and was furious. He beat Florence and drew up a new will excluding his wife from all benefit. Soon afterwards he became ill and Florence wrote to her lover saying that her husband was 'sick unto death'.

This letter never reached its destination. It was intercepted by the household nanny who disliked Florence. She handed it to one of Maybrick's brothers whose suspicions were aroused. They searched the house and found a packet labelled 'Arsenic for Cats'. It also came to light that Florence had earlier on purchased three dozen arsenic fly papers—freely on sale for use in fly-ridden kitchens and dining-rooms—which she said she had soaked to make a preparation for the complexion. Arsenic was believed to clear the skin.

Maybrick unfortunately died and since traces of arsenic were found in his body Florence was arrested and charged with poisoning him with arsenic. As the trial proceeded a great prejudice built up against her not so much on account of the accusation that she had poisoned her husband but because her adultery was publicly revealed. There were traces of other poisonous drugs in Maybrick's body and the defence tried to claim that, with the arsenic, they were all the result of the deceased's self-dosing. Arsenic eating and chloroform-sniffing and swallowing were far from unknown amongst Victorian hypochondriacs, while doses of laudanum which would be considered excessive today were commonly taken for a number of complaints.

However the judge (who later became insane) summed up heavily against Florence Maybrick and the jury found her guilty of murdering her husband. John Theodore Tussaud lost no time in modelling Mrs Maybrick. The figure was placed in one of the small rooms outside the Chamber of Horrors. She stood in a framework of black and red drapery, dressed in black with a Russian cloak of black crêpe over her dress. Her bonnet had long streamers of crêpe and a transparent veil. It was stated that the excellent likeness with golden-brown hair and brown eyes

Mrs Maybrick who was convicted of the murder of her husband in 1889.

had been rapidly modelled because John Theodore did not believe that she would be found guilty and did not start work until the verdict was actually pronounced.

The *New York Herald* which reported the case of American-born Florence Maybrick in detail claimed that John Theodore had descriptions wired to him by an agent in Liverpool and also went to a great deal of trouble to obtain an 'admirable' photograph. The portrait was set up in the exhibition on 11 August and drew an enormous crowd—'like a Bank Holiday' said John Theodore. However, Mrs Maybrick's portrait never actually entered the Chamber of Horrors for her sentence was commuted to life imprisonment and there was considerable public feeling that this attractive and much-tried woman whose hypochondriac husband had put her in financial difficulties as well as deceiving her with a mistress had been convicted more because she committed adultery than because there was conclusive proof that she had killed her husband by poisoning him with arsenic. After fifteen years in prison she was released and returned to the United States, surviving to the age of seventy-six. She retained her place in the 'second room' outside the Chamber of Horrors for five years.

There was one notorious murderer who claimed five victims in a short period of three months in 1888 whose portrait figure was never modelled. This was Jack the Ripper.

Five miserable prostitutes who earned their meagre living in the dark and seedy streets of London's East End were discovered in turn, lying with their throats cut and their bodies ripped and slit open, in the secluded corners to which they had been lured. There was no sign that any of the women had struggled or fought. The murderer knew the East End well for he vanished unseen and left no clues. Queen Victoria was moved to comment on these shocking murders, and the conscience of the public was pricked to such an extent that questions about the poverty and social conditions in the East End were asked even in Parliament.

Letters signed 'Jack the Ripper' were received by a London news agency (Madame Tussaud's possesses one such letter) but the police were totally frustrated. The Ripper's skill in carving up his victims suggested medical knowledge. Wild theories abounded as to the possible identity of the murderer, ranging from the dissipated Duke of Clarence and well-known freemasons to mad doctors and slaughtermen. In years to come other murderers who went to the scaffold for other killings were suggested as possibilities, Neil Cream, George Chapman and Frederick Deeming.

These three murderers would later enter the Chamber of Horrors on account of the crimes for which they were executed, but Jack the Ripper was never modelled though many visitors expressed surprise at this. However, Madame Tussaud's descendants refused to depart from her original policy. Any likeness of Jack the Ripper would be completely imaginary. No one had caught a glimpse of his figure, or even a likely figure, let alone a face. Even today, though one of his victims stands in the Chamber, lurking in the corner of a Victorian street waiting for a client, Jack the Ripper is not there.

In October 1890 just before the newly installed electric light was switched on in the exhibition and bathed the Chamber of Horrors in a dim green glow, John Theodore completed two portraits which *The Evening Standard* thought would certainly focus public attention. The first of these concerned the murder of an Englishman in Canada, a chilling deterrent to those who were being encouraged to emigrate and populate the rich farmlands that awaited them there. Benwell's frozen body, shot in the head, was found by two local farmers near Princeton, Ontario.

Frederick Benwell had met Richard Birchall and his wife travelling from Liverpool to New York. Later at Niagara they discussed entering into partnership in a farm. Birchall had already sold a share in another farm to a newly-arrived Englishman called Kelly and was subsequently alleged to have made two attempts on Kelly's life.

Birchall the entrepreneur extracted £500 from Frederick Benwell and the pair of them went off to inspect a farm in Ontario. Richard Birchall returned from this trip alone. He said the farm proved to be useless and Benwell had opted out. But when the frozen body of Frederick Benwell, shot in the head, was discovered, witnesses came forward to say that they had seen the two men together around Princeton at the relevant time and shots had been heard. Birchall was charged with murder and in spite of an impassioned plea in his defence he was found guilty. The £500 he had obtained from his fellow Englishman and new inexperienced immigrant led him to the gallows in November 1890. The Canadian hangman insisted on using an unorthodox noose so that the execution was by strangulation rather than by dislocation of the neck. A note by John Theodore mentions that the hangman sold the rope (or more likely a part of it) to the exhibition but no trace of this relic survives. The catalogue entry in this murder of a would-be colonist by a fellow-colonist might have been written by the late Madame Tussaud herself, 'Birchall belongs to the category of utterly callous murderers who appear wanting in all moral sense.'

The second portrait figure that particularly impressed *The Evening Standard* was one that halted visitors before a startling innovation. An American, William Kemmler, had been executed by electricity in the prison of Auburn, USA. His crime was the murder of a woman he had persuaded to elope with him. John Theodore modelled Kemmler's head and body from sketches obtained specially from America, and the scientific studies in which he dabbled helped him to reproduce exactly the new instrument of execution.

The electric chair in which Kemmler was seated was placed almost in the centre of the Chamber of Horrors. Visitors had a clear view of its high back and movable leg-rests. A metal cap held the prisoner at the head and another plate was at the spine. The method of strapping and wiring could be closely inspected.

These two new additions provided some extra drama when the green electric lights were switched on. Also a little French prison cell had been constructed to hold a wax model of the French murderer Eyraud. Eyraud, with the help of his mistress Gabrielle Bompard, lured a court bailiff named Gouffe to the girl's apartment. Gouffe, a widower, was known to have a weakness for girls and he was officially involved in bringing bankruptcy proceedings against Eyraud, an army deserter and a business man of disreputable character. Michel Eyraud and Gabrielle Bompard robbed the court bailiff and Eyraud then killed him. Together they sewed the body in a sack, put it in a trunk, and took it to Lyons where it was finally discovered on a riverside site outside the town.

Eyraud and Bompard then fled France but soon after the discovery of the body, when forensic tests and the evidence of witnesses had been pieced together, the police search for them was extended to America as well as all over Europe. In January 1890 the Chef de Sûreté in Paris received a letter from Eyraud written from New York and putting all the blame for the robbery and murder on Gabrielle Bompard. That young lady, however, evidently aware of her former lover's action, presented herself personally to the police in Paris claiming that she had merely been Eyraud's tool and was willing to tell the true story.

Michel Eyraud was arrested in Havana and brought to Paris for trial. He was found guilty and guillotined in February 1891 while Gabrielle Bompard received a sentence of twenty-five years penal servitude. Eyraud was modelled by John Theodore Tussaud before his sentence was passed. He was shown as an anxious and dejected figure sitting on a stool in his Paris cell awaiting his destiny.

Nearby was the effigy of Wright, the Hoxton burglar, who in 1884 was too quick with a revolver when he shot at three constables. He had received three dozen lashes as well as his sentence of penal servitude for life. Wright had not been pleased at the punishment meted out to him. In Court he cried out 'Penal sinks a man to what is worse than the life of a dog . . . *I will not endure it*!' The law was deaf and Wright served his sentence in spite of his objections. He stayed eighty-four years in the Chamber of Horrors.

Mrs Maybrick may have drawn Bank Holiday size crowds to the Chamber of Horrors but her attraction was to be eclipsed by that of another woman killer, Mrs Eleanor Pearcey, who slew

THE HAMPSTEAD TRAGEDY.

MRS. PEARCEY.

A MODEL OF THE KITCHEN, containing the identical Furniture and Fixtures from No 2, Priory Street, where Mrs. Hogg and her Baby were murdered.

LIST OF FURNITURE, &c.,

TABLE, CHAIRS, OILCLOTH, COOKING UTENSILS, CROCKERY, FIREPLACE. GRATE, WINDOW AND FLOORING.

THE TABLE against which Mrs. Hogg was supposed to have been leaning when the blows were struck.

THE WINDOW supposed to have been smashed by Mrs. Hogg in her death struggles.

All the articles contained in the Kitchen have been removed from No. 2, Priory Street, and are placed in exact relative position as found by the Police when they entered the premises.

Mrs. PEARCEY'S SITTING ROOM, with her identical Furniture, Couch, Chairs, Table, Mirror, Carpet, Piano, Ornaments, Curtains, Blinds, &c.

The Piano is the one on which Mrs. Pearcey played whilst the Police were searching her house.

Mrs. PEARCEY'S BEDSTEAD and FURNITURE.

THE PERAMBULATOR in which the Bodies were carried.

CASTS OF THE HEADS OF Mrs. HOGG AND HER BABY, taken from Nature after death.

THE CLOTHES worn by Mrs. Hogg and Baby when murdered.

Mrs. PEARCEY'S RECEIPT in her own handwriting.

THE TOFFEE found in the Perambulator.

The Figures of Mr. and Mrs. Hogg and their Baby are placed in the Ground Floor Gallery.

A catalogue entry detailing the effects of Mrs Pearcey purchased by Madame Tussaud's.

with extraordinary ferocity driven by insane jealousy. This time John Theodore Tussaud had no doubts about the outcome of the trial and was ready. On 24 November 1890 the *Lloyd's Newspaper* reporter wrote:

> 'MADAME TUSSAUD'S Sensation follows sensation at this popular show Mrs Pearcey (or Wheeler) had not been sentenced to death for more than an hour for the cruel murder of Mrs Hogg at Hampstead than Hey Presto! her faithful presentiment in wax was set up in the midst of her late surroundings at the Chamber of Horrors . . . The Tussauds, it seems, had purchased for £200 (which went for her defence) all the wretched woman's furniture, clothing, etc., and there in her little sitting-room she leans on the mantlepiece—the ancient piano, trifling ornaments, pictures, carpets, lounge and chairs complete. Just beyond stand the broken perambulator and even the piece of toffee found therein, while close by, in a showcase, is the cardigan jacket that proved such a silent witness of her guilt, also other bloodstained garments. On a table lie grim waxen casts of the murdered woman's head and that of her ill-fated babe. The kitchen where the crime was committed is being arranged and visitors are flocking by thousands.'

30,000 people are said to have blocked the streets outside the exhibition to view the perpetrator of a crime as horrible as it was unlikely and bizarre. The people concerned in this crime were very ordinary, living in modest comfort in North London. Mrs Pearcey, though her marital status seems doubtful (she was born Mary Eleanor Wheeler), lived alone at 2 Priory Street, Kentish Town. She was friendly with a young married couple (Mrs Pearcey herself was only twenty-four) called Frank and Phoebe Hogg who lived not far off and the husband's sister, Clara Hogg, lived with them. The Hoggs had an eighteen-month-old baby. Frank was a bearded man, quite good-looking in a commonplace way, and his wife was a pleasant-faced young woman.

On 24 October 1890 two policemen patrolling Crossfield Road, Hampstead, were shocked to come upon the body of a woman whose head had been almost severed from its trunk, and nearby was a bloodstained perambulator. A further search of some waste ground produced the corpse of an eighteen-month-old baby.

On that same day, 24 October, Mrs Hogg had taken her baby out in its pram but had not mentioned where she was going. When they did not return at the usual time, Frank Hogg did not appear particularly concerned at their lateness, but his sister Clara began to worry. She went along to consult with the family friend, Mrs Pearcey. By now the discovery of a woman's body in Crossfield Road had become public knowledge. Anxiously Clara Hogg accompanied by Eleanor Pearcey went to the police mortuary. Shocked and horrified as she was to see her sister-in-law's body lying on the slab, Clara Hogg's reaction was nothing compared with that of Mrs Pearcey who went into hysterics and behaved in such a way that police suspicions were aroused and they began a few investigations. They discovered that Frank Hogg had a key to Mrs Pearcey's house and it was evident they had been indulging in a love-affair.

When the police arrived to search Mrs Pearcey's house, they found the kitchen in a shambles with broken glass and furniture, and bloodstains. Mrs Pearcey sat playing her piano while the search was carried on. When questioned about the bloodstains she cried 'Mice! I have been killing mice!' but the slaughter of mice did not explain away the items of bloody clothing and two knives and a chopper in similar condition. Mrs Pearcey herself was searched and bloodstains found on her under-clothes. Letters came to light which left no doubt as to the relationship between herself and Frank Hogg. Mrs Pearcey was arrested.

The 'atrocious circumstances' of what became known as 'The Hampstead Tragedy' brought crowds even to the preliminary hearing in the Marylebone Magistrates' Court. On 3 November Marylebone Police Court was crowded for the second hearing of the case. Ladies and gentlemen were even provided with seats on the Bench. Amongst these personages were one of the attachés of the Chinese Embassy, Viscount Dangan, Viscount Royston, Sir Charles Hartopp, Lord Cardross, Lord Greenock and Sir W. Melville. None of them can have had any personal interest in the comparatively humble people involved but the lure of the macabre was irresistible.

The accused woman was small and insignificant-looking. It seemed inconceivable that she could have hacked and battered to death Mrs Hogg and her baby, piled the inert and blood-stained bodies on to the child's perambulator, pushed them nearly two miles to Crossfield Road and dumped them.

A lady reporter sat in Court for the publication *Pioneer* and observed the prisoner closely; 'the alleged murderess is a quiet-looking little woman by no means handsome—a large chin bold in its curves but not heavy, a very large weak mobile mouth, and large eyes which she continually directs from side to side scarcely moving her head. Otherwise she sat in the dock as motionless as a waxwork at Madame Tussaud's . . . '

The last words of the lady reporter proved prophetic. Mrs Pearcey was brought to trial at the Old Bailey in December 1890. Pleas of hallucination were of no avail. It was clear that Eleanor Pearcey was blindly infatuated with Frank Hogg. She had invited Phoebe Hogg to visit her on 24 October and, whether by premeditation or impulse, had set on her in an absolute frenzy of jealousy, finding the strength to hack her rival and the baby to death and, still sustained by jealous frenzy, to cart their bodies an appreciable distance away from her house. Thereafter her frenzy seems to have failed her for she had made little effort to clean up the kitchen where she performed her onslaught.

Conviction was inevitable. A neighbour had heard screams coming from Mrs Pearcey's house but in respectable discreet neighbourhoods one did not interfere. Another witness had watched Mrs Pearcey pushing a loaded perambulator in the direction of Crossfield Road. Though Mrs Pearcey stoutly maintained she was innocent she was found guilty and sentenced to death. No one will ever know what incident, what

The wax model of Mrs Eleanor Pearcey shown with the piece of toffee sucked by the baby just before she killed it.

words, brought Mrs Pearcey's jealousy to the pitch of insanity, but her lover Frank Hogg extended her no compassion.

Not even the sentence of death could quench Eleanor Pearcey's longing to see Frank Hogg. She begged him to come and see her in prison, but he refused. She even managed to obtain an order which would permit him to visit her and sent it to him. He returned it.

Mrs Pearcey wrote to her solicitor the evening before her execution. After thanking him for his help and support she mentions that Frank Hogg had returned the visiting order. 'It is the last kindness he could have done for me on earth. Will you tell him I forgive him as I hope to be forgiven. But he might have made death easier to bear.'

Frank Hogg could show no pity for a weak-willed woman for whose actions, dreadful though they were, he was in part morally responsible. His sister Clara was able to bring herself to offer a consoling word to a former friend facing immediate death, for Mrs Pearcey ends her last letter to her solicitor with the words 'Just had such a kind letter from Miss Hogg Monday evening, 5.55.'

All classes of Victorian society which had access to art evinced a great appetite for paintings and engravings which told a story. It might be the story of a historical incident, such as the murder of the little Princes in the Tower, or very often the representation of some tense, tragic or sentimental family occasion.

John Theodore had inherited from his great-grandmother a flair for creating tableaux which accorded well with this contemporary taste. Tableaux had always been included in the exhibition since Curtius, Madame Tussaud's 'uncle', introduced 'The Royal Family at Dinner' into his *Salon de Cire* in Paris in the 1780s, and his *Caverne des Grands Voleurs* was also successful with tableaux such as the assassination of Marat in his bath or the scene in a café when Lepelletier, one of the regicides who voted for Louis XVI's death, was assassinated by a Royalist.

There were already tableaux in the main exhibition and the

installation of electric light in 1890 inspired John Theodore to evolve a new dramatic scene depicting the execution of Mary Queen of Scots at Fotheringay Castle in which the doomed Queen lay blindfolded with her head on the block.

At the same time that this striking tableau was unveiled to the public upstairs, down in the Chamber of Horrors the reconstruction of the kitchen and sitting-room of the Hampstead murderess, Mrs Eleanor Pearcey, amounted virtually to a tableau and was having enormous impact. It was partly the realization of this that led John Theodore to a new concept of tableaux specially for the Chamber of Horrors. He would create one in the form of six separate scenes depicting a man's downfall, tragedy and ultimate death as a murderer on the gallows. Its creator also freely acknowledged the influence of the artist William Frith's attempts to rival the morality pictures of Hogarth, and in particular Frith's *The Road to Ruin*.

John Theodore applied his inexhaustible energies for months to his 'The Story of a Crime' or 'The Six Stages of Wrong'. He took immense care over the detail as well as the drama of each of the six scenes that composed the tableau. When they were opened to the public on 15 December 1891 the reporter from *The Evening Standard* wrote 'Six new and artistic "Horrors" have been prepared for Madame Tussaud's show by the skilled hand of Mr John T. Tussaud . . . in every detail Mr Tussaud's work is remarkable for accuracy and realism'. *The Chronicle* called the new series 'grim but extremely realistic'.

While the concept was in tune with contemporary taste 'The Story of a Crime' did involve some departure from Madame Tussaud's policy for the Chamber of Horrors. Hitherto the presentation of accurate likenesses of real criminals had been the rule. The new tableau concerned imaginary characters and an imaginary crime.

It was the story of a young family man inevitably short of money lured into a gambling den by evil acquaintances. Tempted by the thought of easy money he cannot resist the invitation to play. After fleecing their victim the gamblers, three men and a woman, disappear from the room leaving their victim penniless. He has recourse to a moneylender who finally, after demanding the return of a loan and high interest without success, puts the bailiffs into the young man's home while his weeping wife and scared child look on in horror. The desperate victim rushes to the moneylender's office where the cash is kept. Failing to get more time to pay or a further loan he kills the usurer in a fit of frenzy. In the fifth scene the ruined man is shown in the dock standing trial, and in the last he is leaving the condemned cell pinioned and supported by the hangman and warder and preceded by the chaplain who leads him to the scaffold. It was grim and realistic indeed and, in the words of another news reporter, 'could not fail to be very popular'.

In subsequent years there were other special Chamber of Horrors tableaux such as 'The Opium Den' and 'The Coiners'. For accuracy these scenes were based on information that John Theodore obtained from the police. They provided variety in the everthronging, everchanging ranks of murderers and other criminals, but none ever quite repeated the impact and popularity of 'The Story of a Crime'. The six scenes were badly damaged by smoke and water when in 1925 the exhibition was burnt out except for the basement. John Theodore did not revive them when the reconstructed exhibition opened in 1928.

In 1892 John Theodore had another opportunity of reconstructing the scene of a crime (as he had done so successfully with Mrs Pearcey's kitchen and sitting-room). Although the murderer, Frederick Deeming, was tried and executed in Australia his first murders had been committed in England and it was investigation into his past by Australian police that unearthed them and they aroused intense public interest.

Frederick Deeming was a plumber and gas-fitter who worked in Liverpool where he rented a house in a district called Rainhill. He had a wife, Marie, and four children. In October 1891 he left the rented house at Rainhill and it seemed as if the entire family emigrated to Australia, for Marie and the children were not seen again in Liverpool.

Deeming arrived in Sydney alone and began working at his trade. He moved to Melbourne and also took a new wife. She

The last episode of the 'Story of a Crime' showed the condemned man being led to the gallows.

did not remain at his side for very long and police came to look at his house after complaints of an unpleasant smell. They began investigations and found the body of his new wife cemented under the hearthstone. The head had been crushed by a blow with some heavy implement. Frederick Deeming was already 'wanted' in Australia for larceny and was now charged with murder.

The Melbourne press took up his case and set their London correspondents to finding out more about Deeming's background in Lancashire. The Australian and English police were also exchanging information and it was not long before the house at Rainhill was located. Soon located, too, were the bodies of Marie Deeming and her four small children who were thought to have emigrated with Frederick. Instead they were found buried under the cement floor of the fireplace.

In May 1892 less than a year after he had killed his wife and children and left for Australia, Deeming stood trial for murder. He was ably defended by a barrister who later became Prime Minister of Australia but the plea of insanity was rejected by the jury though both his crimes seemed motiveless. He gained nothing by them. It was suggested that he might have been Jack the Ripper though he was still only thirty-eight when he was executed in Australia on 23 May 1892. A crowd of 10,000 people stood outside the prison.

There were plenty of descriptions and published likenesses from which John Theodore Tussaud could set to work on the portrait of this multiple murderer, and he did much more than model a figure. 'The Actual Kitchen' from Dinham Villa, Rainhill, Liverpool, in which the bodies of the hapless Mrs Deeming and the children had been buried was removed intact from Rainhill to the exhibition. Removed too was the identical cement floor that had concealed the bodies, and various other relics connected with the murder were put on display. The figure of Deeming was dressed in 'the actual uniform he wore at Rainhill'. Deeming had often sported an Indian regimental uniform to which he was not entitled. Madame Tussaud's acquired this and a problem was caused when the Commanding

Officer of the regiment concerned happened to pay a visit to the exhibition.

It was on account of a suspected murder and a scenic tableau related to it that Madame Tussaud's were faced with lengthy legal proceedings in 1894 and 1895. The alleged murder, known as 'The Ardlamont Mystery', had an extraordinary and complicated background.

Alfred John Monson was a tutor living in Yorkshire who coached boys for entrance examinations. It seemed a modest and harmless mode of livelihood until in 1890 a Major Hamborough, a retired military man and landowner who was in acute financial trouble, sent his seventeen-year-old son Cecil to Mr Monson for tuition. After a time Monson, in the hope of benefit and gain, managed to embroil himself in the inextricable financial tangles of Major Hamborough's mortgaged estates and the moneylender from whom the Major borrowed.

Disputes arose and Monson and his wife left Yorkshire and went to live at Ardlamont, Argyllshire, Scotland. They took with them Cecil Hamborough over whom Monson appeared to have gained a complete ascendancy. Monson took out a life insurance for £20,000 on Cecil using money he had obtained by false pretences. He also persuaded the boy to instruct the insurers that in the event of his death the money was to be paid to Monson's wife.

On 9 August 1893 Alfred Monson was said to have tried to drown Cecil during a fishing trip by boat. The following day he took the boy rabbit-shooting accompanied by a man named Scott. Monson returned alone saying Cecil had shot himself during the expedition.

The canny Scots doctor who was asked to examine the dead youth asked if the victim had taken out any insurance, to which Monson replied in the negative. However, the insurance company were suspicious when a claim was made and sent in investigators. This resulted in the arrest of Monson on charges of both the attempted murder and the murder of Cecil Hamborough. Monson stood trial at Edinburgh in December 1893 but the judge appeared to favour the accused's defence that he would not have benefited from the boy's death and made the famous statement: 'It is the business of the Crown to prove the case, not for the defence to prove innocence'. The jury returned the Scottish verdict of 'not proven' and Monson walked free from the Court.

The Ardlamont Mystery aroused considerable public interest and discussion. John Theodore Tussaud constructed a scenic representation of the woodland glade near Ardlamont where the unfortunate Cecil Hamborough had met his death by accident or design, and he modelled Alfred Monson in shooting outfit. Monson's figure was placed (where Mrs Maybrick's had earlier been placed) in an ante-room to the Chamber of Horrors but not in it—however still in a location where people had to pay the sixpence extra to see it.

In January 1894 Monson sought an injunction from the Courts to compel Madame Tussaud's to remove the effigy, saying that its display implied he was involved in the death of Cecil Hamborough. After considerable litigation and an appeal Monson lost his injunction and many visitors came to gaze at his wax portrait and the woodland glade tableau.

The following year with Monson's effigy still in its place in the exhibition he took further action and sued Madame Tussaud's for libel. Again many weeks were spent in litigation, affording excellent publicity for John Theodore's work. This time Alfred Monson won but instead of the substantial damages he had hoped for he only gained one farthing compensation. John Theodore was astute like his great-grandmother. Had he placed his portrait of Alfred Monson actually in the Chamber of Horrors cheek by jowl with rows of murderers it might have been a different matter. But *outside* the Chamber the effigy was after all only taking its place amongst those of many who were or had been in the public eye, a position usually considered a compliment rather than defamatory!

During the last years of Queen Victoria's long reign the Chamber of Horrors reached the peak of its fame. While no subsequent criminal portrait drew crowds quite as vast and eager as those attracted by Mrs Pearcey, the Hampstead murderess, there was no lack of crime sufficiently horrible in one way or another to satisfy the taste of the age. Two criminals in particular who took their allotted place in the Chamber seemed to epitomize human wickedness.

The first of these was the compulsive poisoner, Dr Thomas Neill Cream, whose start in life had been promising enough. He was born in Glasgow in 1850 and taken to Canada by his parents when he was still a child. Nothing is known of his upbringing until he became a medical student at McGill University from which he graduated in 1876. While he was not outstanding for any particular brilliance in his medical studies he passed his examinations adequately and left with a degree of Doctor of Medicine, and Master of Surgery. His only peculiarity seems to have been that he was cross-eyed, a defect which did not impair his ability to study.

After graduating he left for Chicago and set up practice. Instead of pursuing the normal course of a young newly qualified doctor he embarked on an extraordinary and unnecessary life of crime which included arson, abortion and finally murder. His motives seem obscure unlike those of his medical predecessor, the mass poisoner, Dr William Palmer of Rugeley, who killed solely for monetary gain.

When Dr Cream gave strychnine to the husband of his current mistress, Mr Stott took the pills trustingly, dying shortly afterwards. Cream then drew attention to his crime by suggesting to the District Attorney that Mr Stott's body should be exhumed and examined. When the strychnine was found Cream and Mrs Stott briefly fled together but she changed her mind and gave evidence against her former lover when he was brought to trial. Cream was convicted and sentenced to life imprisonment but for some inexplicable reason he was released after serving ten years.

In 1891 Cream left Joliet Prison and sailed for England. He still held his medical degrees from McGill University and took rooms at 103 Lambeth Palace Road. With his cross-eyed glance and always wearing a tall silk hat he became a familiar figure especially to the numerous prostitutes who plied their trade in

Lambeth. Suddenly death struck several of these girls. The first to go was Ellen Donworth who fell twisting with pain on the pavement of Waterloo Road after taking some 'white stuff' from a bottle handed to her by a tall gentleman. Ellen could tell no more for she died on her way to hospital. The white stuff she had taken proved to be strychnine.

This mysterious death took place on 18 October 1891. A few days later another prostitute, Matilda Clover, was found dying in her room after taking some pills given to her by a man she knew as Fred. Again strychnine was the killer.

There was a lull in the activities of 'The Lambeth Poisoner', but Dr Cream was not idle. He became engaged to a respectable young dressmaker and had a trip to North America but in the spring of 1892 he was at work again. Two more prostitutes died in hospital in convulsions after taking 'long thin pills' given to them by a man they too knew as Fred.

As he had done in Chicago many years earlier Cream could not resist drawing attention to himself by contacting the police. He complained he was being followed and even offered to name 'The Lambeth Poisoner' for a reward of £300,000. He was arrested in June 1892 on a charge of false pretences but this soon changed to a charge of murder. What Cream did not know was that when he had given pills to another prostitute the previous year she had not swallowed them. She now came forward. Her name was Louisa Harvey and one night she had picked up Dr Cream in the usual way and he had spent the rest of the night with her. When he left he promised her some pills to clear up the spots on her face. She arranged to meet him in a public house where he greeted her with a bunch of roses and then with some 'long pills' which he insisted she must swallow immediately. Louisa was suspicious, and contrived to pretend she was swallowing them whereas in fact she dropped the pills unnoticed on the floor.

When Dr Cream was brought to trial the evidence against him was formidable. Apart from the evidence of Louisa Harvey who had escaped death by her dexterity in getting rid of Cream's pills there was the testimony of the chemist who sold him nux vomica and most damning of all were the seven bottles of strychnine found in his lodging. The jury only took twelve minutes to reach their verdict of guilty. Cream's optician had suggested that the total degeneracy of his behaviour might have been due to the psychological effects of his cross-eyes which had not been corrected in childhood and Cream himself refused to admit guilt.

He was executed on 15 November 1892 and as the bolt on the scaffold was drawn he is alleged to have said 'I am Jack the . . . ' The trap dropped before the sentence was finished but this remark which quickly became public gave an additional interest to the pointless murders committed by 'The Lambeth Poisoner'. Whatever he had meant to say Dr Cream could not be identified as the unknown Jack the Ripper whose savage murders of prostitutes in the East End had taken place in 1888 when he was still incarcerated in prison in America.

The trial of Dr Neill Cream threw some light on the sordid world in which the Victorian prostitute earned her living so close alongside the respectable, secure, complacent environment of the middle and upper classes. The second criminal who seemed to personify wickedness illumined another evil, well known to all, but seldom talked of or even thought of in respectable society, namely the evil of baby-farming.

People knew that unwanted babies, almost always the children of unmarried mothers, even if they survived long after birth, had but short lives under the care of so-called foster mothers. There was no social care for an unmarried girl who produced a baby. Only very rarely could she look to parents or relatives for help. She must learn to support herself and she must put the child somewhere so that she was free to do so.

Mrs Amelia Elizabeth Dyer was a woman who took advantage of the situation in which an unmarried mother was unlikely to find suitable work or even a lodging if she kept the baby with her. At one time Mrs Dyer had been in the Salvation Army. She was separated from her husband and took in children at her house in Bristol. In 1895 she moved to Reading and advertised that she was willing to take in or adopt children. Replies poured in from all over the country and from people in all walks of life. In spite of the strict guardianship of young girls, illegitimate and unwanted children were not confined to the lower orders. Mrs Dyer's minimum charge for adoption was £10, a large sum for an unfortunate girl to scrape together, but her adoption fee went as high as £70 or £100.

It was in August 1895 that watermen on the Thames near London began to make a series of gruesome discoveries of the bodies of babies who had died of strangulation. At first there seemed no clue as to where they came from. Then in April 1896 the bodies of six more infants were found, three in the Thames near Reading, one in the river Kennett and two in a carpet bag in a pool near Reading. One of the bodies was wrapped in a piece of brown paper with Mrs Dyer's Reading address on it.

Mrs Dyer had already moved to another house in Reading but was soon traced. The house was searched and large numbers of letters offering children for adoption, receipts, advertisements and enquiries from parents were discovered. Mrs Dyer had wasted no time in disposing of the babies she took into her house. She had been baby-farming for fifteen years and no one could say how many she had strangled with tape (her usual practice, she admitted) and thrown into the river or otherwise disposed of.

She was charged with murder along with her son-in-law, Arthur Palmer, but she made a statement absolving both him and her daughter from any knowledge of what she had been doing. Mrs Dyer's mother had died in an asylum and she herself had been in asylums several times though it seemed she had retired there more to avoid awkward questions than on account of genuine insanity. In a letter written from prison (which survives in Madame Tussaud's archives) Mrs Dyer said she had no hope of saving her life except through a plea of insanity. However, the jury did not accept this. It seemed clear her motive had been greed and gain. She had taken adoption fees graded according to what she thought the parent could pay and got rid of the babies as soon as possible, some, it was said, within twenty-four hours. Mrs Dyer met her deserved end at

Newgate in June 1896, but it did nothing to mitigate the plight of a mother with an unwanted baby.

Queen Victoria's reign was coming to an end. She survived her Diamond Jubilee celebrations for four years and her life finally closed peacefully in 1901. When she had come to the throne in 1837 Madame Tussaud had been established in London premises for just two years, and the Chamber of Horrors was just beginning its extraordinary growth. Now, when King Edward VII ascended the throne, it was at its zenith.

[6]

The Edwardian Chamber of Horrors

During the first few years of Edward VII's reign, the appearance of the Chamber of Horrors was considerably changed by the acquisition of some extremely large new 'relics'. In 1903 the Old Bailey, in which so many criminals had been tried, and the ancient prison of Newgate beside it were demolished. Some years later, the new Central Criminal Court would rise on the site of Newgate.

There had been a prison at Newgate, originally in the Gatehouse, since the twelfth century. It was rebuilt after the Great Fire of 1666 and again in 1780. Public executions were held outside Newgate Gaol from 1783 until the public spectacle was stopped in 1868 and numerous denizens of the Chamber of Horrors had met their end on its scaffold.

When news of the coming demolition was published John Theodore Tussaud and his brothers hastened there with a catalogue of contents and fittings that were to be auctioned. John Theodore had paid his first visit to the Old Bailey at the age of sixteen and now looked at the long black leather-covered seat on which he had so often sat. He recalled feeling awe and a deep depression of spirits as he listened to the concluding stages of the first murder trial he attended.

There did not seem to be many bidders for the Old Bailey's fittings and its jury box, dock and various other pieces were secured for the Chamber of Horrors at nominal prices. It was a different matter when it came to the selling-off of relics from the grim Newgate Prison. Though it was February and bitterly cold quite a crowd of eager bidders from all walks of life followed the auctioneer about, crossing the prison yard and shivering along echoing dispiritingly bare corridors.

The Tussaud brothers had particular interest in three lots. They wanted the condemned cell from which the notorious robber and highwayman Jack Sheppard had escaped in 1724. They also wanted the cell in which anti-Papist Lord George Gordon had died of gaol fever on 1 November 1793, and they coveted most of all the famous great Newgate Bell which had tolled to notify the citizens of London every time a murderer forfeited his own life in return for the one he had taken. It was rumoured that the metal of the Newgate Bell contained silver, so bidding for it was quite brisk, but John Theodore was pleased to secure it for £100 and there was applause when it was known the famous bell was going to Madame Tussaud's.

The masonry and heavy ironwork of the two cells which fell to Madame Tussaud's had to be dismantled and conveyed to Marylebone Road where they were meticulously reconstructed. The cost of this was much greater than the amount paid for them. They also took up a considerable amount of floor space but the thousands of visitors who gazed at them during ensuing decades, for they survived until the 1970s in the Chamber, amply repaid the initial outlay.

Jack Sheppard, though he had paid for his crimes 179 years earlier, long before Madame Tussaud was born, certainly warranted a place in the Chamber of Horrors even though John Theodore could only model his features from contemporary descriptions and pictures. He was depicted sitting in the original Newgate cell plotting escape. Clockwork mice scurried about the floor. His extraordinary career of crime and his even more extraordinary escapes from prison made his name pass into folk history.

Jack Sheppard was born in Stepney in 1702, the son of a respectable carpenter. Unfortunately his father died leaving a large family and Jack was brought up in Bishopsgate Workhouse. He ran away from a cane-chairmaker who treated him harshly during apprenticeship and was then befriended by a Mr Kneebone, a woollen-draper who had on occasion employed Jack's father. Kindly Mr Kneebone taught the boy to write and cypher (his kindness was later repaid by robbery) and apprenticed him to a carpenter called Owen Wood who also treated him kindly. However, Sheppard frequented a public house, the Black Lion in Drury Lane, where he fell in with two girls, 'Edgeworth Bess' and Poll Magott. Jack's first recorded theft is from the Rummer Tavern in Charing Cross, the tavern depicted by Hogarth in his picture *Night*. Jack stole two silver spoons.

Further thefts led to Jack Sheppard and 'Edgeworth Bess' decamping to Parsons Green where in 1723 he was rounded up as a runaway apprentice, but his master, the carpenter Owen Wood, was misguided enough to plead for his release.

From that time Jack admitted 'I fell to robbing almost everyone who stood in my way' with the aid of an accomplice known as 'Blueskin'. A year later his elder brother betrayed him and he was committed to St Giles' Roundhouse, a lock-up from which he quickly made the first of his skilful escapes.

Immediately Jack returned to his life of continuous crime and in 1724 was in the New Prison from which he made a remarkable break-out. He managed to get free of his leg-irons and cut through a double grille of oak and iron bars and let himself down twenty-five feet by means of a sheet and blanket. He was then faced with scaling a twenty-two foot wall which he did carrying an accomplice on his back.

Free again, Jack Sheppard intensified his career of highway robbery, theft and burglary until he managed to offend, or possibly alarm, one of London's most successful 'fences' who dealt in stolen property, combining this occupation with that of police informer. This man, Josiah Wood, laid information which led to Sheppard's capture on 3 July 1724.

In August Sheppard was tried at the Old Bailey for his countless crimes and condemned to death. Owing to the absence of the Royal Court at Windsor the death warrant was not actually signed until the end of the month. Meanwhile Jack sat in the condemned cell at Newgate Prison pondering his fate and escape. In the nick of time, on 31 August, he was in possession of a file smuggled in by his girlfriends, 'Edgeworth Bess' and Poll Magott. This was all he needed to effect his third break. He fled briefly to Northamptonshire but soon returned to his London haunts and former practices. He carried pistols and inspired so much fear that no one dared attempt his capture though many knew his whereabouts and his crimes.

Eventually one of the turnkeys through whose hands he had once slipped took a posse of armed men to Finchley Common and seized Sheppard and a companion named Page. Now Sheppard was weighed down with the heaviest shackles but still he managed to secrete a small file which was later found in his Bible and a complete set of tools was found in the rush seat of his chair. Had Bess and Poll again used their uncanny skill in smuggling them into the prison? Jack was confined in the strongest part of Newgate Prison and shackled to the floor. On Sunday, 13 September, crowds flocked into the prison chapel in the hope of viewing the notorious prisoner.

Three days later warders tested his shackles at two in the afternoon and left him alone for the rest of the day. When they returned the bird, incredibly, had flown in his most extraordinary escape of all. Somehow Jack had got free of his manacles and snapped the chains that fettered him to the floor. He then succeeded in removing an iron bar from the chimney up which he climbed and with unbelievable strength and dexterity forced several bolted doors to reach the lead roof only to be obliged to return to his cell by the way he had come to get a blanket to let himself down on to the roof of an adjoining private house which belonged to a woodworker. Entering this by a garret window he passed unseen through the house and slipped into the rabbit warren of Smithfield.

He was well provided with money for someone had paid him in advance for his 'dying speech'. For five days he hid in the area, then broke into a pawnbrokers in Drury Lane. He dressed himself in smart clothes, hired a coach and drove past Newgate Gaol with the windows down.

On Friday he went to Clare Market to seek out his mother

with whom he seems to have kept in touch. At the Shears Tavern in Maypole Alley he treated his parent to three-quarters of brandy, then drank himself into a stupor in which condition he was recaptured. There were no more escapes. Jack Sheppard was watched day and night. The turnkeys charged people three shillings and sixpence to have a look at him.

A crowd of some 200,000 gathered to witness his execution and there was a riot over the disposal of his remains that had to be quelled by the military. He was finally buried in the churchyard of St Martin's-in-the-Fields on the site where the National Gallery now stands. Workmen discovered his coffin in 1866. Jack Sheppard's life had only lasted twenty-two years. He was very slender, only five feet and four inches tall and had a speech impediment.

Lord George Gordon whose sallow, emaciated and melancholy figure sat in the adjacent carefully reconstructed cell was a very different character from the compulsive criminal Jack Sheppard. Nothing could have been more unlike Jack Sheppard's than this nobleman's career. A younger son of the Duke of Gordon he had entered Parliament in 1774 and some years later became President of the Protestant Society which was trying to procure the reimposition of certain constraints on Roman Catholics which had recently been lifted by Parliament. In June 1780 a crowd of several thousand marchers proceeded quietly to the Houses of Parliament where a petition to this effect was presented by Lord George. However, the Commons decided to postpone consideration of the demands therein.

In spite of the Protestant Society's calls for calmness and reasonable patience the mood of the protesters became ugly and developed into serious riots that lasted several days. Newgate Prison was burned down with other property. Other prisons were opened and some 2,000 criminals joined the wreckers and looters who were now completely out of control. Finally troops were called and the riots quelled, but at the cost of several hundred lives.

Lord George Gordon was arrested and sent to the Tower. He was tried for high treason in 1781 but acquitted through the brilliant arguments of his counsel, Erskine. It was shown that Lord George had not led the rioters, and had endeavoured as far as he could to prevent violence and calm the situation. For the next few years Lord George continued to act as Protestant champion in various roles and it was even put about that the Pope had tried to have him poisoned and failed.

The misdemeanours that finally brought Lord George to the cell in Newgate Prison, rebuilt after the riots which in spite of his acquittal had become known as the Gordon Riots, were comparatively trivial. Lord George wrote a petition on behalf of Newgate prisoners awaiting transportation for their various crimes, and in this he unwisely made some unfavourable criticism of British justice and Justices. As a result he was convicted of libel in 1787.

He was also in trouble for libelling Marie Antoinette, Queen of France. Lord George took up the cudgels on behalf of Cagliostro, the Italian charlatan who was involved in the conspiracy to discredit the Queen, known as the 'Queen's necklace' scandal. Gordon inserted two paragraphs in the *Public Advertiser* accusing Marie Antoinette of persecuting 'this honest man'. At the time of the 'Queen's necklace' affair Marie Grosholtz (later Madame Tussaud) was working in Princess Elizabeth's household at Versailles and could have heard of these paragraphs which brought Lord George Gordon to trial for libel a second time. He was sentenced to five years imprisonment and a substantial fine and also required to find substantial sureties when he finally came to the time of his release.

By this time Lord George, clearly eccentric and unbalanced, had adopted the Jewish faith. However, his new faith and his imprisonment did not prevent him from leading an agreeable life while confined to his cell. He carried on a voluminous correspondence, practised music including the bagpipes and gave frequent dinner-parties for six or eight people, mingling fellow prisoners with guests from outside. He also gave fortnightly balls which could hardly have been contained within the dimensions of the cramped cell. No doubt through judicious tipping of the turnkeys the dancers were able to resort to the corridors and trip their measures there to the sound of Lord George's bagpipes.

The five-year sentence ran its course but when the time came for Lord George's release he could find no one ready to put down the large sums required as surety for his good behaviour —not surprisingly as it turned out. As the nobleman languished in his small cell, no doubt weakened by long confinement, he contracted the dreaded and ever-rampant gaol fever. To this he succumbed, singing as he died the French revolutionary song 'Ça Ira' once so familiar to Madame Tussaud. King Louis XVI had been guillotined in January 1793, Marie Antoinette who had been 'libelled' by Lord George five years earlier met the same fate in October and Lord George died in his cell the following month, practising to the end the ritual of his acquired Jewish faith.

One hundred and ten years later Lord George's name and some of his exploits, particularly the Gordon Riots, were remembered by the public of the day. Charles Dickens had written of him in *Barnaby Rudge* and he was judged to be a suitable occupant for the newly purchased and erected Newgate cell. John Theodore modelled him as a melancholy figure with no hint of gay dinners and bagpipes playing. The countenance showed the ravages of gaol fever. Lord George was in a different category from his neighbour Jack Sheppard, the compulsive robber, and the ranks of murderers and criminals on whom he looked out from behind bars, but his gaunt form in the authentic cell did not seem out of place in the Chamber of Horrors.

Another large relic was added in 1907 when Madame Tussaud's purchased the treadmill from York Castle, which was no longer used as a prison. The enormous wheel which accommodated a large number of prisoners tramping out their punishment at the same time was far too big for the Chamber of Horrors. Only a segment could be set up but the worn treads and the bowed figure on it gave visitors a realistic picture of the many hundreds of exhausting hours during which prisoners had trodden out expiation of their crimes. 'The branded convict on the treadmill seems poised, awaiting the signal to start the creaking treadmill', wrote an Irish reporter in 1965 more than half a century after the wheel had been introduced into the Chamber. Sometimes prison treadmills had served the useful purpose of raising water, but many were in use simply as a method of carrying out a sentence of 'hard labour' and they turned to no purpose.

The Chamber of Horrors now had plenty of variety with the addition of the Newgate Bell and these other important 'relics' as well as John Theodore's tableaux to break the ranks of convicted criminals. Important visitors seldom hesitated now to include it in their visit. The doughty Begum of Bhopal came in 1911. She appeared unmoved by what she saw except for remarking with an air of some satisfaction as she inspected the guillotine and gallows 'We do not execute in Bhopal'. She did not enlarge on her country's alternative methods of dealing with serious crime.

Two years later George Bernard Shaw was conducted through the Chamber of Horrors after sitting for his portrait with John Theodore. John Theodore was hoping for some witty or biting comment or criticism but was surprised to find Shaw remained curiously silent and reserved as he surveyed the criminal faces surrounding him. It was Charlie Peace's countenance that engaged his attention for longest but he uttered no word on any reflections that were passing through his mind.

Many new figures of murderers and wrongdoers took their place in the Chamber of Horrors during the early years of the new century leading up to the First World War. Many of their crimes won lasting notoriety and the accurate likenesses were witness to the long hours the sculptor sat in Court with notebook and sketch pad observing features, stance and mannerisms, later translated in the studio into a lifelike portrait figure.

John Theodore's eldest son Jack came of age in 1911 and worked full-time in the exhibition and younger brothers were coming on. There were already five great granddaughters of Madame Tussaud who had worked all their lives in the hair insertion and colouring studio and in the wardrobe. This band of talented and highly respectable ladies handled the heads of murderers and their clothing with the same matter-of-fact competence and skill as they did those of royalty and the famous. John Theodore ruled his sisters with an iron hand and it was said they would tremble visibly if he entered their departments with a look of displeasure on his face.

Among the killers whose crimes aroused particular public interest was George Chapman. Some people thought he might have been Jack the Ripper but gave up Ripper techniques for fear that discovery was getting too near at hand and resorted to poison instead. Certainly, just as the Ripper's killings seemed motiveless, Chapman appeared to have poisoned his three barmaid 'wives' for no reason but a wish to kill. George Chapman was in fact a Pole whose real name was Klosowski. He had come to England in 1888 and worked as a barber's assistant in the East End of London. Some colour was given to the Jack the Ripper theory by the evidence given to Borough Magistrates' Court by two Polish witnesses, one the sister of Chapman's first and legal wife.

They maintained that he had told them he had worked as a 'feldscher' in the Hospital of the Infant Jesus in Warsaw. A 'feldscher' was a doctor's assistant, a kind of practical nurse who put on splints, bandages and dressings on the doctor's instructions and therefore had a good knowledge of anatomy and of medicine in general.

A year after his arrival in London, Chapman married his Polish wife and then apparently emigrated to America. Parted from his wife, he appeared again in London in 1895 and again worked in a hairdresser's shop. He came across a Mrs Mary Isabella Spink, a married woman whose railway-porter husband had deserted her taking their child though a second child was born shortly after his departure. However, in spite of her forlorn position as a deserted wife, Mrs Spink possessed a comfortable nest egg which she had inherited.

Chapman, the Polish hairdresser, was quite a striking-looking individual with a bony face, a large upstanding quiff of dark hair and a large drooping walrus moustache. He and Mary Isabella Spink began going out together and finally she went to live with him. Her £600 enabled Chapman to abandon hairdressing and become the landlord of a public house in the City Road where Mrs Spink also lived and helped in the bar. Unaccountably in December 1897 Mrs Spink became ill with stomach pains and sickness from which she died. Her unfortunate death caused no suspicions. The symptoms were common enough in dirty and disease-ridden East London, and could have been caused by a large number of illnesses.

Mrs Spink's ministrations in the bar were missed and the following year George Chapman took on another barmaid, Bessie Taylor, who, like Mrs Spink, was known as 'Mrs Chapman'. Whether some kind of marriage ceremony between them had actually taken place is not clear. It was not until February 1901 that Bessie became ill with similar symptoms to those of her predecessor, and she too died. The doctor could not make any firm diagnosis of her illness but again it did not arouse any suspicions.

George Chapman was now free to engage another barmaid which he lost no time in doing. Her name was Maud Marsh. In due course she developed the same symptoms and was very ill. However, Miss Marsh had a mother, who was not satisfied when the doctor could not account for Maud's sickness and pains. She suspected poisoning and told her own doctor what she thought. Maud Marsh died on 22 October 1902 and, as a result of what her mother had said, the doctor declined to sign a death certificate.

The unfortunate girl was found to have died of antimony poisoning and investigations showed that Chapman had been purchasing tartar emetic from a local chemist. The bodies of his two former barmaid 'wives' were exhumed and also found to have been poisoned.

George Chapman (Klosowski) was found guilty of murder at the Old Bailey and hanged on 7 April 1903. He was quickly in place in the Chamber of Horrors, an object of much public attention for it was said that, when Chapman was arrested, Chief Inspector Abbeline who had been in charge of the Ripper investigations had exclaimed 'You've got Jack the Ripper at last!'

However, there was no evidence that the Pole had perpetrated or been connected with the Ripper murders. Chapman's victims were not prostitutes even if his killings did seem as motiveless as those of the Ripper. The portrait model of Chapman/Klosowski—'this callous criminal' as he was stigmatized in Madame Tussaud's contemporary catalogues—had a long stay of over sixty years in the Chamber of Horrors.

Equally callous though motivated by greed for money was Samuel Herbert Dougal, who within a few months joined Chapman in the Chamber. The victim whose murder brought him to the scaffold was a woman whose incredibly foolish and reckless behaviour would have been incomprehensible to the late Madame Tussaud. Perhaps she might have felt some pity for Miss Camille Holland such as she seems to have felt for Mrs Stewart so long ago in 1829. Both women met their deaths because they were dominated by ruthless and unscrupulous men, a situation that Madame Tussaud had shown herself capable of mastering, though the men she cut out of her life with such determination were neither wicked nor criminal.

Miss Camille Holland was a maiden lady in her late fifties who had every advantage. She even had a faintly romantic air, her friends thought, for she had been born in India of an English father and a French mother. She was still fair, dainty, and pretty and had inherited a comfortable competence from an aunt with whom she had lived for some time. In 1898 she was living in a respectable boarding-house in London, a mode of life adopted at the time by many solitary women who were well off. Camille Holland painted water-colours and composed words and music for sentimental songs. She did not lack acquaintance and was quite attractive to the opposite sex. According to a friend there was always some gentleman ready to escort her when escort was needed though always with the utmost respectability.

It is curious that a woman of attractive appearance (she always took great care to be *soignée*), minor talents which were admired at that period, and money of her own, should never have married. Her sole romance seems to have been at an early

The portrait figure of George Chapman (Klosowski). It stayed in the Chamber of Horrors for over sixty years.

age with a young naval officer who had unfortunately been drowned. His parents had given her a cornelian ring the young man had worn, and this never left Camille's finger. She was a devout member of the Catholick Apostolic Church and with her religious attendance, her hobbies and her innocuous but busy social life she was certainly not a lonely spinster.

Camille's only relatives were two nephews and a niece with whom she corresponded at irregular intervals but on affectionate terms. She did not see them often and they seem to have been hesitant at the idea of seeming to court a rich aunt lest their motive should be misinterpreted as a hope for ultimate benefit. Their aunt was careful with her money and quite a competent business woman.

How such a person as Camille Holland became embroiled with Samuel Herbert Dougal was never clarified. It was believed they had met by chance at the Earl's Court Exhibition. Whatever the circumstances 'Captain' Dougal became a visitor at the Elgin Crescent boarding-house. He was a handsome man in a coarse and vulgar way endowed with an excellent physique, virile with a kind of animal magnetism that made him attractive to women in particular and a skilful approach that often enabled him to 'get round' men who normally disliked him. He used this with women too.

Had the background of this vital and clever man been known to the occupants of the boarding-house, it is doubtful if he would have been so readily accepted as Miss Holland's admirer. She said that he was a widower with an invalid son, a tale that possibly he told her at first or one that she invented as she learned more of his past in order to preserve her reputation.

Samuel Dougal was the son of a man who had worked hard to give him a good education which enabled him to obtain a post in a civil engineering office. He had particularly good and clear hand-writing. However, when he was nearly twenty his dissolute life in his leisure hours had run him heavily into debt. Not wishing his father to learn of his habits Dougal enlisted in the Royal Engineers. He was intelligent and well fitted for clerical duties so he obtained promotion though never to officer rank.

He served for twenty-one years and he retired on a pension of two shillings and ninepence a day with excellent references and the reputation of being a very good clerk.

His private life had been far less exemplary. From the time of his entry into the Army he was notorious among his fellow soldiers for seducing servants and shopgirls whose money he pocketed whenever he could. In 1869 he married a girl who bore him four children and accompanied him to Halifax, Nova Scotia, when his regiment was posted overseas. There she is said to have led an unhappy life until in 1885 she was suddenly seized with pains and died the same day.

This happened in June. Dougal was granted leave and went home to England where he married a second wife in August, a girl with some dowry who accompanied him back to Halifax. Her residence there was short for in October she too died having been taken ill with sudden pains and vomiting. At that period a death in military quarters did not have to be registered with any civil authority and Dougal arranged for his second wife to be buried within twenty-four hours, as he had done with his first. Nobody asked any questions or investigated the sudden deaths of the two women.

He then took as mistress the young daughter of a Halifax farmer. She bore a child and seems to have been much devoted to her lover although he treated her brutally and assaulted her. She accompanied him to England as his 'wife' when he got his discharge but finally returned to Halifax with her child when he threatened to kill her. She posed there as his widow.

For eleven years after his discharge from the Army Dougal lived with a variety of women and sired a number of children while he worked at an assortment of odd jobs. He was living with an elderly woman of some means in Ware and was landlord of a public house in that Hertfordshire town when he was first in trouble with the police.

Dougal failed to get control of his elderly companion's money and some time later a fire broke out at his public house. He had also taken a private house near the inn which shortly afterwards caught fire as well. The inn and the house were insured with different companies but neither would pay. One of them applied to the police for Dougal's arrest for arson. In December 1889 he was tried at St Albans but acquitted for lack of evidence. Dougal acquired a third wife in Dublin in 1892. Three years later he again had a brush with the law being accused of stealing various articles from an unmarried woman with whom he had been living. He stood trial at Oxford Quarter Sessions where he showed great skill in defending himself. His eloquence and his good army record gained him an acquittal.

Next time Dougal was not so lucky. Back in Ireland and employed at the Royal Hospital as a messenger, he had access to the office where the assistant military secretary kept his cheque book. Dougal's clever penmanship enabled him to forge the signature of Lord Frankfort of Montmorency who was signing all documents passing through the hospital. The cheque was for £35. Lord Frankfort spotted the unaccounted-for cheque in the bank statement. Another forged cheque in the name of Lord Wolseley was also discovered. Scotland Yard were informed and Dougal was arrested. Investigations brought him to trial at the Old Bailey for forging Lord Frankfort's signature. He was found guilty and sentenced to twelve months hard labour.

Dougal did not serve his hard labour sentence because, by means of an attempted suicide—which left him unharmed—and apparent melancholia, he got himself certified as insane at Pentonville prison and was transferred to Cane Hill, a mental asylum where his melancholia cleared up in twenty-one days. He was not sent back to prison, remaining at Cane Hill, and emerging at the end of his sentence as a sane person whose conduct during confinement had been exemplary. But the prison sentence had lost him his pension. He had no money and was now fifty. While he made no attempt to support his numerous children, and his wife went back to Dublin on account of his cruelty, Dougal's powers of persuasion were enough to induce his brother to help him. For a time he looked after some house property, but his behaviour soon made his brother get rid of him, and his future appeared bleak.

It was at this point that Dougal met Camille Holland. It is not

Miss Camille Holland who was murdered at Moat Farm in Essex by 'Captain' Samuel Dougal in 1899. Her body was not discovered for four years.

difficult to see how he picked her out amid the throng of visitors at Earl's Court Exhibition, if that is in fact where they met. Miss Holland preserved a youthful appearance. She discreetly tinted her hair, and used equally discreet make-up, which, with her neat figure and smart clothes, made her likely to catch the eye of such a man. She was obviously a single lady of some means, and alone.

Camille's apparently immediate fall for a 'pick-up' of this kind is inexplicable. Certainly 'Captain' Dougal was a fine figure of a man with a military appearance and his appearance had not been marred by a comfortable twelve months stay in a mental ward instead of being exposed to the rigours of hard labour at Pentonville Prison. However, Camille had lived for years in London and travelled on the Continent. She must have been all too well aware of the perils from fortune-hunters that surrounded a lady in her position. Yet she appears to have become completely infatuated, an infatuation which, pierced only by two brief gleams of sanity, lasted until her death.

During the period that Dougal was a regular visitor to the boarding-house Camille Holland took her first step towards death by staying with him for a weekend at the Royal Hotel, Southend, but this venture she justified by saying that the mythological invalid son was there to chaperone and give propriety. It was after this visit that reason momentarily regained its hold on Miss Holland's mind for she informed a sewing woman in whom she was in the habit of confiding that she was breaking with 'Captain' Dougal. He tried to persuade her to draw out her capital and invest it in his name. Miss Holland had hitherto been shrewd and close in the handling of her fortune and Dougal's abortive attempt to get money out of her immediately aroused her alarm.

Alas for Camille! Her extraordinary infatuation overcame her commonsense and in a little while the rift was healed and she was going about with him again. She knew by now that he could not marry her for Mrs Dougal was living in Dublin. On 9 December 1898 Miss Camille Holland left the Elgin Street boarding-house where she had led such a pleasant life ostensibly to be married to 'Captain' Dougal. Some of her fellow-boarders, especially the gentlemen, had their doubts.

They took a house near Brighton, and Camille handed over the rent to Dougal during their two-month stay. Dougal now felt that the time had come for him to take up the life of a country gentleman and wanted to buy a suitable property with Camille Holland's money. He began enquiries and hit on Coldham's Farm, Quendon, Essex, as suitable for his purpose. He instigated negotiations for the purchase to be made in his name. Miss Holland had her second flash of sanity. She made an independent journey to London and had a fresh contract made out in which she, not Dougal, became the purchaser and owner of Coldham's Farm, shortly to be renamed Moat Farm on account of the stagnant moat which surrounded it completely and could only be crossed by a bridge. The contract was signed on 18 January 1899 and there was nothing Dougal could do about it. Although by now she seemed frightened of him as well as infatuated he dared not push her too far. He needed her money.

The pair removed to lodgings in Saffron Walden to be near the house which needed some attention before it could be occupied. Camille took her little dog Jacko, of which she was very fond. There she began to make arrangements to get her furniture out of store and sent to Moat Farm. She also wrote to one of her nephews whose little daugher had died. Miss Holland had been very fond of the child and was expected at the funeral but she did not arrive. Her nephew wrote again telling her about the funeral but he received no reply. Their correspondence ceased. Both nephews seemed to be peculiarly sensitive lest their aunt should think that they hoped to get her money in the end.

At Saffron Walden the Dougals appeared to be a devoted couple. Though Dougal sometimes went off to London and stayed away all night, he always sent a wire and he greeted his 'wife' affectionately when he returned on his bicycle from superintending the work being done at Moat Farm.

In April 1899 Camille and Dougal moved into their new home. It was a remote house at the end of a cart-track leading from several little-frequented lanes. The house was small and neat but surrounded with dark firs and ancient apple trees. In the dreary, sparsely populated countryside it was not a house easy to get to or easy to leave, a curious house for a woman who had lived a busy London life, but Camille, who was after all its owner now, does not seem to have raised any criticisms, or objected to her lover's selection of residence.

Dougal had had it tidied up a bit and some bushes trimmed so perhaps no qualms or apprehensions entered her head as she crossed the spring-fed moat. There was a second moat on the right which connected with a drainage ditch from the farmyard. A narrow garden path led to the house which had a bow window on either side of the door. Miss Holland's furniture, her ample wardrobe, her jewellery and trinkets were installed. She was to live in Moat Farm exactly twenty-one days. For the subsequent four years her body lay in the drainage ditch filled in and planted with trees by Dougal.

Camille Holland's three weeks at Moat Farm were not a pleasant experience. Within a few days she learned from her indignant nineteen-year-old general servant who lived in the house that Dougal had made amorous advances to her. The girl, Florence, was one of the few girls who did not respond. She wished to leave but her mistress, upset and crying bitterly, begged her to stay on. Perhaps it came home to Camille for the first time what 'married' life with Dougal was going to be. She also noticed that no tradesmen's carts called and Dougal always met the postman in the lane.

In May Dougal made a night assault on the servant Florrie's door which she prudently kept bolted, but which threatened to give way. Florrie screamed loudly, Camille came flying to the scene and took Florrie into her own bed while Dougal maintained the girl had only taken fright at the noise he made while trying to wind a cuckoo clock. Florrie again wanted to leave but her mistress's tears again persuaded her to stay. She was a kindly-hearted girl and she was afraid of leaving 'Mrs Dougal' alone with her husband.

Why did not Camille Holland take steps to leave? She was not married to Dougal and although Moat Farm was isolated there were workers around, traps could be hired and there was a train service from Saffron Walden. She would have done well to pack her clothes and jewellery and leave with Florence. Certainly she had burned her boats and her reputation as far as her old London circle of friends and acquaintances was concerned but, in spite of money tied up in Moat Farm, it was in her name and she could sell it so she was still of independent means.

Possibly she would have had to sacrifice her furniture, but that would have been a light price to pay for riddance from Samuel Dougal whose character became more obvious every day. Reverted to being Miss Camille Holland she could have lived a pleasant and comfortable life in some continental watering-place 'for her health' instead of lying dead for four years in a drainage ditch before her body was discovered, yet she seemed unable to save herself.

On the contrary, after two days when Camille refused to speak to Dougal, some sort of reconciliation seems to have taken place. Camille asked Florrie if she would mind being left alone for a short while, not more than an hour, as she wanted to do a little shopping in Saffron Walden. The girl agreed on condition that Dougal was not left with her but this was no problem as he was to drive Camille in the trap. She went off smartly dressed in a dark dress with a fall of lace at the throat and a while sailor hat. Florrie watched them drive over the bridge, the last time she or anyone else in the neighbourhood saw Camille alive.

Florence was horrified when at eight o'clock Dougal returned alone in the trap. He told her that her mistress had decided to go to London and he would meet her the same night. Dougal disappeared several times but returned at midnight saying that 'Mrs Dougal' had not after all managed to get back. Florence who had already written to her mother asking to be removed sat up all night in the locked spare-room which had a window low enough for her to escape from, if necessary.

Next morning her mother turned up in a hired trap, gave Dougal a piece of her mind, and demanded a month's wages and their rail fares. Dougal met her requests without demur. Florrie and her mother packed her belongings and departed in the waiting hired trap. Dougal had already driven off in his own trap and the two vehicles met, Dougal still alone. He whipped up his horse and did not acknowledge the departing servant and her mother. They would not meet again until Dougal was on trial for murder.

The most extraordinary four years followed. Dougal sent for

his wife from Dublin—indeed he had already done so, suggesting she should live in a cottage nearby. He told her he was looking after an estate for an elderly lady. In the new circumstances she moved into Moat Farm and he introduced her to the local clergyman and his wife as his daughter. The cleric had heard of 'Mrs Dougal' but they had not met and he accepted the story that she was away. In her short stay at Moat Farm Camille does not appear to have met any of the local people.

The true Mrs Dougal took charge of Camille Holland's wardrobe and jewellery and soon began to wear some of the things, altered to fit her. In October 1899 she told the clergyman, Mr Morton, and his wife her true status as Dougal's wife and showed them her marriage certificate. She explained that her husband said the lady for whom he ran the place was away yachting. Mrs Morton did not appear to think it odd that Mrs Dougal wore this mysterious lady's clothes and even accepted a shawl and some pieces of music belonging to her.

Dougal soon got tired of work on the farm and found it more pleasant to live on Miss Holland's money, not difficult to arrange as he had her cheque book and had already demonstrated his gift for forgery. When the bank queried a signature he wrote back in Miss Holland's name saying she had sprained her wrist and her signature might appear a little different till it healed. There were no more queries.

By a series of clever forgeries Dougal was able to sell out some of Miss Holland's capital and have Moat Farm conveyed from her name to his. Where a witness was necessary he witnessed Camille Holland's forged signature himself which saved a lot of trouble with her bank and with the solicitors who carried out all the Moat Farm transactions, since to them she had never posed as 'Mrs Dougal'. (The solicitors later went bankrupt.)

During Dougal's first visits to Moat Farm he had talked to an ancient employee of the former owner about the drainage ditch carrying smelly farm effluent to the moat. The old man had explained that it was the only means for draining the farmyard. However, Dougal ordered the ditch to be filled in and planted with trees, a job that was set in motion quickly after Miss

Holland failed to return from her shopping trip. It was soon completed.

By 1900 Dougal decided to get rid of the farm and offered it for sale but there were no enquiries when he advertised it in December. No one enquired either about Miss Camille Holland or the 'first Mrs Dougal' as she was vaguely known during the few weeks she had lived in the neighbourhood. Her little dog Jacko had made its way back to the lodgings in Saffron Walden. The landlady, hurt that she had heard nothing from her former lodger with whom she had been quite friendly, wrote to Moat Farm. Dougal replied telling her to turn the dog out but this Mrs Wisken refused to do. Dougal finally turned up and took the dog away having evaded all enquiries as to where his 'wife' was.

In spite of this very odd situation at Moat Farm, Dougal became popular in the neighbourhood. He was an excellent shot and regarded as a good fellow, liberal in standing drinks. He contributed to a new church clock at Clavering. He had also bought a motorcar and this made him a person of consequence as what he called his 'locomobile' or 'loco' was one of the first seen in the neighbourhood.

What began his downfall were his promiscuous amours which led to paternity claims and affiliation orders. Strange tales about his orgies which included teaching unclothed girls to ride a bicycle began to circulate. Mrs Dougal stood it for a time but in January 1902 left Moat Farm with a labourer with whom she went to live at Tenby. Dougal proceeded to divorce her, a suit which she did not attempt to defend.

Many women came and went at Moat Farm and many of them became pregnant. Gossip mounted. Some remarked that it was peculiar that the 'first Mrs Dougal' (Miss Holland) had never in all this time returned for her clothes or jewellery, or been seen or heard of. Dougal was then foolish enough to contest an affiliation order brought against him by one of the many girls he had seduced. It came to public light that he had been convicted of forgery and served a sentence. It also caused the King's Proctor to rescind his decree *nisi* for divorce. Dougal did not protest at this as his wife had returned to him.

He did not know that the gossip and the two court cases had alerted the local police to make some enquiries about the whereabouts of Miss Holland, once thought to have been Dougal's wife. They traced and contacted her nephews, who had heard nothing since the death of the little great niece, but both her solicitors and her bank were under the impression that they had been steadily in contact with her by correspondence from Moat Farm which she had purchased four years earlier.

A police superintendent interviewed Dougal who said that about three years ago he had driven Miss Camille Holland with whom he had had a tiff to Stansted station. She had taken two bags with her and he had not seen her since. Investigations at the station showed that no ticket for London had been taken that day. The police obtained the last cheque dated 28 August 1902 purporting to have been made out and signed by Miss Holland. One of her nephews stated it was not in her handwriting and it was decided to bring a charge of forgery against Dougal.

After Dougal had received the superintendent's visit he realized his danger but instead of fleeing he went to Bournemouth for a weekend with another girl he had seduced and who was pregnant. Then they went to London and the girl finally returned to Moat Farm. Dougal paid a visit to the Bank of England to change some ten-pound notes. He did not know that these had already been marked and stopped. After endorsing one with a false name and address, the detective on duty at the bank was fetched. On the way to the police station Dougal made a dash for it but turned down a cul-de-sac and was captured. Amongst the valuables found on him when he was searched was a cornelian ring, the cornelian ring worn by Camille Holland's drowned sailor lover so many years ago and which she never allowed to leave her finger. There were other things known to have belonged to Miss Holland in luggage that Dougal and the girl had left at Liverpool Street station. Dougal returned in handcuffs to Saffron Walden and instantly the story became newspaper headlines.

All Miss Holland's possessions were found still at Moat Farm, but where was she? Where had she been for four years without any of her property, personal belongings, cheque book, or money? It took weeks to search the house and farm, during which time Dougal was held only on a charge of forgery. Her little dog, now old and stiff, wandered about the ransacked rooms and the garden and fields scarred with holes and trenches. Dougal, ever bold, threatened to sue the police for damage to his property. Forgery was his only crime to date.

An inspector from London came down and found the local police digging the black mud of the moat. The inspector threw in a stone which did not sink. 'No body would have sunk in that mud,' he said. 'We must look elsewhere.' He discovered from a farm labourer that there was a filled-in drainage ditch. The man who had filled it in was working in Herefordshire but was brought back to indicate the spot where he had started to fill in the ditch. After some hours of digging, the ditch gave up its secret. One of the diggers drew out on his fork, first a piece of cloth and then a woman's boot with the bones of a foot in it.

Camille Holland had been shot in the head and buried in a niche dug in the side of the drainage ditch. Her body had been covered with branches of blackthorn which her lover had cut from bushes growing on the bank of the ditch. These had preserved the clothes on the outer side whereas on the other side they were completely destroyed. Dougal must have thrown Camille's body into the deep end of the ditch, temporarily covered it with blackthorn, and then spent at least a whole night on the actual burial. It was four years to the day after she had set out on her shopping trip that Camille Holland's body came to light.

Dougal was found guilty and executed at Chelmsford on 18 July 1903. He made an appeal to the Home Secretary, stating that the gun had gone off accidentally. At the very last moment on the scaffold Dougal replied 'Guilty' to the Chaplain's question, but the Chaplain was severely criticized for asking this question seconds before the drop was pulled.

Miss Holland was buried at Saffron Walden under a tomb

'Captain' Samuel Dougal being escorted to the Court House, Saffron Walden.

which would have pleased her, with a relief taken from one of her own early paintings representing a charming angel gathering a young girl to her breast. Camille's age was given as fifty-six. Her kind Saffron Walden landlady looked after her little dog Jacko, now blind, until he died when she had him stuffed and put under a glass case which stood on a side-table.

Camille Holland died as the result of her own stupidity, but there can be no doubt that her murderer, Samuel Dougal, ranked among the most despicable and unpleasant subjects ever placed in the Chamber of Horrors. The newspaper *The Standard* described the portrait as 'lifelike' and *The Times* remarked, 'The model of Dougal of Moat Farm was closely scrutinized'.

Crimes whose chief significance lay in their sheer brutality and callousness (nearly always crimes committed for greed and gain) held as much fascination for visitors as those in which human emotions were closely involved. Amongst these brutal crimes one, committed at the end of 1902, aroused general horror. The murderer, Edgar Edwards (sometimes known as Edgar Owens), had a background of insanity which was not belied by his behaviour. The *Bradford Telegraph* reported that Edwards retained his 'sullen vengeful manner' even in the death cell where he awaited execution fixed for 3 March 1903. After conviction of murder he had cursed and raved in his cell, swearing to do his utmost to escape so that it was said that this prisoner was more closely guarded than any previous criminal in Wandsworth Gaol.

Madame Tussaud's catalogue remarked 'the career of this criminal exhibited a life devoted to crime of the most sordid and brutal character'. It was always committed to get money. Edwards was arrested in 1902 in Camberwell where he was attacking a man with a lead sash-window weight. This was not the crime that sent him to the gallows but it was the last attack he ever made.

While searching him in connection with this murderous assault the police found on Edwards several of the business cards of John W. Darby. The Darbys were a young couple with a ten-month-old baby. They kept a greengrocer's shop in Camberwell. The police went along to their shop to make enquiries and were surprised to find no member of the family there and most of the contents missing. Amongst the few things that lay about the police found a window-sash lead weighing eight pounds which appeared to be bloodstained.

Edgar Edwards had recently gone to live in a house in Leyton where neighbours' curiosity was aroused by nocturnal digging in the garden. It was not long before the police began digging too and unearthed the dismembered bodies of John Darby and his wife, and that of their baby. The parents had been battered to death and the infant strangled.

Curiously no one seems to have seen Edgar Edwards in company with his victims so that it was on circumstantial evidence that he was charged with brutally murdering Mr and Mrs Darby and their child, to get possession of the premises and the profitable business that they ran.

Having killed his victims Edwards, again apparently unseen by anyone, cut up the bodies and transported the remains in packing cases to his home at Leyton where he interred them. His house was some six miles distant from the Darbys' shop. Had it not been for Edwards' violent assault on another man with a lead sash-weight, and his purloining of some of John Darby's business cards, which led to his arrest and the discovery that the Darbys had vanished, Edwards might have got away with his multiple murder, though with his violent character there is no doubt that the gallows would have claimed him in the end.

At his trial Edwards pleaded insanity but the jury did not accept this though he had behaved in a peculiar manner throughout his trial. He assumed arrogant airs and often laughed loudly. After conviction he burst into a gale of wild laughter though his manner changed again to 'sullen and vengeful' in his cell. On the scaffold he told the chaplain 'I've been looking forward to this.'

Edgar Edwards, the Camberwell murderer, was placed near Samuel Dougal when the portrait figure entered the Chamber of Horrors, and the two were a focus of public attention for a long time to come. An unconfirmed contemporary newspaper report said that while under sentence of death Edwards made a confession which was placed in the hands of his solicitors, and that Madame Tussaud's had offered £200 for it, while another person made an offer of £100 for the gold-rimmed spectacles Edwards wore. However, Madame Tussaud's records show no trace of any such transaction.

For decades the members of the Tussaud family who worked in the studios had been familiar figures and on good terms with the officials of the Central Criminal Court, and other Courts where serious crime was tried. Their purpose was accepted and they were enabled to place themselves strategically in Court to get the best view of the criminal in the dock. This was essential to maintain Madame Tussaud's original principle that every likeness in the exhibition must be strictly accurate. John Theodore Tussaud had always been passionately interested in photography and had practised the new art as a hobby for many years. According to family tradition, it was early in 1910 that a friendly detective at the Old Bailey (never named by any member of the family) showed John Theodore and his eldest son Jack how a small camera could be fixed into a bowler hat which had a flap cut in the crown through which a photograph could be taken without detection. Father and son perfected themselves in this device and employed it for the first time at the trial of Dr Hawley Harvey Crippen, who was accused of poisoning his wife at the trial in October 1910.

Whether or not the concealed camera helped, the likeness modelled was acclaimed as one of the most successful ever seen in the Chamber of Horrors where the portrait of Crippen still stands, a small figure, his hands on the bar of the dock, his slightly protuberant bespectacled eyes gazing with the intent listening look he wore throughout his trial. Dr Crippen is one of the most notorious murderers in the annals of crime, yet he was the mildest of little men. Even the Inspector who investigated the disappearance of his wife, known by her stage name of Belle Elmore, wrote later, 'There was something almost likeable about the mild little fellow.'

Crippen came of a prosperous family in Coldwater, Michigan, USA, where he was born in 1862. He qualified as a doctor at the Homoeopathic Hospital in Cleveland at the age of twenty-five. It was a period when a craze for homoeopathy was sweeping America. He also gained qualifications as an eye and ear specialist.

He moved on to a hospital in New York and there made an

unfortunate marriage to an Irish girl. It proved to be a stormy union but a son was born. Suddenly in 1892 when she was again pregnant Crippen's wife died of apoplexy. No queries were raised by this unexpected death, and Crippen did not appear greatly grieved at his loss. He deposited his son Otto with his parents who had moved to California and took a post as locum for a New York doctor.

It was in the surgery that he met Kunigunde Mackamotzski. She was the daughter of a Polish greengrocer with a German wife whose determined character she inherited. Kunigunde was proud of her high soprano voice and developed ambitions to become an opera singer. It was the age of grand opera and great divas. She adopted the name Cora Turner and was set up in a flat by a Brooklyn stove manufacturer, a married man, who, importantly for Kunigunde/Cora, paid for singing lessons. She was quite attractive with a round high-cheekboned face and very bright merry black eyes.

Cora and Crippen became friendly and Crippen offered her marriage with a promise to further her singing career. In September 1892 they were married. Not long after the marriage Cora had to undergo an operation which put an end to any hope of children which they both wanted. But for this misfortune the marriage might have been successful. As a mother Cora might have forgotten her singing ambitions and settled down to a family life.

A period of economic depression hit America in the winter of 1893–4. Doctor's bills went unpaid and the homoeopathic fad in America had faded. The Crippens found themselves very short of money. However, though people could not find money to pay a doctor, especially a homoeopathic one, they could and did find cash to buy the patent medicines which were flooding the market. In 1894 Cora persuaded her husband to work for Munyon's Homoeopathic Remedies, a concern which had recently opened an office in New York. Cora also went to work there and at first they were so short of money that they slept in a room above the office. Crippen's new employer found him proficient and intelligent. After some time he was moved to

Portrait figure of Crippen as he stood in the dock.

'Professor' Munyon's head office in Philadelphia where he became general manager and consultant.

Crippen was sent to Toronto to set up a branch of the business, while Cora remained in Philadelphia, not unwillingly for she had resumed her singing lessons. However, when Crippen returned she departed for New York. Her voice was not good enough for opera and she had switched her ambitions to vaudeville, changing her name again to Belle Elmore, the name by which she was known professionally henceforward. She felt the 'operatic sketch' was the right medium for her talent, and spent her money on expensive flashy clothes and jewellery in the hope of furthering a career in the world of vaudeville.

She was still in New York when Crippen was sent to London early in 1897 to open another office for his employer. In August Belle joined him there. She was now a woman of strong personality, full of vivacity and life, domineering and determined to have her own way. In London, Belle made her stage début, not at the Empire, as she had hoped, but at the old Marylebone Music Hall in a mini-opera with an Italian tenor. Their performance was a total failure. None the less Belle persisted and from time to time she got middle-of-the-bill engagements in the lesser music halls. It became obvious that she would never become the top-liner that she craved to be. She blamed Crippen for this and became bitter and recriminatory towards him.

It was on account of Belle's music-hall appearances that Crippen lost his job. Someone drew 'Professor' Munyon's attention to a handbill on which Crippen was named as business manager for 'Vio and Motzski's Bright Lights Company'. Munyon was enraged at the suggestion that there was any connection between his patent medicine business and the music halls. In spite of the esteem and confidence that Crippen had won he was called back to the USA and sacked forthwith. He returned to London unemployed.

During his absence Belle took a lover, making no attempt to conceal the fact from her husband. The object of Belle's

Belle Elmore (Mrs Crippen) when on stage

infatuation was Bruce Miller who played the music halls as a one-man-band. He was big, handsome, flashy, a complete contrast with the quiet mild Crippen. Belle knew that her lover was married and had a wife and children in Chicago.

Crippen accepted it all. He found it difficult to obtain a

permanent post, and his qualifications did not permit him to practise as a doctor in England. At the end of 1901 he joined, as consultant, a concern called Drouet's Institute for the Deaf, which was run by a Frenchman as a mail-order business. In these offices Crippen met Ethel Neave, or le Neve as she preferred to call herself. She worked as a secretary, a quiet ladylike girl, with large grey-blue eyes. From the moment she saw Crippen she took a fancy to him.

One day Belle called at the office and had an angry conversation with her husband. Ethel became convinced that Crippen was not happy at home. Her impression was confirmed when after a second intrusion by Belle and a considerable scene Crippen collapsed and fell off his chair when his wife had gone. Ethel revived him with brandy and kindness. In spite of scenes, nagging and henpecking her husband, Belle was in fact much happier. She had met many of the ladies who were top-liners in the music halls and joined the Music Hall Ladies' Guild which had been founded to help artistes who fell sick or on evil times. Belle was an excellent fund-raiser and worked hard. The music-hall ladies admired her energy and liveliness, but they did not like her husband who they called 'That little shrimp'.

Crippen in turn did not like the music-hall ladies. What a contrast to Ethel le Neve! Not surprisingly his friendship with Ethel ripened. Crippen loathed the charity functions to which Belle insisted he should accompany her. He loved quiet evenings spent listening to a palm-court orchestra with Ethel. But they did not become lovers and Crippen always went home to Belle at night. Belle was well aware of the situation but did not mind.

In the spring of 1904 Bruce Miller abandoned Belle and went back to his family in Chicago. Belle was desolate and her relations with her husband deteriorated. However, in September, she found a new distraction when Crippen decided to move to a larger house—39 Hilldrop Crescent, Holloway. There were several bedrooms and Belle could have her music-hall ladies to tea in the more spacious living-room and give small supper-parties. She redecorated with enthusiasm using much pink, her lucky colour, she said. She only had a daily servant and kept the family table on short commons so that she could entertain.

In the meantime the Frenchman Drouet had been in trouble through the death of one of his patients which caused very adverse publicity and his Institute collapsed. Crippen with Ethel at his side took the opportunity to buy up all the assets for a very small sum and the business now reappeared as the Aural Remedies Company. Ethel kept the books and soon perceived that the company was not producing enough income to meet commitments which included Belle's undiminished extravagances. Ethel wanted Crippen to move out of aural remedies and, noticing advertisements for 'American Dentistry', suggested he should try and set up in dentistry with an American partner.

They found an American partner and 'Yale Tooth Specialists: American Dentists' was established. Crippen put in £250, and they were able to make an arrangement to share offices with the Munyon concern for whom Crippen again did some work as an agent. Belle advised against the dentistry project and was always annoyed when she looked in from time to time on her way to the office of the Music Hall Ladies' Guild. She was irritated by the white-smocked figures of her husband and Ethel, and prophesied doom for the venture which she blamed on Ethel.

Still bored and irritable since her lover's return to Chicago two years ago, and lonely in the empty house all day, Belle decided in October 1906 to advertise in the *Daily Telegraph* for a few paying guests. Her husband agreed. The first to come was a German student, Richard Ehrlich, who wished to perfect his English. Belle still spoke German learned from her German mother. Three more German students came and the house became gay for they all smoked and sang together and drank beer. Crippen neither smoked nor drank and he found himself getting up at six o'clock to do the household chores, greatly increased by the four guests. Belle kept the money they paid for herself. She also took to drinking rather too much brandy and insulting her husband in front of the paying guests all of which, friends noticed, Crippen endured meekly bowing to Belle's temper and never speaking rudely to her.

Towards the end of November 1906 Crippen returned home in the middle of the day unexpectedly and went into Belle's bedroom to find her in bed with Richard Ehrlich, her favourite paying guest. He said nothing, merely going away closing the door loudly. Nor did he say anything later but in December he and Ethel le Neve at last became lovers.

For the next three years Crippen and Belle continued to live at 39 Hilldrop Crescent, and the lovers conducted their meetings in various small hotels. Belle continued to entertain and give little dinner-parties with her husband present and they gave to the world the appearance of a couple living a normal life together. Belle was of course aware of the changed situation with Ethel and she was furious when she came to believe that Ethel was pregnant. Ethel was young and healthy. Belle had always longed for children and this was a thought she could not bear.

Things were made worse by increasing financial pressures. At the end of 1909 the work Crippen had been doing for Munyon's was petering out. The Yale Tooth Specialists needed more capital to keep it afloat and Belle's life style continued to be expensive. All Crippen's sources of income were about to collapse. Belle would not part with her savings or her jewellery of which she had quite a collection, augmented since the days when she and her husband used to invest in diamonds by gifts from admirers and purchases made by herself. Belle thought of leaving Crippen, taking her savings and jewellery with her but she was determined to get rid of Ethel too. She told the ladies of the Guild that Ethel had had an abortion and was a home-wrecker and tried to persuade Crippen to dismiss her.

It was not until 17 January 1910 that Crippen ordered the drug hyoscine from his usual chemist who was accustomed to supplying him with drugs for his various 'remedies'. He ordered a large quantity, five grains. Hyoscine was a drug about which not a great deal was known though it had been used in small doses for many years for quieting mental patients. During his medical training Crippen had seen it used in this way. He had never ordered it before but the chemist, knowing him well, did not question the large amount of the drug ordered and Crippen signed the poisons register for it.

On 31 January 1910 Crippen made a personal call on some music-hall friends, the Martinettis, to invite them to dinner at Hilldrop Crescent that same night. The husband was not well and demurred but Crippen was insistent and finally the invitation was accepted. Belle cooked the dinner herself and then they played whist, the Martinettis leaving about half past one in the morning, though Belle pressed them to stay the night as it was extremely cold. Crippen went and found a cab and he and Belle stood together on the steps as their guests drove off.

Belle was never seen again.

Two days later Crippen left a note on Ethel's typewriter telling her that Belle had gone to America and asking Ethel to hand a packet of letters to Melinda May, the close friend of Belle's who acted as Secretary to the Guild whose office was in the same building. The Committee was actually sitting when Ethel delivered the letters. There were two, both in Crippen's handwriting, and at the end of one he had clumsily reproduced Belle's signature. The letters stated that Belle was handing in her resignation as Treasurer of the Guild and the documents that went with the position because she had been forced to leave for America at short notice on account of the illness of a near relative.

The Guild ladies were shocked, incredulous, and immediately suspicious. From that moment they did not cease their enquiries and it was their persistence in trying to find out what had happened to Belle which was finally responsible for bringing 'that little shrimp', whom none of them liked, to the gallows. They asked more and more questions. Why had Belle not contacted any of them? Why had she not sent as much as a postcard? It was not like their extrovert friend and Treasurer to disappear without a word.

In the meantime Crippen gave Ethel, who appears to have accepted his story without surprise or question, some of Belle's jewellery and pawned the rest. Days went by. Belle had planned to sell programmes at a charity ball at the end of February. The suspicious Martinettis manoeuvred Crippen into taking two tickets and joining their party which included several of Belle's friends.

It was with dumbfounded astonishment that the ladies saw him arrive at the function with Ethel at his side. She wore a pink gown and on her chest sparkled a large diamond sunburst brooch, one of Belle's favourite pieces, well-known to all.

Ethel left her lodgings and moved into 39 Hilldrop Crescent while Crippen told Belle's ever-questioning friends and neighbours firstly that she had become ill in California and then that she had died. To the Martinettis he sent a telegram announcing her death, from Victoria Station where he was about to board a train with Ethel for a holiday in Dieppe.

The news came as a great shock. However, members of the Music Hall Ladies' Guild had managed to prise an address out of Crippen, an address where Belle was supposed to be staying. In fact he gave them the address of his son Otto left behind in California with his grandparents so many years ago. Crippen wrote to his son telling him that Belle had died in California and at the same time the ladies wrote asking Otto to send the details of Belle's illness and death. After some time they received an answer. Otto knew nothing of his stepmother's arrival in California, let alone her illness and death there. He had only heard of this through a letter from his father and would himself like to know what had happened as he had had no communication from Belle at all.

Otto's letter was the beginning of the end. Belle's friends John and Lil Nash had just returned from a music-hall tour. When they saw Otto's letter they decided it was time to go to the police. All Belle's friends were worried and suspicious about her curious disappearance so uncharacteristically leaving all her prized jewellery and clothing behind, and about the presence in her house of Ethel le Neve.

As a result of the information given by Mr and Mrs Nash, Inspector Dew paid a visit to Dr Crippen at 39 Hilldrop

Crescent. He was told a different and much more plausible story that Belle had run off with a man and Crippen had not wished to tell this to her friends and neighbours so had invented the American story. Inspector Dew seemed to accept this. He had a look round and took a statement from Ethel, but as he left he said to Crippen 'Of course, we shall have to find Mrs Crippen to clear this matter up.'

Up till now Crippen had remained calm and unperturbed through all the fuss about his wife's absence and he had been unruffled during Inspector Dew's visit. The Inspector's final words, however, caused him to panic. He told Ethel that they must at once leave for the Continent. What Ethel knew or suspected is a secret she never revealed but she left with Crippen by way of Harwich. They arrived at Brussels and thence went to Antwerp where Crippen had decided they must take ship for Quebec. There, he appeared to think they would be unrecognized, safe, and able to start a new life together. Ethel had bought boy's clothing for herself, evidently not in her usual quiet collected state of mind for she stupidly bought them too small so that the trousers split at the back and had to be held by pins visible at times under the jacket. She cut her hair short. Dr Hawley Crippen and Miss Ethel le Neve became Mr Robinson and his son who was ill and travelling to Quebec for his health.

Meantime Inspector Dew had returned to now deserted 39 Hilldrop Crescent and the garden had been thoroughly dug over. Neither garden nor house yielded any clues to Belle's disappearance. It was not till 13 July, over five months since she had waved goodbye to the Martinettis, that Inspector Dew's investigations turned again to the neat and tidy cellar with its small pile of coal. He had a feeling about the cellar and began probing the brick floor with a sharp poker.

At last he came on a loose brick. Then digging began in earnest. A quantity of human remains came to light, parts of a torso wrapped in a man's pyjama jacket. The head, legs, and arms were missing and all the bones had been removed. There proved to be no doubt that these remains were Belle's and traces of hyoscine poisoning were found. The missing parts were never discovered. How a small weakly man like Hawley Crippen had managed single-handed (for no one could have helped him but Ethel and she was acquitted) to drag to the cellar the stout body of Belle Elmore, poisoned by hyoscine probably administered in her brandy, dismember it, bury the torso, restore the cellar to its clean and tidy state, and carry away and somehow dispose of the missing head, limbs, and bones, remains an unsolved question.

The story of the arrest of Dr Crippen and Ethel le Neve is crime history. The ship's captain had read an account of the cellar discoveries before his ship sailed. Mr Robinson and his son were a conspicuous couple with the 'boy' bursting out of his too-small clothes, and the pair of them clinging so affectionately together. It was the first time the telegraph had been used in the apprehension of a criminal. The captain wirelessed his suspicions to Scotland Yard. Inspector Dew boarded a faster vessel. At Quebec, Crippen and Ethel were arrested before they left the ship.

The trial of Dr Hawley Crippen at the Old Bailey on 1 October 1910 lacked the customary solemnity. The Court was crowded with theatrical personalities as well as many members of the Music Hall Ladies' Guild. The judge, Lord Alverstone, L.C.J., invited Miss Phyllis Dare, actress and postcard beauty, to sit on the Bench with him. It was an extraordinary scene and *The Times* indignantly pointed out that 'such a trial is not in the nature of a matinée'. Hawley Crippen remained aloof, unperturbed in the dock. He was found guilty and his appeal was dismissed.

Ethel le Neve was tried separately on charges of being an accessory after the fact. She was defended with great skill by F. E. Smith, later to become one of the most famous of Lord Chancellors. He represented Ethel as a young, inexperienced girl, fallen completely under the influence and control of a wicked man: a girl who knew nothing and accepted all that Crippen told her and obeyed him implicitly. It was a somewhat curious representation of a young woman in her late twenties,

Portrait model of Ethel le Neve, Dr Crippen's mistress

competent, business-like, who had run the practical side of her lover's employment for years and in her quiet way seemed to dominate him as much as Belle had with her tempers and henpecking. F. E. Smith would not allow Ethel to go into the witness-box and be cross-examined and the jury accepted his defence. Ethel was acquitted.

Her lover was executed on 23 November 1910 and on the same day she boarded a ship for America using another name. She remained there for six years returning to England unnoticed when her sister became ill and died. Ethel went to work where she met her future husband who never knew her story. She had children, grandchildren, and was widowed. She died in her eighties keeping her anonymity successfully to the end.

One cannot but speculate whether she ever took her children or grandchildren to Madame Tussaud's where the excellent likeness of Dr Hawley Crippen gazed from the dock wearing the double-collared grey frock coat and grey bow tie, a replica of the rather flashy garb he had worn at his trial which reflected Belle's taste in choosing his clothes. He gazed intently through his gold-rimmed spectacles and nearby was the dinner-wagon from 39 Hilldrop Crescent which Madame Tussaud's had bought when the contents of the house was sold. Of all the murderers in the Chamber of Horrors few had a more bizarre life story than Crippen.

Frederick Henry Seddon, another poisoner, who joined Crippen in the Chamber of Horrors in 1912 appears to have been motivated solely by an obsessive greed for money. Unlike Crippen whose life story was far from ordinary, visitors who came to Madame Tussaud's to look at the portrait of Seddon after the considerable publicity of his trial and conviction as a murderer, saw a man who might have been their neighbour in any secure and prosperous middle-class inner suburb of London.

Frederick Seddon worked for an insurance company in which he had steadily mounted the ladder over a period of years, for he was industrious, precise, thrifty and exact. In 1910 he was district superintendent for his company with excellent prospects of rising further. He lived in Tollington Park, considered a good neighbourhood, with his wife Margaret and their five children. He was forty years of age.

Making money was Seddon's keenest interest. He never missed a chance of earning a commission or undertaking any small business transaction outside his work from which he could reap even a small profit. Not that Seddon wanted money for any trivial or frivolous purposes. He was hard-working, zealous and uninterested in the more common forms of self-indulgence. His ambition was to own property and already he owned the fourteen-roomed house in Tollington Park in which he lived as well as various other properties all paid for and completely his.

One of the rooms in the Tollington Park house was set aside for use as an office for which he charged his company rent. Some of the rooms were divided by partitions to accommodate the large Seddon family, for his father lived with them and there was a living-in maid as well as the five children to be housed. This cramping was made necessary because Seddon let off the top floor as unfurnished lodgings. Thus, although he owned his home, he was able to make it bring in money almost equivalent to its normal rental value.

In July 1910 the tenant of the top floor was a Miss Eliza Mary Barrow who had answered an advertisement offering the rooms for letting. When she first moved in she was accompanied by two friends, Mr and Mrs Hook, and a small orphaned boy called Ernest Grant who Miss Barrow had adopted. She was extremely fond of this child. Within a month Miss Barrow and the Hooks had quarrelled and the couple departed leaving the spinster and the little boy living on the top floor.

Miss Barrow was an extremely peculiar and unpleasant character. She had lodged with relatives, some of whom lived quite near her new address, and had quarrelled with them, and she had also quarrelled with numerous landlords and landladies who could not tolerate her ill temper and squalid ways. However, in spite of her life style Miss Barrow was far from poor. She possessed some £4,000 in stocks and leasehold property and she loved money, particularly gold sovereigns which she hoarded. She hoarded banknotes too, but it was gold sovereigns that she loved and she brought a boxful of them to her new lodgings at Tollington Park.

This passion for gold and love of money was something she shared with her landlord. It was an extraordinary chance that brought Eliza Barrow, who was only forty-nine in spite of her elderly, miserly ways, to live under the same roof as Frederick Seddon. She paid him twelve shillings and sixpence a week for her lodgings and bought her own food. What services she required were performed not by the maid but one of the Seddon daughters, Maggie. Miss Barrow's income was considerably greater than her expenditure even with a little boy to maintain.

Mrs Seddon did not play a prominent role in the household. She was thirty-seven, quite good-looking and dressed with good taste, but she occupied herself with the lighter housework in the large house and her duties with her children. Everyone in the family seemed rather afraid of Seddon who was cold, hard, and something of a tyrant. He made it clear that he and his business affairs came first in importance.

Miss Barrow had quarrelled and even spat at earlier landlords, but in Frederick Seddon she seems to have recognized a kindred spirit who loved money and in particular handling gold sovereigns as much as she did. He certainly gained considerable influence over his parsimonious lodger for on 14 October 1910, less than three months after she came to live at Tollington Park, she made over to Seddon £1,600 of India stock for the purchase of an annuity. The transaction was made with Seddon personally not with his company, although this handled such matters as part of its business. In January 1911 she assigned her leasehold property, a public house called the Buck's Head, to him for the same purpose and six months later she drew £216 in gold out of her savings bank.

The friendship between Seddon and his tenant grew. She even went to Southend for a few days with Frederick and his wife in August, but at the beginning of September she became ill with a bilious attack. The next day a doctor was called who continued to attend her as her illness did not improve. The doctor wished Miss Barrow to go into hospital but she refused. Maggie Seddon continued to provide the domestic services needed and Mrs Seddon prepared the patient's food downstairs in her own kitchen. She did not use the room that served as a kitchen in the top-floor lodgings. Early in the morning of 14 September Eliza Mary Barrow died. Her illness had lasted two weeks and she had been attended throughout by a doctor who, on being told by Seddon of his patient's death, wrote a certificate without further ado.

Seddon arranged the cheapest possible funeral, telling the undertaker that there was no money available for a grander one and no money to purchase a grave-plot, so Miss Barrow found her last resting place in the public plot although papers among her effects showed that there was a family vault at Highgate. There were no family or friends at the funeral. The little boy Ernest had been sent to Southend with the Seddon children. Three days before she died Eliza Barrow had made a will leaving her furniture, jewellery and personal property to the orphaned child and his sister who had been taken in by another family on their parent's death. She made no mention in her will of other property or cash. Seddon was appointed executor and also given control of the children's inheritance until they came of age. The will was witnessed by Seddon's aged father who was still living with them.

Thus at Miss Barrow's death Frederick Seddon was released from obligation to pay her an annuity in return for the stock and leasehold property she had made over to him and he had control of her personal property. There was no mention of the hoard of gold and bank notes Miss Barrow had always kept in her cash-box. This seemed to have vanished and all memory of Eliza Barrow would have vanished too had not the relations living not far away, with whom she had quarrelled, decided to patch up the rift and make some enquiries about her. They knew her address and were astonished when they learned that she was dead. Mr and Mrs Venderahe were cousins of the dead woman and they were naturally interested in knowing what had become of her property as well as the reason why they had not been informed of her funeral which they would have attended. Seddon told them he had written to them on the day of Miss Barrow's death and showed a copy of the letter, but no missive had reached the Venderahes.

Frederick Seddon explained that Miss Barrow had disposed of her stocks and leaseholds in return for an annuity and he showed her will leaving her personal property to the two orphaned children. As regards cash, only about ten pounds in loose gold had been found in her rooms after her death.

The Venderahes, who knew about the large amounts of cash that their cousin kept by her, became less and less satisfied with the circumstances of her death and her hasty burial in a public grave. In November the body was exhumed and examination showed that a substantial amount of arsenic must have been taken two or three days before Eliza Barrow died.

Seddon was arrested on 4 December 1911 and early in January 1912 Mrs Seddon was also arrested, and charged with being concerned along with her husband in the murder of Eliza Mary Barrow. The prosecution case rested on the theory that Miss Barrow had been poisoned with arsenic from flypapers which Mrs Seddon admitted having purchased because her lodger had complained during her illness that her room was full of flies. There was also an allegation that Maggie Seddon who looked after the lodger had made an earlier purchase of flypapers at the end of August just before Miss Barrow had her first bilious attack.

At the time the sale of arsenic flypapers which had figured in so many cases in Queen Victoria's reign (such as that of Mrs Maybrick accused of poisoning her husband) was still completely uncontrolled. The flypapers were highly dangerous. Usually there were six in a packet and each paper contained enough poison to kill an adult. The packets were labelled 'Arsenical Flypapers' and 'Poison' but could certainly become a weapon in the hands of anyone contemplating a crime. The mode of usage was to place the flypaper in a saucer and cover it with boiling water. The resulting liquid had no taste or smell and was coloured only by the colouring in the paper. It could not be recognized if added to soup or any coloured drinks such as coffee.

The Seddon trial began 4 March 1912. There was enormous public interest on account of the respectable, middle-class status of the accused, the mystery of how they had administered the arsenic, if indeed they had done so, for both pleaded not guilty, and the eminent counsel employed (the Attorney-General, Sir Rufus Isaacs, and Mr Marshall Hall). On 14 March Mrs Seddon was acquitted and Frederick Seddon found guilty and condemned to death. The final drama came when Seddon, making a statement after conviction, gave a Masonic sign, knowing that the judge who had sentenced him was a fellow Mason. Seddon's appeal failed and he was executed on 12 April.

The last murderer to enter the Chamber of Horrors before the outbreak of the First World War in August 1914 was a twenty-two-year-old man called George Ball, or sometimes Sumner, whose callous crime for gain became known as the 'Liverpool Sack Murder', and aroused revulsion throughout that city for its brutality.

The murder might not have been fixed on Ball but for an accident of chance which caused him to be seen just after he had committed it. A ship's steward happened to be waiting in Old Hall Street by the shop front of Bradfield's, the tarpaulin makers where Ball worked with an eighteen-year-old youth called Elltoft. One of the shop's shutters fell down and hit the waiting man on the head. The steward was not injured and a few minutes later a young man who was in fact Ball emerged from the shop and apologized. The steward also noticed a boy who came out pushing a handcart. He joined Ball and the two went off down the street with the handcart.

The next day a sack was found blocking the gates of the water lock in the Leeds-Liverpool canal. When it was fished out of the water it was found to contain the battered body of a woman soon identified by a medallion round the neck as that of Miss Christine Bradfield who looked after the shop connected with her brother's tarpaulin business. The medallion depicted the three wise monkeys, 'Speak No Evil', 'See No Evil', 'Hear No Evil'. Miss Bradfield was forty years old.

The police immediately went after Ball and Elltoft, the employees who had been seen wheeling away a handcart. Elltoft was at home in bed but Ball had disappeared. He was found ten days later, disguised, in possession of the dead woman's watch and with bloodstains on his clothes.

The jury at Liverpool Assizes in February 1914 thought little of Ball's story that a man with a gun had threatened them in the shop, hit Miss Bradfield, and absconded with the takings which were missing. He was condemned to death and confessed his guilt while in the death cell. His young accomplice Elltoft received a sentence of four years penal servitude for being an accessory after the fact.

[7]

The First World War and Disaster by Fire in 1925

When war came on 4 August 1914 attendances at the exhibition dropped dramatically and alarmingly as people adjusted themselves to the shock of war and all that modern warfare involved. Foreign tourists vanished and English people were not at first in the mood for entertainment as men entrained for France. However, as the first months passed there was a change, the flow of visitors began to swell again and their numbers eventually surpassed those of pre-war days, though khaki was now the predominant colour to be seen in the crowds.

Madame Tussaud's became a favourite place of rendezvous and indeed it was often a haven for soldiers arriving on leave from France or on their way to the trenches: a place where hundreds of them went to fill the time while they waited for the train to take them on the next stage of their journey home on leave, or back to the battlefield. The doors of the exhibition were opened at eight o'clock in the morning and John Theodore Tussaud gave instructions to the staff that no weary soldier who fell asleep on the sofas or even on the floor was to be disturbed.

In the great halls upstairs there were battle maps, films, lectures, and new portraits of the heroes and heroines such as Captain Fryatt, Edith Cavell and Jack Cornwell, as well as of all the Allied naval and military commanders. The Kaiser's portrait was there. It was not placed in the Chamber of Horrors but for several months had to be banished from the exhibition on account of the frequent assaults made on it.

When the khaki-clad visitors and their companions wandered down the stairs to the Chamber of Horrors in the basement they entered a dimly lit world where the war did not exist. There were the gallows, the guillotine and the death heads from long-ago revolutionary France. Serried rows of murderers and other criminals gazed fixedly at the soldiers inspecting them, holding their places as if determined to see out any number of years of war.

Then there were the tableaux, the Newgate cells, and the 'horrid' relics such as King Henry IV of France's bloodstained shirt. This might be the Chamber of Horrors but they were very different horrors from those experienced on the battlefronts. There was no noise of whistling and exploding shells: it was quiet and orderly. War could be briefly forgotten down here in the Chamber of Horrors. It must have seemed a remote place, even a refuge from the present, in spite of the character of its occupants.

Only one new figure was placed in the Chamber of Horrors during the years of the First World War. This was the portrait of George Joseph Smith, the 'Brides in the Bath' murderer who was hanged at Maidstone Prison on Friday, 13 August 1915, a year after the war had begun. It was a case so notorious that other calls on the studios had to be set aside to record one evil worthless man's death when so many were being killed in war.

Smith's victims, whether he took their money alone or their lives as well, appear to have been women of almost incredible foolishness, their folly being the more remarkable at a time when women were emerging in thousands to play an active part in the war effort.

George Joseph Smith was a child who seems to have been born with a wicked streak even though his parents were respectable, his father working steadily as a Bethnal Green insurance agent. He was born in 1872 in Bethnal Green, yet at the age of nine he was in a reformatory at Gravesend where he remained until the age of sixteen. George then went to live with his mother but rapidly fell back into criminal ways and served several prison sentences for theft. The last of these sentences, twelve months hard labour for larceny and receiving, he served under the name of George Baker, and the police knew that he was associated with a woman who he placed in various work situations where he induced her to steal for him.

Out of prison in 1897 George went to Leicester where he opened a baker's shop using the name of George Love. It was under this name that he married his only legal wife, Caroline Thornhill, a young girl and friend of a woman who worked in his shop. It is significant that the Thornhill family strongly disapproved and refused to attend the church wedding.

Mr and Mrs Love, as they were known, departed for London. Here Mrs Love went to work, her husband finding situations for her and himself writing the necessary references. Caroline Love, like his previous woman associate, appeared to be willing to work and steal on her husband's behalf in spite of her respectable background. It was not long before she was in trouble with the police. George Smith (Love) managed to evade any connection with his wife's activities on the proceeds of which he lived. However, after about two years Caroline Love, who was working in a situation at Hastings, again fell foul of the police and this time she 'shopped' her husband. He was arrested in London and was imprisoned for two years for receiving stolen goods. When he emerged in the autumn of 1902 he vengefully pursued his wife to Leicester but her brothers succeeded in chasing him out of town. Caroline was alarmed and wished to escape from her husband which she successfully did by emigrating to Canada. She did not see him again until his trial for murder in 1915 for which she was called back to England.

The fact that he had a legal wife even if she had fled to Canada did not deter Smith from finding and exploiting a series of women all of whom had some money on which he managed to lay his hands. Where necessary he did not hesitate to go through a ceremony of marriage using a variety of names.

In the summer of 1908 Smith was in Bristol, where he set up in a small way as a second-hand furniture dealer with some £80 or £90 he had extracted from a widow before abandoning her and not returning. In the same road where his shop was located a Miss Edith Pegler lived with her mother. She advertised for a post as housekeeper and George Smith engaged her. Within a week she had fallen under his spell and agreed to marry him. The ceremony took place by special licence at a registrar's office. This time George Smith used his real name and described himself as a bachelor. Edith Pegler proved to be the one woman with whom he kept a regular contact, always returning to her after his frequent absences. He told her lies, did not support her financially, but she always accepted his explanations unquestioningly. The only things he ever seems to have given her were some clothes belonging to another woman who he had bigamously married and abandoned in his usual style. He told Edith Pegler, who of course believed herself to be Mrs George Smith, that he had done a deal in second-hand clothes.

During his long absences from Edith Pegler, Smith pursued his career of enslaving women and getting hold of their money with such success that he was able to purchase a house at Southend, a useful source of security when he wished to borrow money. George and Edith wandered about a good deal together staying in lodgings in various places. In 1910 they were back in Bristol, and Smith found himself at the end of his financial resources. He had no intention of working and began looking around for some female with a certain amount of means who could be relieved of her money in the usual way. He was, not surprisingly, completely confident of his powers.

In the neighbourhood of Clifton in Bristol he managed to pick an acquaintance with Beatrice Annie Constance Mundy. She was a spinster of thirty-three and better off than most of his previous victims, for she was the daugher of a deceased bank manager. Evidently she was not considered by her family to be very sensible with money for relatives persuaded her to execute a settlement of the money she had received from her father's estate. She had the use of the income, but the capital was secured they thought. It amounted to some £2,000. Smith and Miss Mundy became engaged after only a few days acquaintance. She went with him to Weymouth where they took a two-room lodging and were 'married' at a registrar's office, Smith using the name of Henry Williams, and his status as bachelor.

On the very day of the wedding 'Henry Williams' wrote to his bride's solicitors asking for a copy of his late father-in-law's will. He then discovered the settlement which protected the capital, and found that the solicitors were holding in reserve 'for emergencies' £138 of her income. It did not take him long to get hold of this and having done so he promptly left Miss Mundy, now known as Mrs Henry Williams, leaving her penniless in the lodging they had taken.

George Smith returned to Edith Pegler, paid his debts and for the next year or so they moved around as Mr and Mrs Smith from Bristol, to Southend, to Walthamstow, in each place setting up for a short time some kind of business in second-hand furniture and antiques. Early in 1912 they were back in Bristol. Smith went off again leaving very little money. The business they had set up did not thrive. Edith sold it for what she could get, a mere five pounds, and went to live with her mother. She next saw her 'husband' in the dock.

Whether it was genuine coincidence or whether Smith got wind somehow of Miss Mundy's whereabouts it is impossible to say, but in March he turned up in Weston-super-Mare where Miss Mundy had been staying for some time in a boarding-house calling herself, of course, Mrs Henry Williams. According to the landlady her lodger went out to buy some flowers and accidentally found her long-missing husband 'looking out over the sea'. She brought him back. The landlady, Mrs Tuckett, took such a violent dislike to 'Mr Williams' that she said she was going to send a wire to Mrs Williams's aunt but in the end she did not do so. The couple left the lodgings a few hours later and did not return.

George Smith was in urgent need of money. With incredible effrontery he went back to his so-called wife Miss Mundy's solicitors telling a garbled story as to why he had vanished with her money shortly after their 'marriage' in 1910. It appeared to the solicitors that Mrs Williams was completely under her husband's influence. She assented to and confirmed everything he said.

The couple travelled around for some time and finally at the end of May 1912 came to rest in Herne Bay where George Smith, in the name of Henry Williams, took a lease on a house. He was again in acute need of money and had to seek some means of laying hands on Miss Mundy's capital tied up by settlement. He took legal advice and counsel's opinion from which it appeared that even at his 'wife's' death he would only get it if they both made similar wills each leaving all property to the other. Beatrice Mundy, meekly and apparently without query or suspicion, agreed. The wills were promptly drawn up. Miss Mundy signed her death warrant in signing this will. The date was 2 July.

There was no bath in the Herne Bay house. George Smith did not usually require a bath; in fact in a statement she made later Edith Pegler said that in all the years of his comings and goings as her 'husband' she had only once known him to take a bath. She said he did not like using baths in lodgings that others had access to.

Now however George Smith had a use for a bath. He visited an ironmonger and beat the shopkeeper down on the price from two pounds to seventeen and sixpence. The bath had no taps or fitments. Smith did not pay for it and it was returned four days later. In the meantime, the day after the purchase of the bath, 'Mr Williams' took his 'wife' to a young local doctor only two years qualified saying she had suffered a fit. The doctor prescribed bromide and subsequently paid two visits to the house, finding not much amiss with 'Mrs Williams' and prescribing more bromide.

The next call he received was a note telling him 'Mrs Williams' was dead. He hastened to the house and found her lying in the bath with her head under water. At the inquest a verdict of misadventure was returned, it being concluded that 'Mrs Williams' had slipped under the water while having an epileptic fit.

Immediately after the funeral George Smith got rid of the

house and sold the furniture. In spite of suspicions, enquiries and interference by Beatrice Mundy's family he obtained probate and in accordance with the will that she had signed he emerged from this 'marriage' nearly £2,500 the richer.

Edith Pegler, still of course believing she was Mrs Smith, stayed in Bristol with her mother but had little news of her 'husband'. Now in the summer of 1912 he asked her to join him at Margate. She accepted his story that he had been in Canada and acquired a Chinese image which he had sold at a good profit. They lived together for about a year till in the autumn of 1913 he left her again.

This time he went to Southsea and met a girl called Alice Burnham at a chapel she attended. She was twenty-five and worked as nurse to an elderly gentleman. They quickly became engaged and even visited the girl's parents at Aston Clinton. The visit was not a success. Mr Burnham felt the strongest antipathy to his daughter's fiancé—'a man of very evil appearance'—and the couple left. They were 'married' at Portsmouth, Smith using his real name. At the time Alice Burnham had about £100 in savings and a quantity of jewellery and clothing. George Smith succeeded in turning her completely against her family. He persuaded her to insure her life and make a will in his favour. Like Beatrice Mundy she acquiesced without demur.

In December 1913 the pair went to Blackpool. They declined one set of rooms because there was no bath, but found others let by a Mrs Crossley which had the necessary fitment. Then they called on a doctor where George Smith complained that his wife had a headache after the journey. The doctor wrote a prescription. The following day Alice Burnham asked her landlady, Mrs Crossley, to prepare a hot bath for her. Soon after she had gone into the bathroom Smith went to the landlady saying he could not make his wife hear him. Alice Burnham had her head under water. A verdict of drowning was returned and she was presumed to have fainted and slid beneath the water.

Alice Burnham's mother and brother attended the funeral after which Smith sold all his 'wife's' effects and departed immediately. Mrs Crossley evidently had her suspicions for she

Portrait model of George Smith, the 'Brides in the Bath' murderer with his last victim, Margaret Lofty.

shouted 'Crippen' after him as he departed. Smith returned to Edith Pegler in Bristol saying that he had been in Spain and had done fairly well there. He had no difficulty in collecting the insurance money on Alice Burnham's life.

At the end of 1914 Smith once more left Edith Pegler in Bristol. This time he managed to make acquaintance with Margaret Elizabeth Lofty, an unmarried daughter of a deceased clergyman. She worked as companion to elderly ladies. At the time she was recovering from an unfortunate love-affair in which the gentleman had proved to be already married. She was an easy prey to Smith's spell over women but must have had some doubts over the wisdom of her course of action for she did not tell her mother and sister that she intended to get married. She said that she was going to a new situation and would probably be in London for a few days. On 17 December George Smith 'married' her under the name of John Lloyd.

Margaret Lofty's savings amounted only to about £19, so for George Smith to follow the pattern he had established it would be necessary for her to insure her life. She took out a policy for £700 before they were married. The 'marriage' took place in Bath but immediately after the ceremony they took train for London, 'John Lloyd' having already booked lodgings at Highgate. When they arrived 'Mr Lloyd' asked to look at the bath and remarked that it was rather small but in any case the landlady and the woman who ran the house refused them the rooms as soon as they appeared under the pretext that references were required. In reality both women were alarmed by Smith's 'evil appearance' and did not want him in the house.

He was angry and went in search of other apartments in Highgate. This time it was 'Mrs Lloyd' who asked to see the bath. The same evening 'Mr Lloyd' took his wife to a doctor who prescribed for her. The next day she made a will, visiting a solicitor for the purpose, in which she left everything to her 'husband'. She also drew out all her savings. When she got home in the evening she asked for a hot bath in which she was duly found dead. A verdict of drowning was returned.

This time the pattern so smoothly established by George

Smith was broken. The newspaper the *News of the World* picked up the story of the bride who so tragically drowned in the bath within days of her marriage. Mr Burnham, Alice Burnham's father, read the story and was struck with the similarity of his daughter's death in the bath at Blackpool. Mrs Crossley, the Blackpool landlady who had called 'Crippen' after Smith as he left after Alice's funeral, also read the story.

Both Mr Burnham and Mrs Crossley's husband independently got in touch with the police and investigations began. On 3 March 1915 George Joseph Smith was charged with the wilful murder of Beatrice Mundy, Alice Burnham, and Margaret Lofty. The trial at the Central Criminal Court lasted from 29 June to 9 July, the longest murder trial since that of Dr William Palmer, the poisoner (already an inmate of the Chamber of Horrors), which had taken place sixty years earlier. Palmer poisoned his victims, Smith drowned them. Both murdered for gain.

George Joseph Smith was condemned to death and though he passed his last days in a state of prostration he showed no penitence and made no confession. He was executed at Maidstone on 13 August 1915. A realistic portrait model of George Smith appeared in the Chamber of Horrors together with the bath in which Miss Lofty was drowned and a few other 'relics' from Highgate. The figure of Smith was placed in an iron dock, his clothes an exact copy of those he had worn at his trial.

For those who preferred other things, there were upstairs excellent portraits of three new VCs. In ironic contrast the three war heroes are long-forgotten but George Joseph Smith and the Highgate bath still hold visitors' attention in the Chamber of Horrors.

John Theodore Tussaud was sixty years old when peace came at last. He had carried on the exhibition single-handed with depleted studio and exhibition staff, for five of his sons, who were old enough, served in the armed forces. All these sons returned safely though one had been a prisoner-of-war.

It was a different world to which the soldiers returned and young men were looking for wider horizons. Madame Tussaud's great-great-grandsons were no exception and in the post-war years four of them left the exhibition to pursue different careers. Only one of them, Bernard, carried on the family tradition and worked in the exhibition for the rest of his life. Four of his aunts still worked in the wardrobe and colouring and hair-insertion studios, and his sister Joan joined the wardrobe, working there until her comparatively early death. The Tussaud traditions were maintained.

While the war years had consolidated the position of Madame Tussaud's exhibition as one of London's institutions they left a back-log of work and much needed to be done in the way of rearrangement and refurbishing apart from the production of new portraits as the contemporary scene changed.

The Chamber of Horrors had to take its turn. It was not until 1922 that the ranks of the sixty or more figures of murderers and criminals were joined by a Frenchman, a portrait of one of the most notorious of mass-murderers, the French 'Bluebeard', Henri Landru, yet another who killed for gain alone. Henri Desiré Landru was found guilty of murdering ten women, all widows, and one boy. None amongst his victims except perhaps the boy would have gained much sympathy from Madame Tussaud had she been alive to see her fellow-countryman go to the guillotine. They all sealed their own doom through weakness and stupidity.

Landru was married with a family and lived at Neuilly on the edge of Paris where he ran a business as a dealer in second-hand furniture and cars and other junk. He had been to prison for several swindles. In appearance he was not attractive, being short and bald, with a heavy beard, but his deep-set dark eyes appeared to have a hypnotic effect on women.

It was before the war, around 1913, that Landru hit on the idea of using this influence as a means of gain. From the first it seems that the idea of removing his victims from this world if it appeared expedient was an accepted facet of the plan. He decided to concentrate on widows, attracting them by means of advertisement. 'Widower, aged forty-nine, possessing comfortable income, affectionate, serious, moving in good society, desires to meet widow of similar status with a view to matrimony.' It might have occurred to any woman of sense that a gentleman with the qualifications listed would have no difficulty in finding a second bride without recourse to advertisement. However, a shoal of letters came in response.

Madame Cuchet was a dark good-looking widow of thirty-nine and she was Landru's first choice. She became infatuated with her assiduous wooer. When he went away on 'business' (in fact to his wife and family at Neuilly) he plied her with love-letters of which he kept a store copied from novelettes. He rented a house at Vernouillet and persuaded Madame Cuchet to give up her comfortable flat in Paris and transport her furniture and eighteen-year-old son to the rural retreat. As his fiancée, she parted with substantial sums of money on his promise to invest these profitably for her. He was able to buy a garage at Neuilly.

Before the widow had been stripped of any more, her son André happened to see his future stepfather walking in the Rue de Rivoli in Paris with another lady. He told his mother and she angrily upbraided Landru for taking out another woman when he was pledged to marry her. Landru treated the matter lightly, and in the evening he produced a bottle of wine to celebrate, he said, a good business deal. Neither Madame Cuchet nor her son were seen again. Late that night two passers-by noticed light in the house and thick black smoke belching from the chimneys. Landru was burning the bodies with an oxyacetylene burner. Neither of the passers-by took much notice of what they saw.

The lady with whom Landru had strolled in the Rue de Rivoli was a Brazilian widow, Madame Laborde-Line. She too had answered one of the advertisements (in all over a period of years he placed seven in the press). Calling himself Monsieur Cuchet, the name of his first victim, he followed the same wooing techniques. Soon the widow agreed to let him sell her furniture for which he promised a good price. Then she was invited to Vernouillet and vanished the next day. No one knows exactly what happened there but it is suggested that she too was poisoned with wine, and her body hurled into the swift-flowing

Oise, where the following year the body of an unidentified woman was found some five miles from Vernouillet. In his notebook against the word 'Brésil' Landru entered a net profit of £57.

He had already begun his courtship of an elderly widow, Madame Guillin, who had a legacy of £800 from a family for whom she had worked for years. On hearing Landru's story of a French consulship in Australia to which she would accompany him as his wife, the besotted woman gave him power of attorney to dispose of all her property. She too took up residence at Vernouillet and cut her life short by peeping through the keyhole of a locked attic while her 'fiancé' was out. Like Bluebeard's wife she saw a quantity of women's clothes and shoes, relics of her predecessors at Vernouillet. Uneasy, she questioned Landru who told her they were his mother's things that he kept for sentimental reasons. Although this lulled Madame Guillin's suspicions there was danger that she might gossip and she too swallowed a fatal drink. Her body went into her own new and unmarked trunk which was despatched to Arcachon near Bordeaux, where for several years it was an unsolved trunk mystery. Landru had Madame Guillin's power of attorney and acquired all her property.

His next effort, more ambitious, nearly put an end to Landru's career as a murderer. He went through a form of marriage with a young and pretty war widow who had £10,000. However, she did not like her 'husband's' attempts to make her hand over to him the control of her fortune, nor was she happy about tablets that she found amongst his things. It was by chance she learned from a friend that Landru was known under another name for swindling women. She reported everything to the police. Landru went into hiding. He gave up the house at Vernouillet and through a friend managed to sell its contents.

When Landru deemed it safe to emerge into his dreadful activities again, since he had used a different alias when courting each widow, no suspicious finger seems to have pointed to the second-hand dealer who lived at Neuilly with his family. Then Landru noticed an isolated villa when he was motoring in the forest of Rambouillet. It was to let and the hamlet of Gambais was out of sight of the villa. He took a lease.

Madame Héon was the first visitor. While she had no money she did have some furniture which could be sold. Landru took her to Gambais on a one-way ticket, buying a return ticket for himself. He noted this in his account book. Madame Héon did not stay long at Gambais. The same night she was poisoned and her body incinerated in a large stove that Landru had installed in the isolated villa.

Madame Collumb came next, a woman who should have had more sense for she had a good position with an insurance company, some money and some furniture. On promise of marriage she spent Christmas with Landru at Gambais but on Christmas night died from eating chocolates which he had poisoned. He used acid to make her face and hands unrecognizable and took her body by car to the Channel coast where he threw it in the sea.

By now the newspaper *Le Matin* was publicizing a mystery. A sister of Madame Cuchet, the first victim, had reported to the police the disappearance of both her sister and her nephew after they had gone to live with a man she knew as Raymond Diard at Vernouillet. The police were searching for this man.

Landru read this but felt himself quite safe at Gambais. He picked up a nursemaid who had just been dismissed from her job, calling himself Monsieur Guillet. She went to her former employer's house with a bag to remove her possessions and told both this lady and her mother that she was going away to marry a Monsieur Guillet but would be back in a few days time. She was never seen again. It is not known how she was disposed of but her shoes and some of her letters were later found in the Gambais villa.

It was Landru's next conquest, a forty-four-year-old Madame Buisson, which actually led to his downfall. She knew him as Monsieur Charcroix and much to his surprise and dismay introduced him at her flat to her two sisters, Madame Paulet and Mademoiselle Lacoste. They found him charming. The engaged pair went off on a motor tour ostensibly to visit

Madame Buisson's blind son at Bayonne. She finished up buried in a wood near Biarritz.

Landru was already writing to a Madame Jaume who was separated from a criminal husband who was wanted by the police. She did not have money but Landru invited her to Gambais. At the end of the visit he was to drive back to Paris by a leisurely route through the forest of Fontainebleau. There she took a deadly drink from his flask and was either buried in the forest or thrown into the furnace of a glass factory at Vierzy which was never damped down but left unguarded at night. Landru sold her bits of furniture for seven pounds and entered the amount in his notebook.

It was now 1917 and on a tram a shop assistant, Fernande Segret, got into conversation with a Monsieur Lucion Guillet, middle-aged and bald but with magnetic eyes. She agreed to leave her job and housekeep for him at a little flat in the Rue de Rochouart. She also visited Gambais. During the two years that Landru lived with Fernande he killed two more women. Madame Pascal took her cat to Gambais as she had no one to leave it with. She was never seen again. No trace of her was found but her cat was discovered buried under the garage floor. Madame Marchadier kept a boarding-house in Paris. She went on a visit to Gambais and disappeared. The glass-factory furnace is conjectured to have been her final fate.

Unbeknown to Henri Landru the end had now come. He took Fernande to buy a dinner-service in a china shop in the Rue de Rivoli. By chance Mademoiselle Lacoste, sister of Madame Buisson, was in the same shop. She was sure the man she saw there was André Charcroix who had married her widowed sister and both had vanished. She had been to the police but it was wartime and they were too much occupied with suspected espionage to bother about a missing widow.

Mademoiselle Lacoste left the shop and told her story to the first policeman she could find. He came back with her to the shop and noted the name and address of the purchaser of the dinner-set. In due course the report came to the desk of Inspector Gaffiot whose interest was immediately aroused. He

Portrait figure of Henri Landru, a mass-murderer known as the French Bluebeard.

had a list of women, widows, of small means, who had disappeared after meeting a gentleman of various names who had property at Gambais.

Next morning Monsieur Lucien Guillet was arrested while having breakfast with Fernande Segret. The flat was searched and enough documents were found, including Landru's meticulously kept notebook of expenses and profits, for the case to be handed over to a *Juge d'Instruction*.

This was April 1919 and the wheels of French law grind very slowly. It was not until November 1921 that Henry Landru was charged with eleven murders and tried at the Court of Assize of the Seine et Oise. Throughout those months of public examination the case had been headline news. Landru maintained he was innocent and maintained also imperturbable calm. He gave clever answers to the examinating magistrate, one of the most highly regarded in France, Monsieur Bonin.

At the trial where Landru was defended by a famous criminal lawyer he kept the same demeanour. In the end Henri Desiré Landru was found guilty of eleven dreadful murders. Curiously there was at the same time a recommendation for mercy. However, the appeal was dismissed and on 25 February 1922 the guillotine blade fell.

During the long public examination so fully publicized, scores of women had come forward with stories of how they had been fleeced and swindled by this man who, though he used many aliases, never attempted to alter his appearance. According to the records of the Sûreté his hypnotic eyes and assiduous wooing had deceived no less than 284 women including those he had murdered. The trial had been much publicized in England and Landru's figure attracted many visitors.

The lure of the Chamber of Horrors showed no sign of waning. Early in June 1922 two young daughters of the King of Spain, Princesses Beatrice and Maria Christina, insisted on including it in their visit to the exhibition. They were most interested in the Newgate cells and the Comte de Lorge and his story as well as Marat in his bath—in fact one of the young Princesses went back to have a second look at Marat.

The advertised Whitsun attraction for this year included two totally incongruous portraits. Upstairs was a new excellent likeness of Sir George Williams, founder of the YMCA, and 'just added' down below in the Chamber of Horrors was an equally applauded portrait of Major Armstrong of Hay who was executed on 31 May for poisoning his wife.

So many of the characters who took their places in the sombre basement were actuated by greed and gain but an overdeveloped vanity seems to have been the motive that pushed Herbert Rowse Armstrong into killing his wife, and subsequently trying to dispose of a rival solicitor in like manner.

Herbert Armstrong was thirty-seven when he joined a firm of solicitors in the little town of Hay in Brecon on the Welsh borders. It was 1906 and on the death of the senior partner and his wife Armstrong was able to take over the business entirely. He married a childhood friend, Katherine, and they had three children. The marriage proved to be an inharmonious one. Katherine was a woman of blameless life but she was inordinately strict in her ideas of conduct. No alcohol ever entered the house and smoking was confined to one room. Even if a drink were offered at a dinner-party Katherine would intervene to prevent her husband accepting it.

Herbert Armstrong, a small man, was extremely vain and craved popularity and importance. He could not bear to think he was shown in an undignified and submissive light. His wife must have been a trying companion at times but he did not protest openly or privately.

Herbert Armstrong served throughout the First World War though he did not go overseas. He attained the rank of major, a title which he retained when he returned to civilian life. During his service he had met a widow, named only as 'Madame X', with whom he formed a close and lasting friendship. It is possible this friendship and his wartime freedom from his wife's niggling but strictly enforced prohibitions had an influence on his future course of action.

After the war Armstrong returned to his house, 'Mayfield', in Hay, a house with a garden in which weeds were always particularly rampant. He dealt with these by means of arsenical weedkiller always bought from one local chemist, sometimes in the form of a proprietary brand, sometimes mixed by himself from arsenic powder.

Mrs Armstrong's health had not been good for some time. She suffered from indigestion, rheumatism, and neuritis which prevented her from playing the piano. In July 1920 she made a new will, written in her husband's hand and witnessed by two servants, in which she left everything to her husband. Her previous will had benefited her children more than her spouse.

The local family doctor, Dr Hincks, was a long-established and respected practitioner. Towards the end of August he found Katherine Armstrong's health deteriorating for she appeared to have developed some heart and kidney trouble, and was suffering from delusions. There seemed to be some danger of a suicide attempt and Dr Hincks with another practitioner certified Katherine insane, and she was taken to a private asylum. She remained there for five months during which both her mental and physical health improved considerably.

During her absence in the asylum Major Armstrong contracted venereal disease and was treated by the family doctor. Arsenic played a part in the treatment and Armstrong discussed fatal doses with the doctor. Then in January 1921 Katherine came home from the asylum though she still needed some nursing help. A month later in February she became ill with vomiting and took to her bed. Dr Hincks visited her daily but she became worse and during the morning of 22 February she died. Dr Hincks provided a certificate without demur for he found nothing in her symptoms that could not be related to natural causes.

Major Armstrong survived the ordeal of his wife's death and funeral with equanimity and the village sympathized. He then went off for six weeks' holiday during which, his diary recorded, he indulged in all the pleasures and freedom that the strict views of his wife had forbidden him for so long. He proposed to his friend 'Madame X' but she gave no definite reply though she did spend a day and a night at Hay.

In Hay another firm of solicitors headed by a Mr O. Martin had established itself after the war. Major Armstrong resented the presence of a rival and proposed amalgamation, which was not accepted. The two solicitors were sometimes at odds in connection with their work and social relations between them were not cordial.

However, in October 1921 Major Armstrong appeared to have a change of heart and a wish to become friendly. He invited Mr Martin to tea at Mayfield, an invitation that was finally though reluctantly accepted. Later Mr Martin clearly recollected Armstrong picking up a scone which was among the eatables provided and placing it himself upon his guest's plate. Martin ate the scone. When he got home he was taken very ill and Dr Hincks finally concluded he was suffering from arsenical poisoning. It took Martin some weeks to recover. His wife, who was the daughter of the chemist in Hay and also trained as a nurse, was greatly perturbed. She remembered that a month earlier an anonymous box of chocolates had arrived. Her sister had eaten one and become ill with similar symptoms. The chocolates had not been thrown away and on analysis were found to have been punctured and arsenic inserted with an instrument similar to that which Armstrong used to inject his dandelions and other weeds.

Mrs Martin's father, the chemist, began to think about his sales of arsenic and Dr Hincks became troubled too. His mind went back to Katherine Armstrong's death. He decided to inform the Home Office of his doubt. Mr Martin wanted quicker action. It seemed to him that Major Armstrong, having rid himself of a tiresome wife, was now in a hurry to rid himself of a tiresome professional rival.

In the meantime the body of Katherine Armstrong had been exhumed, examined, and found to contain a fatal quantity of arsenic. Herbert Armstrong was accused of murdering his wife by means of arsenical poisoning. During the trial Armstrong was a perfectly composed witness, explaining the packets of arsenic by saying he made them up specially with the right dose for killing a dandelion. It was suggested that Katherine Armstrong had committed suicide by taking some of the arsenic that was in the house.

In spite of the efforts of a famous defence counsel, Curtis Bennett KC, Armstrong's explanations were not acceptable to the jury. He was found guilty, his appeal dismissed and he was executed on 31 May 1922.

Major Herbert Rowse Armstrong had remained perfectly composed throughout his trial. He made no confession though a newspaper was rumoured to have offered him £5,000. Had it not been for his inordinate vanity which would not permit him to brook a professional rival in the little town of Hay, it seems certain that he would have got away unscathed with the murder of his wife.

The Chamber of Horrors had never been notable for the inclusion of those who perpetrated a *crime passionel*. As in every country, plenty of these occurred between jealous husbands, wives, and lovers but it was in France rather than England that they made the headlines. However, at the end of 1922 one such murder occurred whose emotional background expressed in a series of letters (referred to during the trial as 'deplorable') made it inevitable that Frederick Bywaters and his mistress, Mrs Edith Thompson, should take their place among the poisoners, assassins, and murderers for greed.

Edith Grayson had married Percy Thompson, a shipping clerk, in 1915. They lived in part of a house in Kensington Gardens, Ilford, and had no children. Edith Thompson had a job as manageress and bookkeeper at a millinery concern in Aldersgate, a job which she performed efficiently and with apparent interest. Although Percy and Edith Thompson outwardly lived on good terms they were not a happy or compatible couple. Percy Thompson was not a striking personality and Edith was sometimes an unwilling and unenthusiastic sexual partner which caused acrimony and quarrels and gave Percy a sense of grievance.

Edith was a very different character. Although capable at her job she was a woman of excessive and overheated imagination which found no outlet in her work, her somewhat dull husband, and the home and household duties that she avoided as far as possible. She lived privately in a world of dreams and make-believe. Although not beautiful nor even pretty she had a power of attraction that lifted her out of the commonplace, and it was inevitable that trouble would occur if opportunity arose.

Opportunity did arise in the form of Frederick Bywaters, a young ship's writer who had been acquainted for some years with the Graysons, Edith's family. Frederick was a self-possessed, virile and attractive young man. He became on friendly terms with the Thompsons and in 1921 stayed with them when they were on holiday in the Isle of Wight.

It was almost inevitable that Edith who was now twenty-eight should become infatuated with the young man eight years her junior and an affair between them developed. Frederick Bywaters was often away at sea and Edith wrote to him continuously, passionate dramatic letters about herself, her thoughts, and dreams of bliss with her lover who she could only meet clandestinely when he was home on leave.

Frederick Bywaters kept all her letters though she destroyed his replies. In her letters Edith wrote not only of herself but of her wish to be rid of her husband so that she and her lover could live permanently together. She discussed poisons, implied that she had tried one or two without success as well as powdered and broken glass from electric light bulbs which her husband detected so that she had to desist. She spoke of her husband's unwanted attentions, stirring up the young man's jealousy.

Why, if Edith Thompson was so infatuated and her lover apparently acquiescent, did she not leave her husband and ask him for a divorce? While this was not so easily obtained in 1922 it would not have presented a serious obstacle to their mutual happiness. But, in spite of her protestations to her lover, would such a separation really have suited Edith Thompson's wild imagination and the drama of the dream-life she liked to weave around herself? It is true that she earned herself a good living but what of leaving her comfortable home for the prosaic processes of finding somewhere else to live and the long absences of Frederick at sea? There was little drama in the lives of women who married into the Merchant Navy. The thrills of the passionate love-affair would soon be damped down.

Edith did not take any steps to separate from her husband. She was basically extremely stupid, even unbalanced, and even though the idea may have occurred it was more romantic and dramatic to write continuously about doing away with the obstruction to their happiness. This theme appears to have continued as an accompaniment to their clandestine meetings when Frederick came on leave and she certainly succeeded in working the young man, only twenty years old, into a frenzy of jealousy over the 'rights' Percy Thompson claimed from her.

Against this secret background, possibly suspected by Percy Thompson, their life continued as usual. He went to work; she commuted daily from Ilford to Aldersgate and carried out her work efficiently. Their social life went on as usual.

As usual, that is, until midnight of 3 October 1922. Percy and Edith Thompson had been to a theatre with a relative after work and returned together by train. They were walking along the quiet, almost deserted, street towards their home in Kensington Gardens, Ilford, when footsteps came hurrying after them. It was Frederick Bywaters who had followed them. There was a short altercation, then Frederick drew a knife and stabbed Percy Thompson. He ran off leaving his victim in a dying condition. Edith attempted to give some first aid, then ran to summon help. When she returned with a doctor, Percy Thompson was dead.

There was no possible doubt as to the identity of the murderer. Frederick Bywaters was arrested and Edith Thompson's year-long correspondence with its suggestions of getting rid of her husband was discovered. She was arrested for aiding and abetting the murder. It was suggested that she had arranged it with Bywaters for that very night.

There was little that could be said in Frederick Bywaters' defence except that he had acted under the powerful influence and instigation of his mistress. Edith pleaded not guilty but the letters which created such a public sensation were read out extensively in Court and proved damning.

Frederick Bywaters and Edith Thompson stood in the dock together. He was matter-of-fact, unmoved, and apparently unaffected by his situation and what lay ahead of him. Edith seemed to be in a kind of agonized trance. Her dream-world had crashed round her but she tried to talk of commonplace things when relatives visited her in gaol.

Both were found guilty, both appealed and their appeals failed. They were executed on the same day, 9 January 1923, at different gaols, Bywaters calm and assured, Edith Thompson in a state of collapse.

The wax portraits of Bywaters and Thompson went into the exhibition on 18 December 1922. As the appeals were pending they were placed on a special dais under a canopy in a space leading to the Chamber of Horrors. The likenesses, particularly that of Edith Thompson, were considered extremely realistic and were based on sketches made in the Old Bailey throughout the trial. Both were dressed in clothes similar to those they had worn in the dock. Bywaters wore a blue serge suit and Edith had a fur coat and a black velours hat with feathers.

Many people were shocked at the verdict on Edith Thompson and believed there would be a reprieve. Others believed that it was indeed she who had instigated the crime carried out by her much younger lover. The two figures drew hundreds of visitors and remained in the Chamber of Horrors for fifty-nine years.

The criminals selected over the years to go into the Chamber of Horrors always included a few French citizens, and in the autumn of 1924 they were joined by Pierre Vaquier.

Vaquier was a vain man. Possibly he suffered from the delusion that in poisoning his mistress's husband he was committing a *crime passionel*, the penalty for which under French law was usually comparatively light. Vaquier had no previous criminal record of any kind. He was a Basque, short-statured with thick unruly dark hair and a full moustache and beard. His dark eyes were described as compelling. He was working in a hotel in Biarritz when he met Mabel Theresa Jones, a visitor to the fashionable French resort on the Atlantic coast. She was the wife of a publican who owned the Blue Anchor Hotel at Byfleet in Surrey and during her holiday she came under the spell of those dark eyes.

Neither could speak the other's language but they became friends and then more than friends. When Mabel Jones went home to the hotel in Byfleet in February she was followed by Vaquier. He took up residence in London with the dual object of selling the patent for a new type of mincing machine and pursuing his love-affair with Mrs Jones. They met in London and then on 14 February Vaquier removed to Byfleet and stayed at the Blue Anchor, saying he was awaiting payment for his mincing-machine invention. His clandestine liaison with Mabel Jones appears to have been carried on discreetly and no local scandal was created.

At the beginning of the following month Vaquier paid a visit to London. During his earlier stay he had purchased various chemicals from a chemist in Southampton Row. He explained that he used these for wireless experiments and there was nothing among the items he purchased that was inconsistent with such projects. This time, however, the assistant who had always served him noticed that two items had been added to the list, perchloride of mercury and strychnine. While the perchloride of mercury could be used for experiments with wireless crystals the assistant was puzzled as to how strychnine came into this field. Vaquier said that in France he was well known for his experiments and was able to purchase without difficulty all the materials he needed, even poisons. His persuasions were effective and he was given the perchloride of mercury and also nearly two grains of strychnine, enough to kill several people. The Frenchman signed the register in the name of Wanker and gave his address as the Russell Hotel.

Vaquier returned to Byfleet. Mr Jones the landlord was a heavy drinker and in the habit of taking bromo salts next morning to ease his hangover. On 20 March there was a party at the hotel and as usual the landlord imbibed heavily. Next morning he went to the bar parlour where he kept his bromo salts, mixed himself a glass and drank it down exclaiming immediately 'My God! That was bitter!' His wife took the bottle and put it in the kitchen drawer. Shortly afterwards Jones became so ill that a doctor was called in. While the doctor was with his patient, Vaquier went into the kitchen, took the bromo bottle from the drawer exclaiming 'Medicine, doctor, quick!' The unfortunate Mr Jones was beyond medical aid and died an agonizing death from strychnine poisoning. The bottle of bromo salts was found placed back in the kitchen drawer. It had been washed out but traces of strychnine remained.

It was Mabel Jones, not Vaquier, who now confessed to the affair they had been carrying on since her Biarritz holiday. Vaquier made a statement to the police in which he hinted that the crime might have been committed by a jealous rival, possibly the postman. He also made statements to various newspapers and his photograph was published. The Southampton Row chemist recognized his customer as the Frenchman he had served and produced the poisons register signed J. Wanker, the name by which he knew him. Vaquier was accused of murdering Mr Jones, a man he said he 'loved as a brother'. He also made a wild statement that Mabel Jones's solicitor had asked him to buy the poison and advised him to sign the register in a false name.

Jean Pierre Vaquier was tried at the Old Bailey in July and found guilty. His French advocate tried to organize a petition for reprieve on the grounds that Vaquier felt he had been persecuted and that both English law and his legal advisers had worked against him. Twice during his trial he had exclaimed '*Ils m'ont vendu*!' and when the jury found him guilty he cried 'You have given an unjust verdict!'

It was of no avail. If Jean Pierre Vaquier felt his *crime passionel* merited a less severe sentence than the death penalty he learned that English law was different from French. His French advocate remarked that, though the Lord Chief Justice was right in stating that ignorance of the law was no excuse, something might be allowed for Vaquier's ignorance of English procedure. But the law took its course. Jean Pierre Vaquier had murdered his mistress's husband and he was executed on 12 August 1924.

A murder described by an Appeal Court judge as 'most cruel, repulsive, and carefully-planned' brought the figure of Patrick Herbert Mahon into the Chamber of Horrors not long after the Frenchman Vaquier had taken his appointed place. It was yet another case where the foolishness of a woman led to her horrible death.

Patrick Mahon showed no signs of a criminal future until he reached the age of twenty when he married a pleasant and pretty girl. He was a philanderer and had a charm that appealed to many women. His marriage took place in 1910 and during the next twelve years he faced charges of fraud, embezzlement, robbery with violence, and served five years penal servitude for assaulting a servant girl. In 1922, however, due to his wife's influence Patrick managed to get a respectable job as a sales manager with a firm whose offices were at Sunbury. He was now living with his wife in a West London suburb, where he was a respected and popular figure participating in local activities and his wife was apparently happy and devoted to her husband.

On the staff of the Sunbury office was a thirty-seven-year-old typist, Emily Kaye, a mature woman who had some money of her own. This fact instantly made her attractive to Mahon. She for her part became infatuated with his philanderer's charm, and determined she would become the subject of what she intended to be his last romance. She knew that he was married and had been involved with many other women.

Emily knew too that there was no prospect of speedy marriage but she was willing to live with Mahon. In April 1924, after a romance of some two years, they agreed they would rent an isolated bungalow which Emily had seen advertised. It was on a lonely part of the Sussex coast known as the Crumbles between Eastbourne and Pevensey Bay. Patrick rented the place for a period of two months using the name Walter for the transaction. He also persuaded Emily to sell some of her securities and give him the money. While these arrangements were being made Patrick Mahon's fancy had been caught elsewhere by a woman called Ethel Duncan and in his philandering way he had fallen in love with her. He now wanted to be rid of Emily so that he could pursue his affair with Ethel.

On 24 April 1924 both his firm and his wife thought Mahon was away travelling on business. In fact Emily went to Eastbourne to take possession of the bungalow and Mahon remained for a day in London where he purchased a saw and a ten-inch long knife, before following Emily down to the Crumbles. She was now pregnant and wishing to put her liaison on some permanent footing even if marriage was still out of her reach. She had no idea of her lover's new interest in Ethel Duncan nor that he had actually asked Ethel to come to the bungalow on Friday and spend the weekend with him, an invitation that Ethel had accepted.

During the night after Patrick's arrival at the bungalow, where Emily Kaye was already installed, the couple had a quarrel. No one ever discovered what really took place that night. Mahon claimed that Emily who was strongly built had hurled a coal axe at him. In the ensuing struggle, during which Patrick was knocked unconscious, Emily fell and struck her head on the coal bucket. When he came round, Patrick said, he realized Emily was dead. Knowing that Ethel Duncan was due to arrive in three days he panicked and locked Emily's body in one of the bedrooms. When Ethel Duncan duly arrived she was surprised to find women's clothing scattered about the place but accepted Mahon's explanation that his wife had recently been staying.

Mahon was unaware that his wife at home in their suburban house had become suspicious of his numerous absences. She found a railway-cloakroom ticket and a race card and she was afraid he might again be involved with betting and gambling that would once more lead him into trouble. She decided to hire a private enquiry agent and find out exactly what her husband was up to.

The enquiry agent's first action was to go to Waterloo station and claim the bag that Mahon had left there. When he opened it he found a long knife and women's bloodstained clothing. The agent went straightaway to Scotland Yard. When, on 2 May, Mahon himself came to claim the bag, the police were waiting for him. His explanation was that he had wrapped up meat for his dogs in the clothing. This did not carry conviction and the police were soon at the Crumbles bungalow.

Patric Mahon made no attempt to deny that Emily Kaye had died there. He said he had fitted a new Yale lock to the bedroom in which the body lay so that Ethel Duncan could not look in there, and that he had sent a telegram to himself summoning him back immediately. He and Ethel Duncan left at once together.

Then Mahon had returned alone to the Crumbles and set about disposing of Emily Kaye's body. He dismembered it, put some parts in the fire and boiled some in saucepans. The head he burned and scattered the remains in the shingle over the garden wall. It was never found. The rest of the body he packed in a trunk, a hatbox and a tin and hid them in one of the bedrooms.

Patrick Mahon was charged with the murder of Emily Kaye and his trial at Lewes began on 15 July 1924. For some reason, while he was on remand, he tanned his face with tobacco juice to give himself an open-air appearance, which he presumably hoped would influence the jury in his favour.

He pleaded not guilty, sticking to his story that Emily Kaye had died from striking her head on the coal bucket, but the fact that he had purchased the saw and the knife, and had been extracting her money from her did not help his case. Throughout the trial Mahon remained cold, calm, and unmoved, even when faced with the implements he had admittedly used to carve up the body of his former mistress. Mahon was found guilty. His appeal failed and he was executed on 3 September 1924. According to report he admitted killing Emily Kaye before he went to the scaffold.

The brutal and callous Patrick Mahon was the last new entry into the Chamber of Horrors before disaster struck Madame Tussaud's exhibition. Since her arrival in England in 1802

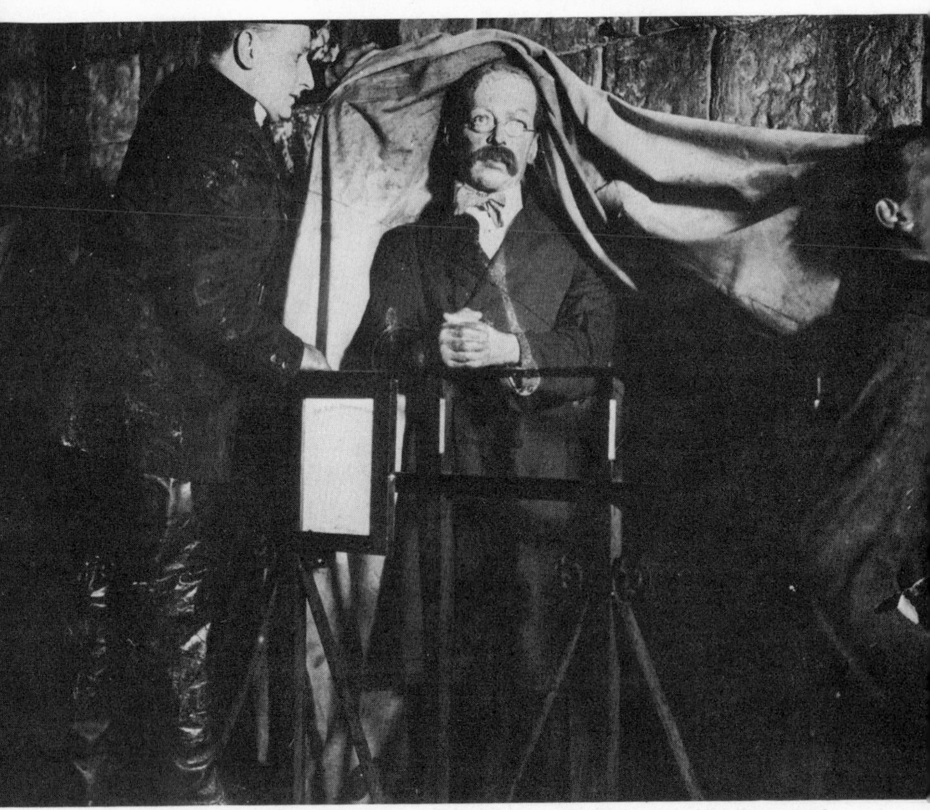

Dr Crippen with a fireman in the extensively damaged basement Chamber of Horrors after the fire of 1925.

Madame Tussaud herself had always been haunted by fear of fire consuming her exhibition. According to tradition she was glad to leave the Lyceum Theatre in 1803, in spite of her success there, because demonstrations of the new gas lighting were to be given in the Upper Theatre.

She passed her fears on to her sons and grandsons so that when the Marylebone building was erected in 1884 extraordinary precautions against fire were taken. Floors were constructed to be as fireproof as possible and hydrants and hoses installed throughout the building. Trained firemen were included in the staff. The strictest safety precautions had been introduced when electricity was installed, new lighting effects added and an electric organ put in.

It was a shock as unexpected as it was terrible when on 18 March 1925 Madame Tussaud's great building, with the exception of the basement, was burned to a shell. The exact cause of the fire and the reason for its rapid spread were never precisely discovered. A wiring defect in the electric organ was the most likely cause and the fire got a hold because the firemen on duty tried to quell the initial outbreak on their own instead of sending at once for the fire brigade.

As it was the fire was already well out of hand when the brigade arrived. Every fire engine in London was rushed to the spot but the conflagration spread with terrifying rapidity. All the great halls and their contents were consumed in the blaze and out of 467 figures only 171 could be rescued.

But the Chamber of Horrors survived though extensively damaged. The hall of murderers in the basement was flooded, water streamed into it. Smoke and dirt swirled, smearing and defacing the figures but the flames never reached the basement. Above it the Napoleon Rooms with all their precious relics, the pictures, and the Waterloo carriage disappeared in the holocaust. 'Many good people have been destroyed in the fire but the devil has taken care of his own,' said John Theodore Tussaud, now aged sixty-seven.

The *Morning Post* gave a vivid account:

> 'Nothing was more gruesome than the interior of the Chamber of Horrors when the blaze was at its height: flaming beams and ashes from above, dense clouds of smoke, and the hissing trickle of the firemen's hoses. Inside the cells of Newgate still confined their grim inmates who stared with the frigid unconcern with which they have faced execution on Tyburn every day except Sunday for generations. From above there dropped hot and sticky remains, blazing fiercely, of the world-famous replicas of all the notabilities and notorieties of the past hundred years . . . royalties and murderers are fused in a common mass.'

When the blaze was finally extinguished great tarpaulins were used to cover most of the figures in the Chamber of Horrors, but one reporter went into the dark basement: 'Wading through three inches of water I struck another match and the gleam disclosed a notice-board "An Opium Den". There lay, oblivious of the inferno of the last twelve hours, two "men" overcome by opium fumes, their features to be seen only sufficiently to make them appear more hideous.'

Was Madame Tussaud's finished? Were the halls of the famous and the grim apartment of the infamous gone forever? People wondered whether the original splendour and the ancient horror could ever be recaptured.

[8]

The 'Horrors' in the Thirties

Madame Tussaud's own indomitable spirit lived on in her great-grandson John Theodore Tussaud, and her great-great-grandson Bernard. They accomplished what must at first have seemed an impossible achievement. Within three years the exhibition was rebuilt, restocked with portrait figures—fortunately many of the moulds stored in the basement had escaped destruction—and somehow the 'original wonder and ancient horror', which many people had feared could not be recaptured, permeated the new building from the first as it had the previous magnificent edifice.

It was a fine structure which arose on the devastated site, higher than the old building, and with a fine double staircase spiralling from the entrance hall. Of course it was impossible to reproduce the gilded carving and stucco and the painted ceilings which had so impressed the Victorians with their grandeur in 1884. None the less it was a worthy and spacious setting for the Grand Hall, the Hall of Kings, the Hall of Tableaux and a section devoted to the sporting and showbusiness fraternity. There was a fine restaurant and a cinema seating 1,800 people. *The Private Life of Helen of Troy* was the first film shown.

As for the Chamber of Horrors in the basement, press reporters at the opening seemed unanimous in finding it more creepy, even more grisly than before. It was approached by a long winding stair like the entrance to a dungeon. The big room with its arched ceiling had a crypt-like appearance. Grim cell-like recesses housed some of the inhabitants, with green lights or 'baleful flickering gleams' piercing the lurking shadows to pick out notorious murderers and criminals past and present.

There was chilling impact in the mass confrontation of so many evil faces with their unflinching stares, for the Chamber of Horrors now housed no less than sixty-seven portrait figures ranging from Victorian to contemporary times. New lighting techniques made it a dark eerie sepulchre weirdly and fitfully lighted, a frightening place, though one reporter wrote caustically 'The present generation abundantly nourished as it is by reading of crime stories and crook plays will of course feel quite at home in its shady groves.' The *Daily Chronicle* reporter found the grouping and display made the new Chamber of Horrors more horrible than the old.

The walls were stained to give the effect of oozing damp. As the visitor approached the entrance the walls were hung with pictures of Turkish tortures including one of a victim being boiled in oil. Mechanical spiders started the unwary by descending suddenly from cobwebs, and on one pillar a large slug left a slimy trail.

Of course, in addition to the ranks of murderers, the relics of the French Revolution were there, the death heads, the guillotine. The Newgate bell tolled and the two Newgate cells had their place as did the scaffold and executioners Marwood and Berry. The cold stare of the criminals could also fix on tableaux of 'The Coiners' Den' and 'The Opium Den' though the typically Victorian six-scene, 'The Story of a Crime', was not restored. Of the 71,327 visitors who came to the exhibition during the first opening week no less than 43,225 chose to sample the 'morbid delights' of the new Chamber of Horrors.

It was only just over a month after the opening that places had to be found in the Chamber of Horrors for two murderers who had committed what was rightly described at their trial as a most foul and brutal crime. One September night in 1927 PC Gutteridge was on patrol at midnight in a lonely Essex lane at Stapleford Abbotts. Later his dead body was found in the lane.

He had been shot three times and with the last two bullets the murderer had shot out his eyes. It was a crime that horrified the entire nation.

Frederick Guy Browne and his accomplice, William Henry Kennedy, were both ex-convicts. On this September night they were seeking to steal a car. Disturbed at their first effort by a barking dog they broke into the garage of a local physician, Dr Lovell, and took his car. Anxious to get out of the district as quickly as possible they were driving at a furious pace through the lanes when they encountered PC Gutteridge. He challenged the speeding car and when it slowed down and stopped he recognized it as Dr Lovell's car but neither of the men in it was Dr Lovell. PC Gutteridge got out his notebook and, as he bent his head over it, a shot rang out and he fell, staggering to the grass verge. As he lay there two more shots followed and deliberately put out his eyes. The men got into the car and continued their journey, abandoning the car near London where it was found with bloodstains on the bodywork and a spent cartridge case on the floor.

Several months passed while police all over the country searched for the two men who had committed this particularly horrible murder. It was four months before Browne was arrested at Clapham, not at first as one of the murder suspects, but for stealing a car. The stolen car and garage were searched and a Webley revolver loaded with bullets was found. The bullets were of the type that had killed PC Gutteridge and a second revolver of the same type was also discovered.

News of Browne's arrest reached Kennedy who promptly made for Liverpool with his newly married young Irish wife. He was taken into custody and found to be carrying an automatic pistol. The two men were charged with the murder of PC Gutteridge. There was no honour among thieves in the case of Browne and Kennedy for, while both admitted having stolen Dr Lovell's car and having been in it when it was stopped by PC Gutteridge, each declared that the other had fired the shots. Whoever fired, if the other had acquiesced he was equally guilty of murder but, while Browne persisted that he had not fired,

Kennedy claimed that he had tried to push Browne away after the latter had fired the first bullet and stood terrified while the constable's eyes were shot out.

A firearms expert proved that the marks on the spent cartridge found in Dr Lovell's car could only have been made by Browne's Webley revolver and the bullets found in the victim's body must have been fired by the same gun. It was a case that established the science of forensic ballistics as a means of detecting crime. Both men were convicted of murder and executed at different prisons on 31 May 1928.

It was in April the following year that the British Instructional Film Company made a film entitled *The Chamber of Horrors*. It was first of many films featuring 'the Horrors' in one way or another. Bernard Tussaud, who had personally modelled many of the criminals now occupying the Chamber, felt that the time was ripe to extend its appeal by gradual stages throughout the early thirties, giving particular emphasis to historical crime and punishment. He envisaged tableaux depicting such subjects as the murder of Thomas à Becket, and portraits of historical assassins, while still retaining the majority of the portraits which had been in the Chamber since Madame Tussaud's own time. Of course new outstanding criminals would be added from time to time so that the exhibition was always updated.

Along these lines Bernard modelled the 'Torture of the Hooks', a former Algerian punishment in which the victim was suspended by a hook in the stomach at the Barbizon gates of the city of Algiers. This figure was hung in the Chamber of Horrors and revolved slowly.

A copy was made of an iron cage, the original of which was found in the moat of the castle of Hilazzo in Sicily. This cage contained a skeleton. The cage had been used in medieval times for convicted prisoners who were in holy orders and could not be executed. Suspended outside the castle walls the prisoner ultimately died of hunger, thirst and exposure.

A flogging or whipping tableau was based on an eighteenth-century print. Public flogging of both male and female prisoners outside Newgate or the London Sessions House had continued into the early nineteenth century.

A smaller but grisly relic was the skull of Mrs Nicholson, a demented woman who in 1784 had tried to stab King George III as he alighted from his carriage in St James's. The knife she used was placed by the skull. Mrs Nicholson was not executed for her attempted regicide but finished her life in Bedlam lunatic asylum. These additions gave variety and proved popular with visitors, as did a series of dioramas depicting numerous medieval tortures used to force confessions from hapless prisoners.

There were some lighter moments. In June 1931 an earthquake hit London and Madame Tussaud's building was quite severely shaken by this shock. The only casualty, however, was Crippen whose head split in two. One half lodged on his shoulder while the other crashed to the ground. Charles Peace had an 'outing' in 1935 when his figure was loaned for a Crime Club lunch at which many distinguished personalities gathered.

Bernard's plans for the Chamber of Horrors evolved slowly for political events: the rise of Hitler, the Abdication, the Coronation of King George VI and Queen Elizabeth put great pressure on the studios. Hitler was not relegated to the Chamber of Horrors until the Second World War although soon after he was modelled and put on show the figure was smeared with red paint and a placard 'Mass-Murderer' hung round his neck by some angry visitor.

All this work for the main halls did not mean that no new 'subjects' took their place in the Chamber of Horrors during the 1930s. The trial of Sidney Harry Fox caught the public interest because it was his mother that he murdered for gain. Matricide is not a common crime and both mother and son were exceptionally peculiar individuals. Wild rumours circulated round the trial that Rosalind Fox had consented to her own murder to get money for her son and that she was not in fact his mother at all but an old mistress.

Rosalind Fox had married a railway signalman and had several children before she left him for a railway porter. Sidney

Harry was her fourth and last son and possibly the child of the porter not the signalman. The boy himself had other ideas. He believed or pretended to believe that he was the illegitimate son of a noble father. He had an aptitutde for mimicry which enabled him to pass as a public schoolboy, and a positive genius for forgery.

Sidney was the apple of his mother's eye. He grew up a thief and a forger and spent his life in and out of prison but his mother supported him and even appears to have been his confederate in his misdeeds. She willingly accompanied him to luxury hotels without luggage knowing that they would leave without paying any bill. Sidney boasted that he was a homosexual and only used women in order to get their money.

His career of crime had started early when he stole some charity money. The theft was reported to the police and he was birched. None the less he was able to enter domestic service and became the devoted houseboy or page to old Sir John and Lady Leslie who called him Cupid because of his looks. He was still only sixteen but his tastes required money. He stole some silver and managed to extract her savings from an elderly housemaid. He was found out and dismissed but the Leslies did not prosecute because he had given them such devoted service.

Sidney then got a position in a bank where he exercised his talent for forgery, but again escaped prosecution on condition that he joined the Army. He became a cadet in the Royal Flying Corps. He then had the idea of visiting an elderly relative of Lady Leslie who lived at Brighton, and passing himself off as a Leslie grandson. He knew many details about the Leslie family so deception was not difficult. Finally he asked the old lady to cash a cheque for him. She did not have money in the house but sent him with her maid to her greengrocer who obligingly handed over the money. The cheque came back marked 'No Account'.

It was unfortunate that an Assistant Provost Marshal of the Eastern Command was staying in Brighton and discussing cases with the local authorities. He learned of the young man Fox who had cheated the greengrocer. It seemed he might be the same Fox who had been devoted servant to Sir John and Lady Leslie.

Enquiries were set in motion and Mrs Rosalind Fox was traced and interviewed. She referred to her son as 'Lieutenant Fox' and mentioned that he was a member of the Royal Automobile Club. It was at this club, of which Fox was not of course a member, that he was arrested. He admitted that he had stolen the cheque book and got three months hard labour.

Sidney Fox did his First World War service in England and made friends with many officers more highly placed than himself. He emerged with a pension of eight shillings a week. Two spells in gaol for forgery and fraud followed but the two elderly Leslies still took an interest in their former devoted page and while he was in prison arranged for him to be taught carpentry.

It was to no avail. Sidney Fox returned to fraud and forgery and was in and out of prison, always welcomed back by his mother. She worked as a cook or charwoman when he was in prison. When he was free she joined him moving from luxury hotel to luxury hotel always decamping without paying the bill.

His mother had somewhere made a friend of an Australian woman, Mrs Morse, a lady of some means. Mrs Morse and Mrs Fox set up home together sharing a flat in Southsea where Sidney Fox was of course always welcome. In spite of his preferred homosexual habits he started a relationship with his mother's friend, Mrs Morse. Sidney embarked on this to him distasteful relationship (Mrs Morse appears to have been quite infatuated) with a view to laying hands on his mistress's money. Since this might take some time and he was impatient he decided it would be simpler to take out a policy of £3,000 on her life and persuade her to make a will in his favour, which she did readily. Shortly afterwards Mrs Morse awoke to find her room filled with gas. There was a disused gas tap behind a chest of drawers and this was found to have been turned on. Sidney Fox knew of the gas tap which he said must have become turned on by the movement of the chest. The incident gave Mrs Morse food for thought and she decided to break up the Southsea establishment. Before Mrs Fox and her son left the flat he stole some jewellery from a locked drawer. Mrs Morse reported the loss and the theft was traced to Sidney who returned once more to prison for a spell of fifteen months. Mrs Morse, thoroughly alarmed, went back to Australia. She presumably destroyed the will she had made in Sidney Fox's favour but he hopefully retained a copy of the will and the life policy which he carried around with him.

While Sidney was serving his latest prison sentence his mother was taken care of by the Board of Guardians and because of ill health was placed in an infirmary in Portsmouth. In March 1929 her son took her away from this hospital and they resumed their itinerant life together in luxury hotels. Mrs Fox made a will in favour of her youngest son and a few days later he took out an accident policy on his mother's life.

The pair continued their normal life style of swindling one high-class hotel after another and if this temporarily failed relied on the pawn shop and their few possessions to see them through. However, Sidney was growing tired of this mode of life. He decided he would like to settle down in comfort, even luxury. Mrs Morse's husband had begun divorce proceedings against her, having learned of his wife's liaison. It is possible that Sidney Fox may have considered going to Australia if he could raise the money and there winning over Mrs Morse as a source of income. But for the moment life had to follow its usual pattern.

In October 1929 Sidney Fox and his mother arrived in Margate. They had no luggage, only a brown paper parcel, yet were able to book in at the Metropole Hotel. They appeared to be an adoring mother and a devoted son. They looked most respectable. Mrs Fox was now silver-haired. She shuffled, supported and aided by her son, for she was suffering from paralysis agitans. The manager had some doubts about their lack of luggage—they did not even have any nightwear as it turned out—and he rendered their account every day but he did not tell them to go.

After a few days Sidney Fox told the manager his mother was

not well. The rooms they occupied were unheated and it was the manager himself who suggested they should move to a pair of intercommunicating rooms, one of which had a gas fire. A doctor was called but could find little wrong with Mrs Fox. He prescribed a tonic. Sidney made a brief trip to London where he extended the accident policies he had taken out on his mother's life.

The Foxes had booked in at the Metropole on 16 October. It was on the evening of 23 October that Sidney Fox ran downstairs in his shorts shouting 'Fire!' His room was found to be full of smoke and the communicating door with his mother's room was shut. That too was filled with smoke, black smoke, and it was only with difficulty that the body of Mrs Fox was located and dragged out. A doctor was sent for and found that she was dead. He signed a certificate that she had died from shock and suffocation but because it was a violent death there was an inquest at which the Coroner returned a verdict of accidental death. The cause of the fire was not established. It was suggested that Mrs Fox had accidentally set alight a newspaper she was reading.

After his mother's funeral Sidney Fox left the Metropole Hotel without paying the bill and went to London. He could now draw the money for which he had insured Mrs Fox's life, and with it go to Australia. The way seemed clear. It was an insurance company official who brought about Sidney Fox's downfall. He noticed that the policies would have expired just twenty minutes after the hour at which Mrs Fox met her accidental death. He was suspicious and instituted enquiries. These brought to light Sidney's hotel frauds and also the fact that the fire in Mrs Fox's room must have been started deliberately. It was never discovered exactly what her son used to cause so greasy and dense a black smoke. The body of Mrs Fox was exhumed and on 9 January 1930 Sidney Harry Fox was charged with the murder of his mother.

At his trial there was conflicting medical evidence as to whether she had died of asphyxiation or heart failure due to the fire. In the end the jury found Fox guilty of murder. Throughout the trial he had remained calm with no signs of emotion. He made no appeal against the verdict and made no confession of guilt. He was executed on 8 April.

The case had received much publicity on account of the unusual nature of the crime and the bizarre relationship between mother and son and the extraordinary life style they had managed to carry on for so long. When the portrait of Sidney Harry Fox made its appearance in the Chamber of Horrors it did not fail to attract a throng of curious visitors.

Madame Tussaud's acquired some of Fox's clothes and the model was dressed in a suit he had once worn. A reporter asked to examine it more closely and wrote 'Obviously the once almost too smart lounge suit was "off the peg" or made by a cheap tailor: the meretricious tie-pin probably cost a few pence'. Fox also wore an Old Etonian tie which he used to flaunt and which is still in Madame Tussaud's possession. However, this tie soon had to be removed from the figure. Fox had never been to Eton and it was spotted by an Old Etonian who raised strong objections.

Another figure clothed in the suit actually worn at the time of the crime was that of Alfred Arthur Rouse, the perpetrator of the 'Blazing Car Murder' for which he paid the penalty in 1931. 'Own clothing' always had a fascination for visitors. It was another case with bizarre features on account of Arthur Rouse's extraordinary involvement with women to whom he referred as 'my harem', and the fact that the identity of his victim was never discovered.

Rouse's family background was creditable. He was born in 1894, one of the three children of a respectable hosier of Herne Hill. Owing to family disruption when Rouse was six years old the children were placed under the care of an aunt. The boy was educated locally and as he grew up showed intelligence, keenness and industry. He was vain for he was good-looking, had a persuasive tongue and a number of social accomplishments. He played several musical instruments and had a pleasing baritone singing voice though his speaking voice was high pitched and unattractive.

When the First World War broke out Rouse had been working for five years with a soft furnishing concern in the West End but he immediately enlisted. Before he was sent to France he married an equally respectable young woman of twenty-three, three years older than himself. Arthur Rouse only spent a couple of months in France for he was severely wounded. His injuries included a head-wound, but he was there long enough to sire a son who was brought up by his French mother. His wounds took a long time to heal but as a patient he was brave and cheerful. In 1918 he was discharged from the Army as unfit for further military service and returned to his wife.

As Arthur Rouse had good looks, a ready tongue, and was hard-working and ambitious he obtained a number of jobs without difficulty, always bettering himself when he changed employment. Finally he became a commercial traveller earning the then very satisfactory wage of £500 a year. His regret and that of his wife was that they had no children.

Life as a commercial traveller took Rouse around the country and the gifts which enabled him to succeed also enabled him to seduce women. His conquests were numerous and he referred to the collection of women to whom he paid regular visits as 'my harem'. Unfortunately a number of these liaisons led to pregnancies and applications by the mothers for maintenance orders. Rouse never denied paternity though his payments against the orders were extremely irregular.

Mrs Rouse, living comfortably in the small house he had begun to purchase in Finchley, was not aware of these liaisons. In 1920 Rouse seduced an Edinburgh girl, Helen Campbell, fourteen years old, who worked as a domestic in a house that he frequently visited. By the time she was fifteen Helen Campbell had produced a child in a home for unmarried mothers but this infant only survived a few weeks. Rouse renewed the liaison and when in 1924 Helen became pregnant again he went through a wedding ceremony with her in an Islington church and set her up in a house in Islington. The girl firmly believed that she was the only Mrs Rouse. A son was born the following year. Helen went out to work to help support the child for she got little from her 'husband'. A disagreement arose between them and Helen left, but finding herself in financial difficulties applied to the Courts for maintenance for the child. Again Rouse admitted his responsibility and expressed a great love of children.

The real Mrs Rouse learned of this affair and met Helen Campbell. A somewhat curious arrangement resulted. It was agreed that the boy should be taken into the Rouse home and brought up there. Mrs Rouse treated the child with every kindness.

Her husband had been pursuing his career as a seducer. He had two daughters by a local servant for whose support he again became liable under a maintenance order. A more difficult situation arose in Monmouthshire where a Miss Ivy Jenkins was expecting his child. Her father was a colliery proprietor and she told her parents that she and Rouse had been married.

In spite of his good income, the support of all these children and the expenses involved in keeping other members of 'the Harem' happy, together with his normal expenses at home in Finchley, was becoming a heavy financial drain. Mrs Rouse learned more of her husband's infidelities and though outwardly they remained on good terms they were considering a separation and selling the house in Finchley where Rouse was a popular member of the community. His vanity led to bragging and talking about his conquests with other commercial travellers he met on the road. He realized that this was laying himself open to blackmail where his employers were concerned. Altogether Rouse had got himself into an impossibly involved situation likely to lead to serious trouble. These were the circumstances in which Arthur Rouse seems to have hit on the idea of disappearing in some way that would suggest his death. The plan he eventually evolved to achieve this object was brutal and callous.

It was late on 5 November 1930 that two young men, cousins, were making their way home to Hardingstone near Northampton after attending a bonfire party in the town. It was an easy walk but as they turned off the London-Northampton road into Hardingstone Lane two unusual things caught their attention. The first was the figure of a man apparently climbing out of the ditch at the corner. He was well dressed, hatless, and carried an attaché case.

The second unfamiliar sight was a red glow behind the hedge some distance along the lane. 'What is the blaze?' asked one of the young men addressing his cousin but it was the hatless man now just behind them who replied 'It looks as if someone has had a bonfire.' Then the man reached the main road and appeared to be hesitating as to which direction he would take. It was a bright moonlight night and the cousins could observe him clearly.

When the two young men came nearer to the glow they realized that flames were leaping from a small blazing car. One of the young men ran ahead to call his father who was the village constable and with the aid of another constable and buckets of water the flames were extinguished. It was then seen that the car had not been empty. A badly charred body was sprawled across the front seat. At first it was thought this must be the remains of the owner but the curious appearance of the hatless man who had emerged from the ditch and the fact that the position of the remains indicated that the body had been thrown down on the seat rather than lying in a fallen position aroused suspicions. This was not a simple disaster of someone trapped in their burning vehicle.

Arthur Rouse, who had hesitated on the main road, hitched a ride back to London and visited his wife for a brief time. He then headed by coach for the home of Ivy Jenkins in Monmouthshire where he said his Morris Minor had been stolen.

The press publicity given to the burnt-out car and its unknown victim together with the clear description provided by the two young men of the figure who had mysteriously appeared from the ditch made Rouse realize that the Jenkins family might soon become suspicious and start asking questions. He beat a hasty retreat from the house and took a coach to London. To catch this a neighbour drove him to Cardiff and on the way Rouse made some indiscreet remarks. These remarks led the neighbour-driver to contact a Cardiff journalist who promptly advised the police.

Plain clothes men were waiting on Hammersmith Bridge and boarded the coach on which Rouse was travelling. He was taken to the police station where he told his story. He said that he had picked up a man who said he wanted a lift to Northampton. Wishing to get out of the car after the long drive he turned down Hardingstone Lane and told the man to fill the petrol tank from a can while he was away. The man asked for a cigarette, but Rouse had none and gave him a cigar. The next thing he knew was that his car was ablaze. He panicked and ran towards the main road. He knew nothing about his passenger nor what he had done to start the blaze. Later on Rouse made an unwise remark to the police about the troubles he was having with his 'harem'.

There were detailed investigations and finally Arthur Rouse was charged with the murder of an unknown man. The main prosecution points were that the car had deliberately been set on fire and there was evidence that the carburettor had been tampered with. Also the position of the victim's heavily charred body indicated that it had been thrown on the front seat.

Furthermore a mallet with hairs on it had been found some yards from the car. From this it was deduced that Rouse had stunned the unknown man outside the car and then pushed him into it before setting the vehicle ablaze with the can of petrol. Indeed, had the young men not attended the bonfire party in Northampton and thus witnessed Rouse leaving the lane and the burning car, it is extremely probable that his disappearance plan would have succeeded. He must have ascertained that the man he picked up was not likely to be missed, probably a tramp, and the body would be unidentifiable anyway.

It was a complicated case that took eleven days to try with much press coverage. The jury returned a verdict that Rouse had deliberately murdered the unidentified unfortunate he had picked up. Motive was clear enough, since by then Rouse most earnestly desired to disembarrass himself of the personal and financial problems caused by his relationships with women.

With a new identity he was confident that his gifts would enable him to start again. He pleaded innocence but perhaps the fact that he told so many lies to so many women helped to swing the verdict against him.

Murderer Reginald Ivor Hinks was unusual in that he was described as 'modelled from life', a rare circumstance in modern times. A particularly callous 'ne'er-do-well', he met a divorcée, Constance Bullen, who had one child, and persuaded her to marry him. His interest lay in the inheritance that would come to her on the death of her father, aged eighty-five, who lived in Bath. The old man was cared for by a male nurse who was quickly sent packing by Hinks who also made his wife leave the house. Hinks undertook the nursing duties and forced his father-in-law to take long walks which he hoped would result in the old man's collapse and demise. When this did not happen he planned a murder that could be passed off as suicide.

He put the old man's head in a gas oven, bruising it in the process. When he rang the firemen he mentioned that any bruise found on the head had occurred after death when he extricated his father-in-law from the oven. Medical evidence proved otherwise and Hinks was executed in May 1934. Hinks was not a very long-stay occupant of the Chamber of Horrors. Five years later he was taken out.

With the threat of war ever increasing and so many political naval and military personages to be modelled or remodelled for the main exhibition not a large number of new 'subjects' appeared in the Chamber of Horrors during the late thirties. The last new entry before the outbreak of war was the portrait of Dr Buck Ruxton convicted of two particularly gruesome and horrible murders. Dr Buck Ruxton, a native of Bombay, who had qualified in Bombay and London and after changing his complicated Indian name set up a successful medical practice in Lancashire in 1930. With him lived the woman who passed for his wife though in fact they never actually married. Ruxton had a legal wife in India while Isabella Ruxton was a divorcée having formerly been married to a Dutchman, Van Ess.

The Ruxtons, who had three children, led a stormy personal

Portrait figure of Dr Buck Ruxton convicted of the murder of his wife and a nursemaid, whose dismembered remains were found in various gullies in Scotland.

life. Buck was a man of excitable nature with an uncontrollable temper. He was violently jealous of his wife, accusing her quite wrongly of affairs with other men. Police had been called to the house on more than one occasion and maidservants who had left the household spoke of his threatening actions towards his wife with revolvers and knives. However, in spite of their resounding quarrels, the couple always made up their differences.

In 1935 the household staff consisted of Mary Rogerson, a pleasant girl who spent most of her leisure time with her parents, and an assortment of cleaning women who came in at various hours to attend to the heavier chores.

In September of this year Ruxton in one of his outbursts accused Isabella of an affair with the son of family friends with whom she had recently made a trip to Edinburgh. A few days later Isabella Ruxton disappeared in peculiar circumstances. She had driven herself to Blackpool to meet her two sisters and look at the illuminations with them. She left them at about eleven-thirty at night to drive home and no one other than her husband saw her again. At the same time Mary Rogerson vanished. Her parents soon raised the alarm for the girl had never gone away without telling them and if she was on holiday she wrote regularly.

Dr Buck Ruxton's behaviour during the days following his wife's disappearance and that of his nursemaid, neither of whom were seen after 14 September, was strange in the extreme. He explained their absence by saying that his wife was in Blackpool and the nurse on holiday. He had a badly-cut hand which he explained he had suffered while opening a tin of fruit for the children and he asked some friends, the Andersons, if they could care for the children while his wife and the nursemaid were away. The regular cleaning women were told not to come and instead he enlisted the help of a patient, a Mrs Hampshire, and her husband to strip the house and take up the carpets in preparation for decorators to come in. The Hampshires noticed what appeared to be many bloodstains as they went about this work and Dr Ruxton gave Mrs Hampshire a suit with a bloodstained waistcoat and a bundle of bloodstained carpet which she tried to wash at home. The doctor said he had lost a great deal of blood from the severe cut inflicted by the tin-opener and the Hampshires appear to have accepted this explanation without query.

It was on 20 September 1935 that a visitor to Scotland was passing over a bridge which spanned a gully near Moffat. Looking over into this gully the lady was horrified to see what appeared to be a human arm protruding from a bundle of wrapping in the ravine below. She hastened to summon her brother who informed the police.

A number of parcels were retrieved from gullies which, when assembled, proved to contain the remains of two women. All marks of identity had been removed, also fingers and thumbs and in one case teeth were missing—Isabella Ruxton had noticeably prominent teeth. The bodies had been meticulously dismembered into small pieces. Mrs Hampshire later recalled that while she and her husband were stripping down the house two bedrooms had remained locked. Behind those locked doors lay two bodies, that of Mrs Ruxton killed by her husband in a fit of unbridled temper and that of Mary Rogerson who had witnessed the murder.

Skilled and detailed forensic work on this collection of gruesome remains built up a volume of evidence pointing to the guilt of Ruxton. He was charged with the murder of Mary Rogerson and then on 5 November with that of Isabella Ruxton. It was for the latter murder that he actually stood trial at the Manchester Assizes.

At the trial medical evidence was minutely put to the jury as the prosecution painstakingly established identification of the two bodies. One extraordinary feature of the evidence was the report of a 'Cyclop's eye' discovered among the remains.

Cyclopia is an unusual malformation very rare in humans, more often found in pigs. Both eyes are fused together and appear as one eye in the middle of the forehead. The condition is usually accompanied by other malformations and the victim usually dies within hours of birth.

It was impossible to say whether this extraordinary eye came from a human or an animal. It appeared to have been preserved in such a way that it could have been an anatomical specimen. Buck Ruxton was known to have been interested in ophthalmology. If he had possessed such a specimen he might have made use of the preserving fluid while cutting up the bodies and poured out the eye with the fluid. However, no evidence could be produced that the accused man had ever possessed a specimen of a 'Cyclop's eye'. The judge in his summing up seemed to consider the eye to be an accidental finding which had no significance in the actual facts of the case. The presence of this object, which could have proved Ruxton's guilt without question had he been proved to possess it, remains a complete mystery.

It was a long and complicated trial during which over a hundred witnesses were called. Dr Buck Ruxton himself was the only defence witness. Protesting his innocence he gave way to frequent hysterical outbursts. The jury found him guilty, and appeal failed, and Buck Ruxton was executed at Manchester on 12 May 1936. It was later revealed that he had confessed to both murders in writing stating 'I killed Mrs Ruxton in a fit of temper. I was mad at the time. Mary Rogerson was present at the time. I had to kill her.'

[9]

The Second World War and After

When the war broke out in September 1939 John Theodore Tussaud, Madame Tussaud's great-grandson, was eighty-one but still active in the exhibition which he had already seen through a world war and a disastrous fire. His son Bernard was fifty-three. Remembering the losses of the fire Bernard found an empty barn in Hertfordshire and removed as many moulds as he could to comparative safety. As in the First World War no figures were taken away for it was intended that the exhibition should carry on as it had before.

For a time it seemed as if the new war would do what even the fire had failed to do—close down Madame Tussaud's entirely. The black-out, partial evacuation of Londoners, fear of airraids and other war conditions caused attendances to fall drastically. But true to the spirit of the foundress the exhibition including the Chamber of Horrors remained open. The restaurant continued to serve food and the band played from seven o'clock to ten o'clock in the evening. A figure of Adolf Hitler had of course been in the exhibition for some time. Now Bernard hurriedly set about modelling Goering.

The optimism and determination of Madame Tussaud's great-grandson and great-great-grandson was justified, as her own had always been in time of crisis. It was not long before attendance figures began to rise again as people adjusted themselves to war conditions and many returned to London. They needed entertainment, and once again soldiers on leave or waiting in London on their way to active service made a visit to Madame Tussaud's a priority.

The early stages of the war were quiet, 'the phoney war' as it was called. Bernard and other members of the studios were seen haunting Whitehall to get a personal glimpse of political and Services personnel as they came and went. No one had time to give sittings and there were minor difficulties. Medal ribbons for example were very difficult to obtain. There were sixty-eight portrait figures of murderers and criminals in the Chamber of Horrors, as well as the relics, tableaux and dioramas. There was no time to add to this already formidable array.

Then Hitler's blitz and the Battle of Britain began. The zeppelin raids of the First World War had left Madame Tussaud's unscathed but the blitz was another matter. On the night of 9 and 10 September 1940 a direct hit destroyed the cinema and the restaurant was badly damaged. The wall of a mould store was adjacent to the cinema. It had not been possible to evacuate its contents. The wall collapsed and hundreds of moulds, likenesses of the great and the criminal alike, crashed into the bomb crater and were irretrievably smashed. Moulds of 295 male heads and 57 female heads were lost.

The effects of dust, dirt, flying rubble and glass made havoc in the building though few of the figures were seriously damaged. The portrait of Hitler, not yet removed to the Chamber of Horrors in the basement, was one which, ironically, was hardly affected. The Chamber of Horrors itself suffered from blast and dirt. Only two of its occupants sustained no damage at all and one of these was Crippen who had also survived the fire in 1925. The *Eastbourne Herald* mentioned that the exhibition's large white cat, Paul, which had been a familiar figure around the place for six years was found safe after the bombing lying on the figure of Crippen in the Chamber of Horrors.

Although no lives were lost, and no person injured, overall damage in addition to the destroyed cinema and shattered restaurant forced Madame Tussaud's to close until December when it reopened 'much as before', said one reporter. Crowds

Hitler was moved into the Chamber of Horrors after the outbreak of war in 1939. With him are other German 'war criminals'.

now came in again for as *The Star* remarked 'London without Madame Tussaud's has been rather a blank'. A visit paid by King George VI and Queen Elizabeth to inspect the bomb crater had also stimulated interest in the catastrophe.

As the war continued and restrictions became more and more stringent, difficulties naturally increased, affecting the main halls and the Chamber of Horrors alike. Clothes rationing was one problem. Since the modelling of portraits never halted, the supply of coupons doled out to Madame Tussaud's was totally inadequate. Soap rationing cut off the supply of fine curd soap used for cleaning the figures and washing their hair, but even in the Chamber of Horrors the high standards of maintenance laid down so many decades ago by Madame Tussaud herself were adhered to as far as possible. A criminal's garb might not appear the picture of elegance but it received the same regular cleaning as more meritorious figures and hair and faces underwent the same maintenance processes. The supply of eyes which had come largely from Continental manufacturers and the bundles of real hair also from Continental sources were extremely difficult to procure. It was Bernard's sister Joan who now wrestled with the problems of the wardrobe.

When the exhibition reopened after the bombing the 'war criminals' Hitler, Goering, Goebbels, Ribbentrop and Mussolini were put in the Chamber of Horrors but it proved impossible during the war years for Bernard to add portraits of those executed for murder or imprisoned for serious crimes. However, the existing array proved sufficient attraction. Few wartime visitors especially the soldiers from overseas countries left the exhibition without penetrating down the stairs into what the French called *La Chambre Sinistre*.

The post-war years brought no immediate easing of all the problems, in fact a few new ones were added. For example when the National Health Service was established all the supplies of fine plaster needed for making moulds were requisitioned and allocated for medical use. The Tussaud family finally succeeded in persuading the authorities that Madame Tussaud's exhibition was of immense value as a tourist attraction and dollar-earner. Sufficient material was then grudgingly released for use in the studios.

There had always been a good scattering of French 'subjects' in the Chamber of Horrors and the first new figure to be placed in it after the end of the war was that of a Frenchman, Dr Marcel Petiot. Dr Petiot was a mass-murderer who took advantage of the conditions in occupied France to kill for gain. He was never a participant in the French Underground Resistance Movement, but he callously pretended to be involved in order to lure victims to his house.

While the Germans occupied Paris Dr Petiot managed to retain a house he had owned for some time in a quiet respectable neighbourhood near the Étoile. It was in March 1944 that his neighbour, Monsieur Marcais, became aware of black and evil-smelling smoke issuing from the chimney of 21 Rue Lesueur. Other people living around confirmed the nasty character of the smoke and said it had only started fairly recently. No one seemed to know anything about the owner of the house but a card pinned to the door gave another address. The police telephoned Dr Petiot there and told him a fire in his house had been notified. The doctor said he would come immediately.

In the meantime the fire brigade had arrived and broken into 21 Rue Lesueur. They emerged rapidly saying the house was full of corpses. In the cellars they had been shocked to find human remains, several heads, a smouldering body and another body slit from head to groin. When Petiot arrived he descended to the cellar and calmly looked round at its grisly contents. He explained to the police that the cellar was now being used as a secret execution chamber by members of the French Resistance. The police believed this story and allowed Dr Petiot to leave without further questioning.

This Dr Marcel Petiot, who had so suddenly come into the limelight, had been born in 1897 and orphaned in his mid-teens. At the age of sixteen he began robbing letter boxes. He was found out but escaped punishment and was able to begin a study of medicine which he continued until his call-up for military service. During this he was wounded, one foot being seriously injured by a grenade. Again he fell into trouble stealing drugs from a casualty clearing station and selling them to drug addicts. Once again he got off lightly as his wound was thought to have caused 'mental debility'. Petiot was given psychiatric treatment and an honourable discharge from the army with a life pension.

He resumed his medical studies and in 1920 held a post in a lunatic asylum where he wrote a book that gained him a doctorate. The following year he set up practice at Villeneuve-sur-Yonne. Here his dark handsome looks and genial manner enabled him to build a prosperous practice. In 1917 he married a girl from the same district. He was a popular figure, participating in local politics as a convinced socialist, and also playing his part in social activities.

Yet there were a few rather curious incidents in which the popular and public-spirited doctor was involved. Before his marriage his servant girl, who he had seduced and made pregnant, vanished without trace. One of his woman patients kept a local shop where she was known to keep considerable sums of money. She was found murdered and robbed. Local gossip associated this tragedy with Dr Petiot's name and tongues were not silenced when his chief accuser, who was under treatment for rheumatism, died after taking some tablets prescribed by Dr Petiot. Dr Petiot conducted the autopsy himself and certified death from natural causes. Later the file concerning this death was found to have disappeared.

Petiot decided to remove to Paris and he set up a practice in 1933 in a house not far from the famous Madeleine church in central Paris. He advertised his modern equipment including X-rays by means of a broadsheet which he circulated. Three years later he was arrested for stealing from a bookshop but discharged with a recommendation to seek psychiatric treatment. He was not struck off the medical register.

He continued with his practice until the outbreak of war when he set up as a private dope pedlar, his professional position enabling him to supply drugs. In 1942 one of his customers was picked up by the police. She was a young girl and she involved her lover, Van Bever, who in his turn stated that Dr Petiot was the source of the drugs—a charge that the doctor firmly denied. The young man, Van Bever, vanished without trace, while he was on bail.

Then a Madame Kahid disappeared. Dr Petiot had been treating her daughter for drug addiction and the girl's mother accused him of supplying excessive quantities of drugs to the girl at well above the normal prices. She threatened to expose him unless he mended his ways. Madame Kahid arranged a meeting with the doctor and subsequently she disappeared. Of course it was wartime in occupied Paris and sudden disappearance was not an unusual thing. Dr Petiot was not questioned, though in connection with the case of young Van Bever he did receive a suspended prison sentence and a fine in spite of the disappearance of this young man.

Dr Marcel Petiot had bought the house near the Étoile in the Rue Lesueur in 1941. He had a number of curious alterations made, such as sound-proofing a windowless room and constructing a high wall which obscured the courtyard. The furnace was repaired and put in good working order. A consulting room was arranged at the end of a passage.

The Germans had been occupying France for two years and there were many people, especially Jews and Communists, who were very eager to get out of the country. Various individuals began setting up arrangements by which such flights could be secretly organized and one of the names whispered around as one who could help was that of Dr Marcel Petiot. But he could only be approached by appointment at his consulting room at 21 Rue Lesueur.

One such client was so uneasy after his first interview that he did not attend a second, but most of the frightened people who came to the consulting room were eager to grasp at any opportunity. Dr Petiot related the cost of an 'underground trip' to his clients' means. He also suggested that they bring with them jewellery, cash or any negotiable securities. Among those who wished to escape were some of his patients.

No one knows exactly what happened to the victims when they finally arrived at the doctor's house equipped for their dangerous journey. Possibly he gave them a lethal injection in the guise of a vaccination. Possibly he took them into the windowless sound-proofed room to wait and asphyxiated them there with a lethal gas. They ended up in quicklime in a pit dug in the yard behind the high concealing wall, or else in the furnace. Petiot, who used the name of Dr Eugène for these operations, cleverly timed his murders for periods when both the Gestapo and the French police were fully occupied and had no time to pry into his doings.

Nevertheless the Gestapo, the German police, were aware of the doctor's activities though they had no idea of the fate of the escapers listed on their files as having vanished. They blackmailed a Jew into acting as 'stool pigeon' to report on the methods of this supposed escape route but the Jew too disappeared. The Gestapo assumed he had taken advantage of the opportunity to flee himself. However, they had sufficient evidence and they arrested Petiot for having aided escapers in return for money. In May 1943 he was put in prison and remained there for eight months. The police picked him up at his house near the Madeleine and did not bother to take a look at 21 Rue Lesueur. Petiot had arranged for the transfer to the country of a collection of suitcases and clothing belonging to his victims.

In 1944, after the firemen's grisly discoveries, the French police began intensive and secret investigations. In the end it was the transfer of quicklime from Auxerre where Petiot's brother lived to 21 Rue Lesueur which provided the final link. Also the brother appeared to have a much larger income than his business as a radio repairer warranted.

On 31 October 1944 Dr Marcel Petiot was arrested. He consistently maintained that the bodies discovered in his house were those of Germans or collaborators seized by the French Resistance group to which he belonged. But the people he named as his superiors in the group proved all to be dead and the code name of the group which he gave was unknown to the

Resistance. Petiot insisted to the last that those he had helped had got away and he knew nothing of their fate once they had gone.

His trial in March 1945 was lengthy. Petiot was accused of the murder of twenty-seven persons. Amongst the evidence brought against him were a large number of suitcases, trunks, packing cases and parcels containing belongings of those he had purported to smuggle out of the country. It was claimed that in cash and valuables he had netted no less than the equivalent of a quarter of a million pounds from his murders. During his trial Dr Petiot was alternately in a blithe mood, given to outbursts of bitter fury, or querulous as he sought in vain to prove himself a patriot who had only destroyed France's enemies and helped her citizens to escape the German occupation. He was found guilty and his appeal met with no success. Dr Marcel Petiot was executed on 26 May 1946. He made no confession and went to his death like the earlier French mass-murderer, 'Bluebeard' Landru, whose portrait figure he joined in effigy in the Chamber of Horrors.

In the autumn of 1946 Bernard Tussaud spent a period of three weeks observing the murderer Neville Heath in Court. It took him six weeks finally to complete the figure which was moved into the Chamber of Horrors one hour after Heath's execution. Had the prisoner received a last-moment reprieve, Bernard told reporters, the head would have been melted down and the figure broken up. In the event his anticipatory work was not wasted but there was one point on which Bernard was adamant. He had served himself in the RAF during the First World War and he would not allow the model of Heath to wear the RAF tie that the murderer had so often flaunted. The wardrobe had to provide a blue tie with white stripes from their stocks.

Like so many of Madame Tussaud's criminal 'subjects' Neville Heath was a personable man. His square firm face, bright blue eyes, military appearance and pleasant persuasive manner belied the long record of offences he had committed before he turned to murder. When Heath killed he did so not for gain, jealousy or revenge but to satisfy a horrifying sadism.

Heath joined the RAF when he was twenty years old but soon deserted and was dismissed for absence without leave. He then turned to fraud, obtaining credit by posing as Lord Dudley. When prosecuted he admitted numerous frauds but escaped lightly for he was only put on probation. Later he was sent to Borstal for housebreaking and forgery. Other dishonesties followed but when war broke out in 1939 he joined the Royal Army Service Corps and gained a commission. As an officer he was posted to the Middle East but his stay there was of short duration. He was court-martialled, cashiered, and shipped home for false pretences and a forged cheque.

On the way back to England Heath slipped his guard at Durban and using a false name managed to join the South African Air Force in which he rose to the rank of captain. While in South Africa he married and had a son. He was seconded for a time to the RAF but back in South Africa he finished up with another court martial and was dismissed from the service for various offences. His wife divorced him for desertion.

It was in February 1946 that Neville Heath returned to England but he did not change his ways. Again he posed as Lord Dudley, also as Lieutenant-Colonel Armstrong, wearing decorations to which he was not entitled. He was caught and prosecuted, but up to this time his criminal record was free of acts of violence. It had been rumoured in South Africa that he had made attacks on women but if this were true none of them had lodged any complaint.

Four months later, in June, Heath took a double room at a Notting Hill Gate Hotel, signing the register in his real name but giving himself the rank of lieutenant-colonel. A girl spent the night there with him but she came to no harm and returned home. He had promised her marriage to induce her to spend the night with him.

Heath stayed on at the hotel and a few days later spent the evening at a Kensington club with a woman named Margery Gardner. They had met before. She was a married woman some years older than Heath and promiscuous in her habits. She made no demur about returning with him to his hotel, leaving the club after midnight.

The next day the chambermaid found the door of Heath's room locked and could get no response to her knocking. Finally at two o'clock the assistant manageress went with a master key. The room was dark and when she drew the curtains she saw that one bed was empty. In the other bed she found a naked girl, dead, her ankles bound and her arms folded behind her. The body was horribly mutilated including the marks of lashes from a whip which the post-mortem revealed had been made with a diamond-weave thong. No noise had been heard in the hotel during the night except the sound of a door slamming at about half-past one in the morning, which could have been made when Heath left the room and secretly made his exit.

Neville Heath went to Worthing to the girl who had recently spent the night with him under promise of marriage. She introduced 'Lieutenant-Colonel' Heath to her parents as her fiancé. He made an excellent impression until they read his name in the newspapers in connection with the terrible murder at Notting Hill. Heath slipped away and went to Bournemouth.

On Sunday 23 June while still at Worthing he wrote an extraordinary letter to Superintendent Barratt at Scotland Yard. In it he explained that Mrs Gardner had for financial reasons agreed to sleep with a client on the night she was murdered. Heath had given her the key of his room and said she could make use of it until the early hours of the morning when the man would have departed and he in his turn would join her. He did this, he wrote, and found Mrs Gardner's body. He was afraid to go to the police so collected his belongings and left the hotel.

Having arrived in Bournemouth, Heath assumed the name of Group Captain Brooke. He took a room at the Tollard Royal Hotel. When he had been some ten days in Bournemouth he made the acquaintance of an ex-Wren, Doreen Marshall, who was convalescing at the Norfolk Hotel. She joined Heath at his hotel in the evening and dined with him there. Soon after midnight, when Heath seemed somewhat tipsy and Doreen

Marshall looked rather pale and drawn, she asked the porter for a taxi to be called but this was countermanded by Heath who said they would walk to her hotel. He told the night porter he would be away for half an hour but Doreen said no and that it was only a fifteen minute walk. She obviously wished to be rid of Heath's company as soon as possible.

At what time Heath did return to his hotel was never established for he entered his bedroom window by means of a ladder standing nearby. At the Norfolk Hotel it was forty-eight hours before anyone missed Doreen Marshall. She had dined with Heath on the evening of 3 July, a Wednesday, and was not notified to the police as missing until Friday. Heath telephoned the police and called at the police station to identify a photograph of the missing girl. At the police station he was recognized as the man who was being sought in connection with the brutal murder of Margery Gardner and he was detained.

He asked for his coat which was fetched, but before it was handed to him the police searched the pockets and found a left-luggage ticket. This related to an attaché case which contained a whip with a diamond-weave thong and a stained scarf which had presumably been used to gag Mrs Gardner. She was an able-bodied woman experienced in relations with men and it had seemed curious, until this scarf came to light, that she could be attacked and murdered in a hotel room without screaming for help.

It was not until Monday evening that the naked and mutilated body of Doreen Marshall, slashed with a knife, was discovered in a little-frequented part of Branksome Chine. When questioned Heath claimed that he had walked as far as the pier with the girl and watched her cross the road and enter the gardens.

The man with convictions for fraud, housebreaking, theft and forgery, who had been three times commissioned in the Services and three times court-martialled and dismissed, was now charged with the murder of Mrs Margery Gardner. The killing of Doreen Marshall was not mentioned until introduced by defending counsel to support the plea of partial insanity.

However, the medical evidence called to try and prove insanity was demolished by the prosecution. The jury was not convinced and brought in a verdict of guilty. On 26 October Neville Heath was executed. His effigy still stands in the Chamber of Horrors today.

The figure of John George Haigh, the 'Acid Bath Murderer', was another which was carried into the Chamber of Horrors within a short time of his execution on 10 August 1949. It was dressed in a copy of the clothes that Haigh had worn in the Magistrates' Court, fawn-grey lounge suit, cream poplin shirt, red tie and brown shoes, and it was placed in company with Neville Heath, Buck Ruxton and Marcel Petiot.

However, this attire was soon changed for in his last hours Haigh made several requests. An inordinately vain man, he wished the clothes he had worn at his trial to be presented to Madame Tussaud's where he felt sure he would soon be on view. When the clothes were received Haigh was re-dressed in a green hopsack suit, green socks and a red tie with green squares. He had asked that the trousers should be meticulously pressed. John Haigh was quite familiar with Madame Tussaud's exhibition. It was said that he used to take his girlfriends, to whom he always behaved with propriety, either to concerts of classical music or to Madame Tussaud's.

Queues formed to see the new entrant in the Chamber of Horrors. When someone remarked on the morbidity of the crowds Madame Tussaud's spokesman replied as she herself might have done 'No, it is a natural interest to see if murderers like Heath and Haigh look like other people, and how can anyone decide better than by seeing them as they are!' Madame Tussaud's 'uncle' Curtius had though exactly the same when he had founded his *Chambre des Grands Voleurs* long ago in Paris in 1783.

It is not surprising that the murders committed by Haigh, a cold and pitiless man, aroused exceptional public interest. The man himself was an enigma. Even the prison officers and chaplains liked him and he appeared to enjoy being a focus of public interest at his trial, unaffected by his dreadful crimes.

John George Haigh was the son of a couple who belonged to the strict Plymouth Brethren sect. His mother was forty years old when her only child was born, in 1909. He was brought up in the austere and narrow tenets of his parents' beliefs and not allowed to mingle with other children. The family lived at Outwood Colliery where his father worked as a skilled electrician. It was only two miles from Wakefield and, curiously enough, his parents allowed him to sing in the Cathedral choir taking part in High Anglican services, which were otherwise abhorred by Plymouth Brethren. The boy was extremely musical and intelligent at school, where his teachers reported favourably on his pleasant manners. His contemporaries with whom he was not allowed to mix outside school called him 'Chinky' because of his narrow eyes and he was fond of pranks of a harmless nature. His teachers failed to notice the boy's aptitude for forgery.

By the time Haigh was twenty-five he had the appearance of a well-to-do young man driving an expensive sports car, but this asset was not the fruit of industry. His money was coming from fraudulent hire-purchase deals and the selling of non-existent cars. About this time he married a girl whose parents were on the music halls. It was a match disapproved of by both sets of parents and none of them appeared at the registry-office wedding at Bridlington. Haigh's charm and ingratiating manner always assured him of plenty of girlfriends but sex did not seem to interest him.

He had only been married eleven months when he was arrested and sent to prison for fraudulent dealings. His wife faded from the scene but Haigh's parents, in spite of their strict creed so alien to their son's way of life, maintained close ties with their son who always kept in touch with them.

When Haigh came out of prison in 1935 he went to London after a brief spell in a dry-cleaning business at Leeds. Three years later he was sentenced to four years penal servitude for false pretences. In Dartmoor he took the opportunity to study chemistry and law in the prison library, studies which may have given him the knowledge he displayed in his later crimes. He worked in the tinsmith's shop where sulphuric acid was used and is said to have experimented with small animals brought in by prisoners who did field work to observe its destructive properties on flesh and bones. In 1941 he got another prison sentence of hard labour for stealing.

On the outbreak of war in 1939 Haigh managed to evade his call-up and only did some fire-watching so was free to answer an advertisement he noticed in a show-business paper. It was inserted by a Mr McSwan who had made a considerable amount of money out of pin-table saloons, a business which he ran with his son Donald. Now living comfortably in Wimbledon Mr McSwan decided to advertise for a chauffeur/secretary. John Haigh replied and, always pleasant mannered, he got the job. He did so well that he was promoted to be the manager of a pin-table saloon in Tooting.

Such steady employment did not really suit Haigh. After a time he left and set up as a phoney solicitor under different names taken from the law list. He moved around operating in a number of localities. His method was to advertise shares for a quick sale at below market prices in order to clear up the estate of a mythical deceased person. Such is the credulity and greed of the public that cheques poured in. The senders never saw any share certificates.

It was in 1944 that he met Donald McSwan in a pub. They had parted on friendly terms and now Donald confided to Haigh his anxiety to evade military call-up. Haigh, who had himself been successful in this, volunteered to advise and was welcomed by the McSwan parents. The old man had now retired from the pin-table business. Next Haigh decided to set up his own business as a repairer of pin-tables, and rented a basement in Gloucester Road for the purpose. Donald McSwan called a number of times to discuss his own problem and on 9 September 1944 John Haigh battered his unsuspecting visitor to death with the leg of a pin-table. Haigh's stores included acid for pickling. He found a water-butt on a disused site and took it to his basement premises. There he heaved Donald McSwan's body into the butt and poured in acid with a bucket.

Haigh told Donald's parents that their son had, on his advice, gone away to avoid his call-up papers. He posted them a forged letter purporting to come from Donald who gave no address on account of his fugitive situation. Haigh wrote more forged letters to the McSwan parents asking them to send money, which he collected but the sums were not large.

The remains of Donald McSwan had been poured down a drain in the Gloucester Road basement when the acid had done its work. Now Haigh persuaded the old couple to visit him in his workshop. They were disposed of in the same way as their son.

Posing as Donald McSwan with a forged power of attorney Haigh disposed of the properties and securities owned by Mr McSwan thus getting himself about £4,000. No one seems to have noticed anything suspicious or even queried the disappearance of the McSwan family.

By now John Haigh had moved into the Onslow Court Hotel, a respectable place with a number of fairly well-to-do resident old ladies. He was well liked and provided them with extra rations, which they did not question, using the McSwan's ration books. However, Haigh was now betting and money was always tight. He answered an advertisment inserted by a Dr and Mrs Henderson offering a house for sale in Ladbroke Square. The Hendersons were a worldly couple, fond of night-life and sophisticated but this did not prevent them becoming friendly with Haigh when he put in an offer for the house. However, after a time when the money was not forthcoming they sold to another bidder but still remained on friendly terms when they removed to Fulham.

Haigh joined them on a holiday in Brighton. He had now moved his workshop to premises at Crawley that were, in fact, little more than a shed with a yard. One day he drove Dr Henderson to this workshop from which the doctor did not emerge again. Haigh fetched Mrs Henderson telling her that her husband had been taken ill in Crawley. She too was never seen again, alive or dead.

By means of a forged letter of authority Haigh sold the

Hendersons' car and other assets and got possession of their Fulham house. In that year (1948) he paid £7,000 into his banking account.

Mrs Henderson owned a crocodile handbag which he sold to Mrs Durand-Deacon, one of the elderly residents at the Onslow Court Hotel who did not ask any questions as to where the bag came from. She would be Haigh's last victim. Mrs Olive Durand-Deacon, a lady of sixty-nine, was the widow of a colonel and enjoyed a comfortable income of about £1,000 a year. Her table was next to Haigh's in the hotel dining-room and she was friendly with him. He escorted her to literary lunches. She appreciated the extra rations he sometimes provided and did not think to ask where they came from, any more than she asked about the handsome handbag she had bought, paying only ten pounds.

During conversation Haigh interested her in the idea of plastic fingernails which he said he was starting to manufacture at his workshop in Crawley. He invited Mrs Durand-Deacon to drive down with him and look at his work. She agreed and on a cold winter day, 18 February 1949, she left the hotel wearing a Persian lamb coat, her pearls and other jewellery, and carrying a red plastic handbag.

She did not return. Haigh had shot her in the back while she was examining some samples of plastic fingernails in the workshop, whose contents included a large vat and carboys of acid. In spite of her weight—she weighed fourteen stone—Haigh managed to get her body fully clothed except for her fur coat and jewellery into the vat and he pumped in acid with a stirrup pump. He added the red plastic handbag, having removed the money.

When Mrs Durand-Deacon did not return to the hotel her friend Mrs Lane became worried. She questioned Haigh who said he had waited for her but she had not turned up. The next day Mrs Lane decided to go to the police and report her friend missing. Haigh offered to go with her. Four days later when he had sold Mrs Durand-Deacon's jewellery and taken her fur coat to the cleaners (the ticket was found in his workshop) he emptied the vat into the yard behind his Crawley premises. There was no convenient drain as there had been in Gloucester Road but Haigh was confident that all traces of Mrs Durand-Deacon had disappeared. He was questioned at the hotel and the Sussex police paid a visit to the Crawley workshop. They found a revolver and ammunition, the carboys of acid, and protective clothing, as well as the ticket from the cleaners who had the Persian lamb coat. This interested the police as they knew she had been wearing a lamb coat when she disappeared.

Forensic experts were called in and the soil outside Haigh's premises removed for examination. He had been wrong in thinking no trace of his victim remained. Mrs Durand-Deacon's dentures were found and positively identified by her dentist. The strap of her red plastic handbag survived the acid as well as various other damning fragments. On 2 March John Haigh was arrested and charged with the murder of Mrs Olive Durand-Deacon. He made a full confession after his arrest and also described how he had murdered the McSwan family and Dr and Mrs Henderson. He was confident he would be found insane and sent to Broadmoor. He embellished his story with lurid details claiming he had drunk the blood of each victim before putting them in the acid bath.

People queued all night in bad weather to get seats at the trial at the 1949 Summer Sussex Assizes at Lewes. After John Haigh's execution they also came in crowds to Madame Tussaud's to see the effigy of this extraordinary and callous man. They still gaze at it today, the portrait of one of the most notorious murderers in the annals of crime.

Throughout the 1950s no major changes were made in the structure of the Chamber of Horrors. The chilling impact of the eyes of dozens of murderers, together with the French revolutionary relics, the gallows from Hertford Gaol, and numerous other gruesome relics, had sufficient appeal to maintain the flow of visitors.

There were, of course, new entries and among them was a figure in a reconstructed room which rivalled that of John Haigh as an attraction. Some 13,000 people were reported to

The portrait figure of John Reginald Christie in a reconstruction of his squalid kitchen in Rillington Place. He put three of his victims' bodies in an alcove and papered over it.

have crowded past the tableau of John Reginald Christie in his squalid kitchen during the first four days after it was set up. Rillington Place is a name that has long disappeared from the street maps of London and few could identify today the house in which Christie killed his victims, but his effigy in his kitchen can still be seen in Madame Tussaud's.

Like many of the inhabitants of the Chamber of Horrors John

Christie was born into comfortable circumstances. His father, a skilled carpet designer in Halifax, was a man of many good works but also a disciplinarian in the Victorian mould. He had a violent temper which his children feared. The mother, who had been considered a 'beauty' in her youth, enjoyed amateur theatricals in the intervals of bearing seven children of whom John Reginald who arrived in 1908 was the fifth.

He was a puny and ailing child and his father who liked a 'manly' boy displayed little affection for him. To compensate his mother was over-possessive, over-cosseting and as John Reginald's sisters were all of a dominating nature he grew up in his Halifax home under a predominately feminine influence. This may have produced in him an innate and unrecognized dislike and even fear of women.

He was about eight years old when he made his first acquaintance with death. His grandfather died and he was taken to view what looked to him like a wax dummy rather than the somewhat alarming old man he had known. From that time the child was fascinated with death and took to playing for preference in the graveyard.

John Christie was well educated, and sang in the church choir. He became an assistant scoutmaster, but as a young man he was not an impressive figure. Slight and not very tall, he had pale blue eyes, gingery hair and exceptionally small feet. However, in 1918 when he was eighteen and a half he enlisted in the Army. His companions found him even-tempered, even jovial, and liked him for his ready smile. He showed no outward interest in girls but at nineteen was reputed to be consorting with prostitutes.

An exploding mustard shell put him in hospital. Christie always said he was rendered blind for three months and dumb, but his records show no lasting conditions of the kind. Nonetheless in subsequent years Christie did lose his voice from time to time and speak in a whisper. He was demobilized in 1919 with a small disability pension.

Back in his home town of Halifax the young man tried several jobs and began courting a homely unassertive girl, Ethel Waddington, whose family was known to his parents. They were married when both were twenty-two. The marriage was not an entire success on account of Christie's sexual deficiencies but Ethel was not a demanding girl and they appeared normally content.

But inwardly John Christie was craving excitement. He was working in the Post Office and his restlessness led him to steal postal orders. He was found out and sent to prison. He and Ethel had only been married eleven months. He was again in trouble in 1923 for false pretences and violence and there were stories that he was again frequenting prostitutes. His family disowned him and it was Ethel who suggested a move to Sheffield where she had relatives. The move was not a success. There were quarrels and then Christie left alone for London.

Having arrived in the capital he was knocked down by a car, injured, and spent some time in hospital. In the autumn, when he was sent to prison again on charges of larceny, he had no employment and no fixed abode. For the next nine years he led a double life. In spite of his prison record he was successful in getting jobs and by day appeared to be an ordinary, quiet, industrious clerk. At night he was to be found in low-class cafés and mingling with prostitutes and criminal elements.

Christie again showed signs of violence in 1929. He was living with a prostitute who tired of him and told him to clear out. He took up her son's cricket bat and split open her head causing an injury which, though he pleaded accident, got him six months in prison. It was during this spell in gaol that Christie wrote to his wife who was still in Sheffield and had not seen her husband for nine years. She earned her living as a typist, but was lonely and agreed to come to London.

John and Ethel Christie set up house in Notting Hill. He got work as a ledger clerk but when Ethel visited her Sheffield relatives or other opportunity occurred he slipped away to mingle in the world of petty criminals and prostitutes with which he was already so familiar. He was neurotic and hypochondriac and constantly visited his local doctor for minor complaints.

In 1938 they moved to the ground floor flat at 10 Rillington Place, Notting Hill. The house was small and run-down though it contained three flats. A patch of garden went with the Christie's flat and a washhouse, used for storage, backed on to their kitchen. Off this washhouse was the only lavatory, used by all the tenants and with access only from outside by way of the Christie's kitchen. Christie was unsettled, restless, conscious of the total failure of his life which had begun in prosperity.

War was looming and in the summer of 1939 he volunteered and was accepted as a special constable in the War Reserve Police. Incredibly no check was made on his record. Posted to Harrow Police Station he proved himself efficient and enjoyed his work. This did not prevent him starting an affair with a young woman who worked at the police station. Her husband was away serving but unexpectedly returned. Finding Christie with his wife in the room where she lived he beat-up and threw out the surprised lover.

It was after this that Christie took to murder which in ten years time would bring him to the scaffold. Ruth Fuerst, a seventeen-year-old nursing student, left her training on the outbreak of war to work in a munitions factory and in all probability eked out her earnings as a part-time prostitute. Somewhere, possibly on his beat, she met John Christie. Ethel was away in Sheffield and Ruth was invited to Rillington Place. She never came out. After intercourse Christie strangled her with a rope.

His wife was due home and he had to get rid of the body quickly. He removed loose floorboards in the front-room, put the girl's body and her clothes in a depression beneath and cleaned up the bedroom. Ethel Christie brought her brother home on a brief visit. That night he slept in the sitting-room only yards from the body beneath the floorboards.

Next day, when Ethel's brother had departed and she was at work Christie dug a grave in the garden in full view of the neighbours, having hidden Ruth's body behind junk in the washhouse. No one who used the lavatory that day noticed it. When dark had fallen Christie told his wife he was going out to the lavatory. He put the body in the already prepared grave and threw earth over it. Next morning he raked the patch evenly and burned Ruth's clothes in a dustbin incinerator.

At the end of the year Christie obtained release from the police force and went to work in a radio factory. In the canteen he felt attracted to a thirty-one-year-old spinster, Muriel Eady, a highly respectable woman who lived with an aunt and had a steady boyfriend. Christie took her to Rillington Place several times to have tea with Ethel.

In 1944 Ethel departed on another Sheffield visit. Her husband's desire for Muriel Eady grew urgent. He told Muriel, who suffered from catarrh, that he had a special device for treating the condition and hinted that his police experience had given him a knowledge of medical matters.

Finally Muriel accepted Christie's offer to try the gadget. In October she called at Rillington Place. Christie gave her a cup of tea, and having positioned her carefully in a chair he handed her a screw-topped jar which contained some Friar's Balsam. There were two holes in the lid accommodating two rubber tubes. From one of them Muriel inhaled Friar's Balsam but she could not see that the other led behind her chair to a gas point. When she was unconscious from the coal-gas Christie had intercourse, strangled her and, as with Ruth Fuerst, buried her body, this time fully clothed, in the garden.

Both Ruth and Muriel were reported to the police as missing. Not much effort was made to find Ruth. She was known to frequent a fringe world where people often moved away. Muriel was a different matter. Her friendship with Christie was known but there was nothing, no motive, to connect him with her disappearance. It was the time of flying bombs and finally it was assumed that she must have been killed when one of these fell on London. Often no body was found after these incidents.

Christie left the radio works and tried a job at the Post Office but his early theft of postal orders was discovered and he was dismissed. Ethel had given up her job and spent more time at home. Christie paid frequent visits to his doctor and obtained certificates of unfitness for work.

In 1948 a new tenant came into the top flat. The middle flat was unoccupied, its tenant, old and blind, being in hospital. Timothy Evans, the new top-floor occupant, was a young man, semi-literate and of low intelligence. His nineteen-year-old wife, Beryl, was pregnant. After her baby was born she became friendly with Ethel Christie. When Beryl found herself pregnant again she did not want the child and told her friends, including the Christies, that she wanted an abortion which at that time was illegal. Her husband did not agree.

Meanwhile Christie had been to the Borough Council and complained that his flat was damp and delapidated. The landlord was ordered to do repairs including plastering the washhouse and replacing skirting and boards in the hallway. On 31 October the builders moved in and the repairs took some time to complete.

Beryl Evans and her husband quarrelled about the abortion she wanted and she said she would leave and go to her father. At the same time she made a private arrangement with Christie that he would abort her—he had mentioned his medical knowledge—the next morning, in her flat, while Timothy was at work.

No one knows exactly what happened that morning but Timothy Evans returned to find his wife dead. Christie said something had gone wrong and that he would dispose of the body on account of the illegality of the abortion, probably down a drain. The feeble-minded Evans accepted this and the two men moved Beryl's body into the empty middle flat. One of Beryl's friends persistently kept calling and Christie, who always opened the door, told her that Beryl had left.

Evans was bewildered and distressed about the care of the baby. Christie said he would find someone who would take it in and look after it. The baby disappeared. He had strangled it as he had strangled Beryl. Then Christie persuaded young Timothy Evans to sell up his furniture and move away, since both his wife and baby were gone.

Christie had taken Beryl's body wrapped in a blanket and tablecloth into the washhouse and hidden it behind boards the workmen had removed from the hall floor. He had also concealed the baby's body in the washhouse. No one making use of the lavatory nor the workmen who stored their tools in the washhouse noticed the bundle.

An unexpected development followed. On 30 November 1948 Timothy Evans walked into a police station and said he had found his wife dead and put her body down a drain. Then he made a confession that he had killed her, later withdrawing this and accusing Christie of the murder. On Friday, 2 December, the police searched 10 Rillington Place and discovered the bodies of Beryl and the baby in the washhouse.

Christie, a witness at the trial of Timothy Evans, denied responsibility. He convinced the Court of his innocence. Timothy Evans was found guilty of the murder of his baby and hanged. It was a conviction that has aroused controversy ever since in view of later happenings.

Now John and Ethel Christie were the only tenants living at 10 Rillington Place until in August 1950 a new landlord, a Jamaican, let the upper floors to fellow-countrymen. This upset both the Christies who disliked their new neighbours. Both became highly nervous and relations between them worsened.

Christie's urge for sex and to kill was growing strong again. Hitherto he had been able to commit his crimes without his wife's knowledge or suspicion because she had been away from home. Now she seemed to be about the place all the time. He could bring no one into the house. Ethel was becoming a nuisance, an obstruction, and she must be removed. Christie gave notice to his employers and on 14 December strangled his wife while she was in bed. He put her body under the sitting-room floorboards in the same depression he had used for that of Ruth Fuerst, and put some earth over it. He told friends and neighbours that she had gone to Sheffield. He wrote to her relatives there at Christmas saying that Ethel's rheumatism prevented her from writing herself and he sent them the customary small Christmas present.

John Christie was now unemployed and in need of money. He sold all the furniture in the flat for a few pounds to the same dealer who had bought Timothy Evans' furniture. Nothing was left in the flat but an old dirty mattress and a deck chair with rope strands, two other chairs and a kitchen table. Living in this squalor the money from selling the furniture tided him over. He also forged his wife's signature to get her small savings.

In mid-January Christie called in at a Paddington public house where he met two prostitutes. One, Kathleen Maloney, he had met before. She was drunk and willingly accompanied him to 10 Rillington Place where she met a fate similar to that of Muriel Eady, killed with a new gas contraption Christie had devised. He wrapped up her body and stowed it in an alcove behind a cupboard in the kitchen.

A few days later another prostitute, Rita Nelson, who was pregnant went home with Christie. Possibly he had promised her an abortion. She died by the same procedure of gassing and strangling and joined Maloney in the alcove in the kitchen.

There was a pause of almost a month before Christie murdered his last victim, Hectorina Maclennan. She and the unemployed man with whom she was living were looking for a flat. They went with Christie to 10 Rillington Place and spent three uncomfortable nights there. The following night Christie told the man, Baker, that he must leave but Hectorina could stay on if they could find no other shelter. Next morning Hectorina went out to meet Baker, but Christie asked her to come back and see him later. Hectorina agreed, telling Baker when she left him, where she was going. She returned to 10 Rillington Place and finished up in the alcove.

When she did not reappear Baker went to Rillington Place looking for her but Christie declared he had not seen her. The two men had a cup of tea in the kitchen. Baker noticed a curious smell but gave no more thought to it.

It was in mid-March that John Christie decided to leave the flat. He had carefully papered over the alcove in the kitchen concealing its horrifying contents. Ethel's body was still under the floorboards and the other bodies safely buried in the garden.

When Christie left the landlord gave one of the other tenants permission to use the now vacant kitchen. The man cleared out a good deal of rubbish and then went over the walls looking for a suitable place to fix a bracket. Tapping around he noticed that the paper-covered alcove sounded hollow. He picked a hole and shone a torch into the space behind.

John Reginald Christie was wandering in London, destitute and homeless. As he leaned over Putney Bridge he was recognized by a policeman as the former occupant of 10 Rillington Place where such horrors had been discovered, the bodies of three prostitutes in the alcove, that of Ethel Christie under the floorboards and those of three women and a baby in the garden. It was on 1 April that Christie was taken to the police station for questioning and he was tried for murder three months later. The defence pleaded insanity but the jury found him guilty and he was executed on 14 July 1953.

The trial raised doubts as to whether Timothy Evans had in fact murdered his wife Beryl. He had confessed to it, had been tried, found guilty and executed, but could it not have been John Christie who strangled Beryl Evans and her baby and hidden them in the washhouse? The answer has never been established. Christie's figure in his squalid kitchen is still seen in the Chamber of Horrors today, the killer of six women and possibly a seventh and her baby.

In the same year that the Christie tableau brought visitors flocking in Miss Beatrice Tussaud died suddenly at the age of seventy-eight. Like her three sisters she had worked all her life in the hair and colouring studios, first under her father who could remember his grandmother Madame Tussaud, then under her brother John Theodore, and after his death she saw her nephew Bernard take control.

During more than half a century hundreds of wax heads had passed through the hands of the Misses Tussaud. They inserted the hair and reproduced the complexions of kings and criminals alike. While they did so tea was brewed in the studio in a silver plated Victorian teapot as if in a drawing-room. As old age crept on and there were no members of the family available to take their place they reluctantly trained successors from outside. They did not relish imparting their inherited skills and secrets.

One of their trainees said many years later when she was in charge and training young people for the job herself that it was more in spite of than by means of the Misses Tussaud that she had managed to learn her craft.

Neither Beatrice nor her sisters ever spoke publicly about their work except in the most general terms. They recorded nothing of the exhibition in which they spent their long working lives. Did these quiet, unmarried ladies accompany the male members of their family into the criminal Courts and sit during murder trials observing hair colour and the way it grew and the skin tones and textures they would reproduce if the accused were found guilty or did they rely for accurate results entirely on what they were told and sketches and photographs? We do not know for the Misses Tussaud inherited not only their great-grandmother's skills and devotion to the exhibition but also her reticence.

At the end of the last century the introduction of an accurate and full-scale model of the American electric chair in which Kemmler was executed had stimulated immense interest in the Chamber of Horrors. It was in 1960 that an equally accurate reproduction of the gas chamber was constructed as used in the execution at St Quentin prison, California, of Caryl Chessman. He was executed in May of that year, twelve years after sentence of death had been passed on him. Chessman had a long criminal record of robbery, kidnapping and attacks on women. His execution was postponed eight times and while he was in prison he wrote four books. He survived the judge who sentenced him and when his execution was finally carried out it aroused a furore of comment and criticism widely reported in British newspapers. It was said that some sixty witnesses peered through the 'portholes' of the gas chamber while the execution was taking place.

Attitudes towards the punishment of crime had been slowly changing for decades. The concept of remedial punishment and rehabilitation was replacing that of retribution alone. By the 1960s the climate of opinion on the use of the death sentence had changed considerably and it was clear that in the foreseeable future execution for murder would be abolished. No hangman had been modelled for the Chamber of Horrors since Berry sat to John Theodore Tussaud. In 1960 Harry Allen who would be the last public hangman in the British Isles consented, like Berry, to be modelled from life. The work was done by Bernard Tussaud, son of John Theodore and great-great-grandson of Madame Tussaud.

The last figure of an executed murderer to be placed in the Chamber of Horrors was that of James Hanratty, whose conviction has been the subject of much controversy. One evening in 1960 in the summer month of August a married man and a girl were sitting in a car parked in a field near Slough. They were disturbed by a man who knocked at the window and threatened them with a gun. He said he was on the run and, climbing into the back of the car, ordered Michael Gregson to drive on. Eventually the unwelcome passenger ordered the car into a lay-by on the A6 road. Gregson moved when the gunman asked for a duffle bag to be handed to him, and was killed with two shots. The gunman raped the girl, Valerie Storey, then fired several shots into her body. He left the bodies both apparently dead in the lay-by and drove off. The car was later found abandoned but someone had seen and taken notice of it being driven by a man. The gun which fired the fatal shots was discovered on a London bus.

However, Valerie Storey was not dead though paralysed and she was able to give a detailed description of the killer. One characteristic was his singularly blue staring eyes. The police finally issued an Identikit picture which did not resemble the description of the man who had been spotted driving Gregson's stolen car.

In a hotel room occupied by Hanratty the night before the murder, cartridges which fitted the murder weapon were found, though Hanratty was no longer using the room. The occupant was a man named Louis Alphon. It was the widow of the victim, Michael Gregson, who felt certain she recognized the killer of her husband in the street, her intuition based on the descriptions she had read. Hanratty was known as a petty criminal and the police arrested him and put him on identity parade. The other men lined up included Louis Alphon. Valerie Storey positively identified James Hanratty as the killer.

The question of identification made the trial difficult as Hanratty did not resemble the Identikit picture that had been issued and he claimed an alibi. He said he was in Liverpool at the time of the murder but refused to name witnesses to support this claim. Later he said it was at Rhyl, not Liverpool, where he had been at the time but again produced no witnesses to corroborate.

The jury was out for nine hours before finding James Hanratty guilty and he was hanged, still protesting his innocence, on 4 April 1962. The verdict aroused a great deal of public discussion and dissension. For a time the figure of Hanratty with its icy staring blue eyes and ginger hair had a placard with a large question mark placed beside it.

There were few effigies in the Chamber of Horrors whose originals had not been convicted of guilt, but in 1963 they were joined by an assassin who had never stood trial. On 22 November 1963 in Dallas, Texas, the President of the United States, John F. Kennedy, was killed by a sniper's bullet. Lee Harvey Oswald, a twenty-four-year-old Texan, was arrested and accused of the murder. As he was being transferred to the city police headquarters Oswald himself was shot and killed by a bullet fired from the watching crowd by Jack Ruby, a fifty-two-year-old night club owner. Ruby said he did it to spare Mrs Jacqueline Kennedy the ordeal of a trial. The shot was fired at point-blank range as Oswald walked down a ramp flanked by detectives to an armoured car that was to take him to prison. It was all a far cry from the attempted assassination by poor Dennis Collins, modelled by Madame Tussaud herself in 1832, the disabled sailor with a grievance over his tiny pensions who had stood in the crowd and hurled a stone at King William IV at Ascot races.

In 1965 the death penalty was abolished in the United Kingdom by the Abolition of the Death Penalty Act. Since 1783, first in Curtius' *Caverne des Grands Voleurs* in Paris and then from 1802 in Madame Tussaud's Separate Room which became the Chamber of Horrors, it was the portraits of *executed* criminals which had formed the vast majority of the 'subjects'. Now there would be no more of these.

Strangely enough the fact that the addition of new figures to the Chamber had ceased did not appear to diminish the fascination which drew visitors down the winding stairs. After all, where else but in the Chamber of Horrors could one see and muse on the faces of dozens of murderers, as well as contemplate historic relics of crime and punishment? From time to time the existing figures were regrouped, rearranged, and of course kept clean and in good repair. Even the Victorian murderers looked as if they had been modelled only yesterday.

Bernard Tussaud, the last member of the family to work actively in and control the studios, died in September 1967 at the comparatively early age of seventy-one. Apart from a break during the First World War his life had been dedicated to the exhibition. Bernard had sat through many a trial at the Old Bailey noting the features and appearance of the criminals he then modelled so accurately for the Chamber of Horrors. Now there was no Tussaud left working actively, but all the same Madame Tussaud's original traditions and principles were carried on in every aspect of the exhibition.

The Chamber of Horrors was not allowed to become static. Decades earlier Madame Tussaud's grandson, Joseph Randall, had tried to introduce a new name and concept, the 'Chamber of Comparative Physiognomy'. Now in the 1960s the protrait figures of murderers and criminals were reassembled according to types of crime they had committed. Visitors could study and compare the faces of poisoners, those who had killed for greed or gain, the assassins, the women murderers like Mrs Dyer and Mrs Pearcey and the perpetrators of *crimes passionels*. Was there a common factor to be discovered in the faces of those who committed similar killings? The shudder induced by the spectacle of so much evil still remained.

Later the Chamber was again reorganized and the portraits of some forgotten Victorian criminals removed while others were gruesomely accommodated in coffins tilted upright against the walls, but basically the Chamber of Horrors had remained unchanged since its refurbishment after the fire of 1925. The time was coming when, in accordance with Madame Tussaud's firmly-held principles of updating and the changing tastes and outlook of a public familiar with appalling horrors from their daily newspapers and television, the massed stare of murderers was not enough.

In 1979 the old Chamber of Horrors was closed down for a few weeks while a complete reconstruction took place.

[10]

The New Chamber of Horrors Opens in 1980

The New Chamber of Horrors was opened in April 1980 completely redesigned with modern sound and lighting effects. The dungeon-like atmosphere which had been the setting since 1884 was swept away. It was a new Chamber of Horrors yet in essence it was unchanged, exercising the same peculiar fascination that has drawn visitors for 200 years.

There is no place for concocted horrors. If Dr Curtius and Madame Tussaud herself could stroll through the new surroundings they would feel at home in a place where accuracy of likeness and presentation still prevail as they did in the *Caverne des Grands Voleurs* in Paris in 1783 and during Madame Tussaud's entire lifetime.

History still combines with the criminal and macabre. Madame Tussaud's own bloodstained reminders of the French Revolution, the guillotined heads and Marat stabbed in his bath are still the root of the Chamber of Horrors. Those instruments of death: the guillotine, the gallows from Hertford Gaol and the electric chair are joined by other methods of execution. There is the garrotte, used chiefly in Spain from the seventeenth century and last used in the early 1970s. Gary Gilmore, who chose to die by firing squad in Utah, USA, in 1977 after refusing to appeal against the death sentence, by a special technique is shown before and after the shooting.

In the electric chair is Bruno Hauptmann, who was executed in 1936 at Trenton State Prison, New Jersey, USA, for the

Portrait figure of Bruno Hauptmann in the electric chair. He was executed in 1936 for the kidnap and murder of the Lindbergh baby.

kidnap and murder of the Lindbergh baby. The baby was the son of Colonel Charles Lindbergh, the aviator famous for his solo crossing of the Atlantic. In March 1932 the baby was taken at night from his cot in his parents' isolated country home in New Jersey. A ransom note demanding $50,000, later increased to $70,000, was found. The kidnapper, using a false name, arranged a meeting with a Dr London who had appealed through a New York newspaper, begging the kidnapper in the name of humanity to reveal where he was hiding the child. The child's night clothes were sent as proof that the person demanding the ransom had in fact taken the baby. At a second meeting Colonel Lindbergh handed over the ransom and was directed to go to a boat at a place on the Massachusetts coast where he would find his son. The father found neither boat nor baby there.

In May 1934 the child's body was discovered buried in a shallow grave not far from the Lindbergh home from which he had been taken. The kidnapper was finally identified when he paid a petrol-station attendant with a banknote known to have been part of the ransom money. Police traced the driver, of the car through its registration number. The driver, Hauptmann, was arrested in September 1932.

Hauptmann, German-born and once a soldier in the German Army, was an immigrant. In his garage the police found some $11,000 from the ransom Colonel Lindbergh had handed over. Hauptmann, who pleaded innocence of the crime, was tried and convicted of the kidnap and murder though he insisted the money was stored on behalf of someone else who was never identified or traced. In April 1936 he was executed. Some people still hold the opinion that Hauptmann was not in fact the kidnapper and murderer of the Lindbergh baby.

The Chamber of Horrors has always been an eerie place. Now there is a reconstruction of a dark, narrow, cobbled Victorian street, a sinister alley where the effigy of prostitute Mary Kelly, last victim of Jack the Ripper, leans waiting for custom at the door of her sordid room. In a dim passage the body of Catherine Eddowes lies bloody and mutilated by the invisible Ripper, while patrons drinking in the Ten Bells are disturbed by the sound of screams and running feet.

Charles Peace crouches there with his tools of burglary while body snatchers Burke and Hare stumble in the semidarkness with a bundle inert and heavy on the way to the hospital dissecting room. Over all the Newgate Bell tolls its warning of execution.

Some earlier murderers appear as they were originally presented: Crippen gazing with his rather prominent blue eyes from the dock, Ethel le Neve beside him; Mrs Pearcey with the baby's pram and other effects bought by Madame Tussaud's after her trial; George Smith with the bath where his last 'bride' lies drowned; Christie in his squalid kitchen in Rillington Place; Haigh, the 'Acid Bath Murderer', wearing the clothes he bequeathed to Madame Tussaud's before his execution; and the sadistic Neville Heath.

Since 1965 when the death penalty for murder was abolished in the United Kingdom, the sentence for murder has been life imprisonment. Portrait figures of present-day criminals convicted of murder and in prison custody are placed in a modern prison setting with the sound of rattling keys, locking and unlocking, echoing around them. The crime of murder has always covered a wide spectrum which has been reflected in the Chamber of Horrors since its beginning. The more recent portraits continue to reflect this.

The Hosein brothers of Asian origin, who kept pigs and a few other domestic animals on a farm in the remote Hertfordshire countryside, conceived the idea of kidnapping for ransom the wife of a newspaper magnate. They followed the Rolls-Royce which he often used to a house in Wimbledon, unaware that it was another newspaper man and his wife who lived there. In December 1969 the brothers broke into the house and kidnapped the woman they believed to be the wife of the magnate. Ransom demands by telephone and letter followed with threats of killing her if the money was not paid. In accordance with a written instruction money was left in a telephone box. The kidnappers who waited in a car in the vicinity of the telephone box did not realize that they had been seen. The police traced the ownership of the car which belonged to the elder Hosein. In it was found the exercise book, pages of which had been used for some of the letters. Fingerprints confirmed that the Hoseins had handled it. The Hosein brothers were arrested and convicted of murder though neither the body of the victim nor any trace of it was ever found. No one but the brothers who have remained silent knows exactly what happened to the kidnapped woman, how she died and her body was disposed of, probably on the pig farm, possibly dismembered and used in the pig food.

Graham Young, compulsive poisoner, had been sent to Broadmoor, the mental hospital used for criminals judged to be mentally impaired, for the murder of his stepmother and an attempt to poison his father, sister and a friend. After nine years he was released. Young obtained a job in a factory where in his capacity of teaboy he poisoned six workers, two of whom died. Young came under suspicion after the illnesses and deaths. When searched by the police he was found to have in his pocket a lethal quantity of the poison (thallium) that had been found in the ashes of one of the dead men. After arrest he admitted administering poison to six persons though at his trial in July 1972 he pleaded not guilty. The jury decided otherwise and he was sentenced to life imprisonment.

The Kray brothers, twins, were convicted of two East London gangland murders in 1969, while one of the most horrific killers of recent times, Donald Neilson, known as the 'Black Panther' on account of the black hood he wore as disguise when committing many robberies, was another kidnapper. He seized a seventeen-year-old girl from the home of her wealthy parents near Kidderminster and demanded a ransom of £50,000. Meanwhile he kept his victim hidden in a system of underground drainage shafts of which he had made a careful study for this very purpose. The girl's body was eventually found in March 1975, naked, and with a wire round the neck, hanging in one of the shafts. Neilson managed to evade the police for nine months, and was finally arrested in December 1975. In June the

Portrait figures of Charles Manson and three girl members of his 'family'. They used the blood of their murdered victims to smear slogans on walls.

following year he was tried not only for the murder of the young girl he had kidnapped but also for the murder of three sub-post-office officials by shooting. He was convicted on all four counts.

In a tableau setting are Charles Manson and three shaven-headed girls, members of the Manson 'family'. This was a group of hippies, drop-outs, drug-takers and practisers of free love who had formed a commune at a ranch not far from Los

Angeles. Charles Manson, leader and 'father', disseminated among his followers his senseless maniacal hatred of any form of established society.

On the night of 9 August 1969 a group headed by Charles Manson broke into the home of a Hollywood film director and killed his pregnant wife and four other people. The next night Manson and his followers repeated their action at the home of another Hollywood couple, both of whom they murdered. The victims were shot, stabbed, and clubbed, and the murders were made the more horrible as Manson and his followers used the blood of their victims to smear slogans such as 'Pig' and 'Nothingness' on the walls.

Manson and three of his girl followers were tried for the six murders. The prosecution called Manson 'one of the most evil, satanic men who ever walked the face of the earth'. A death sentence was passed on all four who were found guilty of these mindless and revolting crimes. However, the death sentence was not carried out and their penalty was changed to life imprisonment.

Why has Madame Tussaud's Chamber of Horrors survived two centuries when countless exhibitions of torture chambers and instruments of horrible death have come and gone? There are many reasons. There is always what Sir Roy Strong has called 'man's fascination for a safe experience of the macabre', and man's perennial interest in crime and punishment.

Charles Dickens, looking at the ranks of murderers in 1860, exclaimed '*What* a horrible place!', and went on to say 'There is Horror in the very unpicturesqueness of this aspect of crime—crime in coats and trousers being more horrible (being nearer to us) than crime in doublet and hose'.

But perhaps it was the shrewd old Duke of Wellington who put his finger on the answer. When asked why he often visited and gazed on the effigies in the Chamber of Horrors, he replied: 'Well, do they not represent *fact*?' Dr Curtius and Madame Tussaud would have nodded agreement.

Index

Names in bold type (thus **Robespierre**) refer to people who appear as exhibition models